The Crack between the Worlds

The Crack between the Worlds

a dancer's memoir of loss and faith

MAGGIE KAST

RESOURCE *Publications* · Eugene, Oregon

THE CRACK BETWEEN THE WORLDS
A Dancer's Memoir of Loss and Faith

Resource Publishing
A Division of Wipf and Stock Publishers
199 W. 8th Ave., Suite 3
Eugene, OR 97401
www.wipfandstock.com

ISBN 13: 978-1-60608-777-0
Manufactured in the U.S.A.

Scripture quotations are from the Revised Standard Version of the Bible, copyright © 1946, 1952, and 1971 by the National Council of the Churches of Christ in the USA. Used by permission. All rights reserved.

Material in chapter 20 was first published as "Liberal Catholicism" in *America* 196: 15, April 20, 2007, © 2007. All rights reserved. Reprinted with permission of America Press.

Material in chapter 15 was first published as "Dancing in Sacred Space: Some Reflections on Liturgy and Performance" in *Religion and the Arts* 4, no. 2 (2000). Reprinted with permission of Koninklijke Brill, N.V.

Material in chapter 16 was first published in the *Sun Magazine* and later in *Love You to Pieces,* edited by Suzanne Kamata. Reprinted by permission of Beacon Press, Boston.

Excerpts from Muriel Rukeyser's "Dream-Singing Elegy" reprinted by permission of International Creative Management, Inc. Copyright © 1973 by Muriel Rukeyser. Excerpt from Sylvia Plath's "Child" in *Winter Trees* reprinted by permission of HarperCollins Publishers. Copyright © 1972 by Ted Hughes.

Excerpt from Maxine Kumin's "After Love," copyright © 1970 by Maxine Kumin, from *Selected Poems* 1960–1990 by Maxine Kumin. Used by permission of W.W. Norton & Company, Inc.

The author acknowledges permission to quote lyrics from Si Kahn's song "Borders." Copyright © Joe Hill Music (administered by MCS Music America, Inc.). All rights reserved. International Copyright Secured. Used by permission.

Permission is also acknowledged to quote from Jean Ritchie's song "Cool of the Day," © 1968, 1971 Jean Ritchie Geordie Music Publishing Co. ASCAP; from Anita Silvert's song "All Roads Converge," Balancing Act BAM-003; and from Tom Conry's "Anthem," Oregon Catholic Music.

Lost in the Stars. Words by Maxwell Anderson. Music by Kurt Weill. © 1946 (Renewed) Chappell and Co., Inc., and Tro-Hampshire House Publishing House Corp. All Rights Reserved. Used by Permission of Alfred Publishing Co., Inc.

For Eric and all of our children:
Richard, Byron, Anton, Tom, Stefan, Natasha, and Erica

Contents

Acknowledgments

SPECIAL THANKS TO THE editors of the following journals in which some of these chapters originally appeared, sometimes in different form: *ACM/Another Chicago Magazine*; *America Magazine*; *Image Journal*; *Kaleidoscope: International Magazine of Literature, Fine Arts and Disability*; *Nimrod International*; *Religion and the Arts*; and the *Sun Magazine*. Portions of the chapters "Dancing in New York" and "Still Dancing" were first printed in *Contact Quarterly Dance Journal, A Vehicle for Moving Ideas*, vol. 24, no. 2 (Summer–Fall 1999), and vol. 25, no. 1 (Winter–Spring 2000). "Joyful Noise," a version of chapter 16, was reprinted in *Love You to Pieces: Creative Writers on Raising a Child with Special Needs*, edited by Suzanne Kamata (Boston: Beacon Press, 2008).

I'm grateful to Christopher Noel, who critiqued an early version of the manuscript, and to the members of my writing group: Rosellen Brown, Garnet Kilberg Cohen, Tsivia Cohen, Peggy Shinner, Sharon Sollwitz, and Sandi Wisenberg, who critiqued the material chapter by chapter. Janet Steen edited the book, and Laurel Richardson, Ron Moline, and Carolyn Walker reviewed the whole manuscript near the end, making invaluable suggestions. Amy Davis, Meg Cox, and members of the Writers' Workspace of Chicago offered indispensable support and encouragement, while Suzanne Kamata and Vicky Forman, both writers and parents of handicapped children, reached across miles and an ocean to share stories. Carol Sickman-Garner copy-edited with precision and care.

Gratitude and respect to Father Jack Farry for supporting liturgical dance at St. Thomas Apostle and, on one occasion, dancing himself. Organist Thomas Weisflog conceived the organ-and-dance concerts at this church and codirected them for three years, with Father Jack's encouragement. HMS Media videotaped the concerts, and William Frederking photographed them, providing enduring records that are artworks in themselves.

Vermont College's MFA program taught me to write near the end of my dancing time, and I owe special thanks to Abby Frucht, David Jauss, Ellen Lesser, and Sharon Sheehe Stark for their painstaking critiques. Thanks to the Ragdale Foundation, whose residency nurtured the evolving book, and to the Illinois Arts Council, whose Literary Award affirmed both the work and the journal (*ACM/Another Chicago Magazine*) that published an early chapter.

Finally, thanks to all the people, living and dead, whose stories have shared time and space with mine: parents, teachers, children, colleagues, and friends. I've changed a few names for the sake of privacy; any other distortions arise from the fog of memory.

PART ONE

1

The Other Side

FOR THE LAST TWENTY-ODD years I have gone to Catholic Mass almost every Sunday, as believer and skeptic, supporter and critic, seeker and sought, trying to be faithful to the experience that brought me to the Church in the first place. I've clapped and sung at gym masses, where lay preaching is common and children dance to guitars and tambourines, and I've yawned through somber, poorly attended masses in irreligious Catholic countries. When I've least expected it, I've discovered myself in the presence of the holy, perhaps at a small community mass in a spare, white room with no music, no statues, a single branch in a vase suddenly trembling and radiant, cracking to reveal the splendor of its making.

I received the sacraments of Baptism, Confirmation, and Communion at the Easter Vigil in 1982. But nothing can give me a Catholic childhood, reflective patent-leather shoes, nuns with rulers, or fish on Fridays. Nothing can infuse me with the Roman Catholic culture of my city, Chicago, with its division into Polish, German, and Italian parishes, its struggle to be a religion of the powerful as well as of immigrants. For me these ethnic traditions are no less foreign, and just as Catholic, as the rattling sistrum and drum of the Church's Ethiopian Rite, with its women ululating "le, le, le, le, le" on a single, high note. In other parts of the world, the Church struggles with its converts over such cultural issues as polygamy and ancestor worship, but my cultural baggage is no less strange. In some ways, I am as alien to the person sitting by me in the pew as a South Sea Islander on a pig hunt.

My search for God and entry into the Church were vibrant, if conflictual, parts of my thirty-year marriage to Eric, a man twenty-two years older than I. With his death in 1988, my spiritual fervor weakened, displaced by grief that threatened my stability. At fifty, I found myself a single parent of a ten-year-old girl and a mentally handicapped seventeen-year-old boy, as well as two college-aged sons, and I devoted myself to the needs of children, to therapy, and to my work, teaching dance and choreographing. I dropped out of church committees, like liturgy planning, as I struggled to be a person and a mother without being a wife. But I continued to make and direct dances for churches, as part of worship or as concerts, and I tested the waters of the Mass each Sunday, searching for the immersion of my initial baptismal plunge.

Thirteen years later, the children on their own, I moved to Chicago's North Side and found myself without a parish. I hoped to find one with the rich, up-to-date liturgy of my first church, St. Thomas the Apostle, on Chicago's South Side, with its inclusive language, occasional lay preaching, enthusiastic folk-style music, and intellectually solid theology. I'd been wandering, disappointed, for a couple of years when I stumbled into the gym mass at St. Gertrude's on the first Sunday of Advent.

Four nests of greenery were arranged throughout the open space, each one supporting a candle at waist height, and a blue drape hung behind the improvised altar. At the beginning of Mass, the tiniest children circled in the center. Those who could manage fire held lighted tapers, and those too young had candles with paper flames. As the choir sang "O Come, O Come, Emanuel," they processed to the first candle and lit it.

The children's action was dance without dancing, if "dance" is taken to mean deliberately elaborated movement. It was all the children could do to get to the candle and light it without setting each other's hair afire. They were simply performing the liturgical action of kindling light, and there was no room for self-conscious gesture, performed for its own sake.

The world hushed; I took a sharp breath and felt myself settle into remembered layers of meaning, as the old story of hope and expectation unfolded in the gestures of the youngest tellers. I knew that I would be at St. Gertrude's as more children were added each week, dancers accumulating with the candles, the light building until it breaks into the dark of Midnight Mass on Christmas Eve, radiating from the cradle to defy winter's gloom. I had found a home.

For the first time since my years of intense mourning for Eric's death, I was released from an endless waiting game. I sensed a playful God, one who might be hiding but whom I could seek, one from whom I would no longer hide. As my faith flickered back into life, I began to reflect on its strange journey, sometimes rescuing me when I didn't even know it existed and other times getting confused with my own desires and ambitions, just when I thought it was strongest.

As I slipped into this community, I began to suspect that the story was bigger and more complex than a door opening and slamming shut within ten years. I scribbled pages and pages freehand on a yellow legal pad, recalling the time when each Sunday was an expedition into the virgin territory of faith. At first, the writing was just "telling," the page a substitute for Eric's listening ear. Then the page began to speak back to me, showing me things I'd forgotten or hadn't suspected, revealing connections among childhood, adolescence, early religious experience, and its distant ripples in my present life.

On March 12, 1977, when I was thirty-nine, I flew with my husband, Eric, and three of our children to Jamaica for spring vacation, leaving our six-year-old, disabled son, Stefan, with my parents in D.C. We speeded in a rental car on the unaccustomed left side of twisting roads, trying to reach our hotel before dark. Swerving to avoid an oncoming truck, we hit the embankment, rose for a weightless moment, then tumbled and rolled. Stillness. Something heavy pinned my right shoulder.

"Are you on top of me?" I asked. Shouts approached, and someone righted the car, dumping Eric back behind the steering wheel and revealing my three-year-old daughter, Natasha, beneath me, limp, blood streaming from her neck, teeth broken. Baby teeth, I told myself, just baby teeth. Up the embankment I saw nine-year-old Tom, thrown from the car but uninjured. "Where's Anton?" I asked.

"We've turned him over," said a stranger's voice, "and he's all right." Thrown out the downhill side, he'd fallen in the ditch beneath the car. As we raced in a jeep over dirt roads toward a hospital in the tiny town of Santa Maria, I found myself bargaining. "If I can have this one thing . . ." To whom? Not God. I was pleading with anything or anyone that could transcend harsh, material reality, that could reverse the flow of Natasha's life, her body seeming to liquefy as it threatened to slip from my lap. Anton, eleven, wept muddy tears on the seat across from me, while Tom pushed me back into my seat each time the careening jeep jiggled me to the edge. "If I can have this one thing, then . . ." What? I had nothing to offer in return, nothing but my impotent wish. I craned my head toward the driver. "Please hurry," I begged over the motor's racket. My baby's eyes rolled up in her head, and someone screamed into the wind—my husband. I knew his doctor's eyes had seen a sign. "If I can have this one thing..." I'd never pleaded for anything before.

Attendants rushed Natasha into one treatment room and Anton into another, while Tom remained among the local families in the small, crowded waiting room. Eric and I stayed with Natasha as darkness invaded the room with the speed of tropical night. The nurse listened to Natasha's heartbeat, then passed the stethoscope to Eric at his request. With two hands pressed together, she began rhythmic compression of the baby's chest, then listened again. I went out to the waiting room to report to Tom. Eric checked the other treatment room, but Anton's diagnosis would have to wait for a bigger hospital. We hurried back to Natasha. The nurse compressed the baby's chest more slowly, then took the stethoscope from her ears, drew back, and pulled the sheet from the foot of the gurney up over Natasha's face. I pulled it down to kiss her stomach, her lips, and her face, counting: she'd lived for three years, two months, and fourteen days. Raising my hands, I grabbed the neck of my shirt to tear it but couldn't quite inhabit that traditional gesture of grief. I pulled the sheet back up over Natasha and went out to tell Tom.

My living children tugged at me, pulling me back from the abyss. Anton was hospitalized in Kingston after a lurching ambulance ride across the mountains, Eric fearing that Anton had a ruptured spleen. Children in the waiting room stared fearfully at my white hair, dyed red by Natasha's blood. Neither Eric nor I suffered more than a black eye, and Anton was only bruised and battered. Hair filled with gravel, he raved and flailed, semiconscious, and then slept, sedated. We went to a hotel. Tom, nine, bore the brunt of grief undiluted by a struggle for physical healing.

"It's hard," he said, the next morning, "to wake up to the sound of you crying." Eric and I drew Tom into the circle of our embrace, amazed at how little it helped. Food turned to cardboard in my mouth, feeding myself an outrage against one who couldn't eat. We wandered around the hotel pool, violated by sun and air, and yet we took one step, and then one more, and then one more. After Anton's torn eyelid had been repaired and a cast put on his badly sprained ankle, he left the hospital and flew with us back to Washington. There we picked up Stefan and returned to Chicago.

The week after, I went back to work at the Body Politic theater complex in Chicago, where I taught modern dance and choreographed for my company, the Chicago Contemporary Dance Theatre. I tried to collect myself and focus on the work, to let its rhythm carry me. The moment I became involved, the knowledge of loss came charging back, as though punishing me for forgetting. I wondered if I would ever be able to simply eat an egg, drink a glass of wine, take a walk, or snuggle for a night of sleep.

A week later, distraught, I grabbed pad and pencil and descended alone to our bright yellow kitchen, the light reddened by reflection from the dark orange ceiling. Pots and pans hung from hooks, collected from college apartments and garage sales, trips to the Maxwell Street market and the Salvation Army. Here, as the children were born and grew, Eric and I had had long dinner conversations by candlelight. Here the little boys had retired to *platzies,* blanketed corners where they could rest after eating when adult dinner took too long, until their father roused them to extinguish the candles with a copper snuffer while he sang the Austrian national anthem, loudly and off-key, then agreed to "carry both," as they demanded, one in each arm, to bed. Here I'd taught the boys to cook, standing them unsteadily on chairs at the counter and giving them potatoes to peel and carrots to wash, holding one hand between them to stop a push while stirring rice into onions on the stove, keeping one eye on my third son on the floor. And here on another stark night, I'd come to realize that Stefan, the baby on the floor, would only slowly learn to walk or speak, would never read or write or hold a job.

When Stefan was newborn, we'd called him "Zen baby" for his peaceful nature, marveling at how little he cried. Soon we began to worry about his floppiness and failure to sit up on time and started weekly visits to speech and occupational therapists. Eric defended him against the experts' tests, hanging onto his conviction that Stefan was special, perhaps even holy. "Developmentally delayed," said the social worker to whom we talked while Stefan had speech therapy. Eventually I said the dreaded word: "retarded." By that time, he was three and couldn't walk. A name couldn't make it any worse than it already was, I thought. I wanted to say the word before someone said it to me. More than anything, I hoped Stefan would never hear it, would never know this harsh fact about himself. "Retarded, retarded," I repeated to myself. A "retard" was a discard, but "retarded" was all right, I thought, just a fact about a person. We listened to the news about Nixon's wrongdoing on the radio while Stefan played on the floor, lying on his stomach and propping himself up on his hands. I'd said the unacceptable word to Eric, and he'd shared my embattled joy that Stefan would never be able to accomplish any serious evil.

Now Stefan was six, and I rued the sense of security I'd felt when I faced the fact of his condition, my false conviction that I'd paid my dues and earned safe passage for all my children. The weird orange light shimmered in the night kitchen, and my once solid, settled innards seemed all water, as fluid as my daughter had been the day she flowed away. The body's mostly water. Eighty percent? Or is it 98? I wanted to disgorge my watery self, pour it out, turn inside out, sink into earth. The light bounced harshly from walls to lined yellow pad. Natasha had been my only girl. Not only flesh of my flesh, but my kind of body.

Newborn, her sucking mouth had called forth a rush of milk and made my womb contract, seeking its former size. While I nursed her, I read Adrienne Rich's *Of Woman Born* and felt the intimate dialogue between mother and child of which she speaks.[1] Natasha's whole self sucked with such effort that her forehead shone, and my throat ached with her yearning. My old ideas of womanhood began to shift and heave, ruptured by the intense efforts of this woman-child. Her mouth, my nipple, my womb, her microscopic eggs like seeds inside her: body called to body with coursing waves of sensuality. My womb: her former home; her womb: my future, as echoes of ancestral births called to the children Natasha and her children would bear. If she was so wonderfully made, then so was I. I loved her length and the tidy seam of her pubis. Her blue eyes always seemed to ask, like Princess Lise, as she died in childbirth in *War and Peace*, "I love you all, and have done no harm to anyone, and what have you done to me?"[2] It seemed, impossibly, as though Natasha's birth had been a grief foretold.

The pencil, the pad, the chasm that separated me from Natasha. Where was she, and what did "gone" mean? I thought vaguely of physical laws of conservation of matter and energy. The *g* sound nudged my mind, not the hard *g* of "girl," but the soft *g* of the woman she would never become: generate, vagina, her generous being. Being? Without being, nothing. No thing. But she had never been a thing. How could she cease to be? Genesis, the vegetating vegetation where the car had rolled, my stomach divulging. The words bounced around the kitchen, flitted along the curtains, and slid to rest on the paper, capturing images of tropical seed, fruit, and juice. I pictured Natasha in evanescent flight, a fragile bird once trapped, set free in an explosion of time, and myself crashing into the brick wall of brute fact.

For years before the accident, I'd dreamed of houses with an "other side." I'd enter a childhood home, like the house on Dumbarton Avenue where we lived when I was ten, in Washington's Georgetown. I'd pass the piano room that would later be my bedroom and then climb the stairs to the second floor, where the living room looked out through French doors to the long, narrow garden. I'd continue up to the third floor and enter my bedroom, glance out the window at the garden and take a peek at the neighbors' flowers, then pass through a dream door into a room I'd never seen before. Sometimes it was a living room furnished with the clean lines of Danish modern, much like our own, and sometimes cluttered and cobwebbed, full of old dishes and rusty tools. Other rooms led from this one on and on into rooms ever new and mysterious, occasionally narrowing to nightmare constriction, sometimes opening to vistas of lake and meadow. How could I have missed this up to now?

As I grieved that night in the yellow kitchen, those other rooms opened to me. The air filled with paradox, reality and dream exchanging roles like a pair of linked tumblers doing somersaults. Life could be stifled in the tropics as easily as fruit burst from the trees. Weeds could grow through concrete, unstoppable, yet no one could hold Natasha's ebbing life. I began to feel—to hope, to believe?—that I would meet her again someday. The love that bound us together felt stronger than the harsh fact of separation, strong enough to crash through that wall.

Everything was different. Before the accident, I'd approached my dance company's studio timidly, always parking facing south, toward home, as though that could ensure my return to a safe haven. Upcoming performance seasons always threatened to reveal my inability, the hollow at my core. What if I failed to produce new work? Feeling undeserving of studio and theater, I walked with my head down, eyes on the floor. Now I strode into the theater, fearless, and addressed the tech director.

"I want a platform built in that corner, a raked platform to simulate a mountainside." I imagined the dancers as Jamaican women with jugs on their heads, descending a mountain at daybreak, necks swaying, innocent of what the day would bring.

"Sure, we can do that," said the tech guy. "You mean you want to change the theater to the diagonal?" He indicated the skewing of banks of seats to face the mountain.

"Right," I said, walking to the opposite corner. "This'll be front."

"Do you want it to fill the whole corner?" he asked, starting to measure along the wall.

"Yes, so the dancers can descend along a winding path." I began to visualize a slow accumulation of bodies, starting from the top, a sort of six-person version of *La Bayadère,* the classical ballet sequence that starts with one person doing an arabesque and backbend and builds to twenty or thirty, each entering from up center and winding back and forth downstage. "Can we have an entrance at the back?" He explained how he could mask an entrance and allow the dancers to enter at the mountaintop. I paid no attention to what it would cost, for I'd forgotten how to worry. Mountains and theater seats, success and failure had lost their importance. The worst thing had already happened, and nothing else mattered.

Sights and smells and tastes, perceptions that I had considered "real," now seemed a shimmering, changeable surface, but what the underlying reality might be, I didn't know. Whatever it was, it united me with Natasha, no matter how far beyond the trees she'd flown or how unknown she was to flesh or fruit or seed. Her vivid, continuing presence contradicted my faith in empirical fact, my secular upbringing, and drew me to the edge of the world I'd known. As I peered beyond, the horizon receded, suggesting there was more than I could see, an "other side" to the world like the other side of the house. Maybe she'd be running ahead of me, like when she took my father's hand and dashed into a field, chasing her brothers on a tractor, saying, "Wanna ride, wanna ride, wanna ride!" Maybe she'd be in my arms, every inch of me welcoming every inch of her. I didn't know. But somehow, somewhere, I'd meet her once again. My critical self said "Illusion of a grief-stricken mother," but the feeling remained, strong and real as pinched flesh. I had no idea what to do with it.

2

Dance Was My Religion

Maggie Kast, about thirteen years old. Photo by Vern Blaisdell

I COME FROM NO traditional religion. I grew up without prayers before bed or grace before meals, no Bible in the house and no Christianity in Christmas, no matter how much generosity and joy. In our family, what you saw was what you got, and life was a series of problems to be solved by your own effort and ingenuity. If I needed a rock or a fortress, it was there in the person of my father, a short and solid figure with large, balding skull, white hair and beard, big paunch, and strong arms covered with black hair.

Daddy looked like Santa Claus. Children who saw him on the street rejoiced that the jolly saint was real after all. I never even considered whether Santa might be real or lamented his absence; I had Daddy. His care for his women and his smells of sweat and whiskey defined reality. There was nothing behind or beyond his deep, storytelling voice or his belly, and I would be out of line to search for more. Long before my birth, he'd rejected the moldy basement smell of Sunday school at the Congregational church where his mother played the organ, as well as the conservative, narrow thinking of his small Wisconsin town. A structural anthropologist, he studied the rituals and myths of native peoples but did not believe in the reality of any object of faith. Even the word "atheist" was too sectarian for Daddy, who did not posit a deity to be denied. Believe in me, he seemed to say, and in no other. For quite a while, I did.

Mama's parents were German Jews long since converted to Unitarianism and uncomfortable with their Jewish origins. Mama rejected not only this background but also the stormy household of her childhood, where her father's explosions of temper were followed by inappropriate sexual overtures. Of course, I did not know this as a child. To me Mama was my dark-haired, straight-nosed, beautiful mother, the one who sang sweet, sad songs to me and sexy songs at parties, the woman my father loved more than me.

The winter I was ten, she stayed in bed for weeks on end with a low-grade fever, and Daddy said that she had some kind of flu. Her illness dragged on, and Dick, a family friend and physician, offered to help find the cause. Dick was over six feet tall, a burly, blond army officer, Daddy's drinking companion. I liked his deep voice and chuckle and had been attracted to him as long as I could remember, long before any adolescent awakening. Even at six, when we lived in a second-floor apartment on Washington's Swann Street, I would lie in my spool bed, staring out the window at the fire escape, and think of him with the same pleasure I took in my favorite colors, turquoise blue and pink, the ice cream sodas I bought with my twenty-five-cent allowance at the drugstore downstairs, and the fairylands made of clouds I explored between sleep and waking.

One Sunday when Mama was sick, Dick came to our house on Dumbarton Avenue, entering through the back door on the second floor, jovial and ruddy from the cold. Daddy took him upstairs to see Mama, and I followed, lagging behind. Unsure whether it was all right to go in, I peered around the corner into my parents' bedroom. Dick sat on the edge of the bed, back to me, drawing blood from Mama's arm, while she reclined on pillows in a bed jacket, eyes downcast and head turned away. I focused on her face, eager to know what she felt. Pain? Some romantic stirring? Surely this must be a poignant moment, Dick and Daddy both attending to her, caring for her, Dick inflicting pain in order to help. When the men were gone, I couldn't resist asking.

"Did it hurt?" She shook her head vaguely, "No." I wanted more but suspected I was treading on forbidden ground, asking her to describe the mix of pain and secret pleasure I imagined. Shame turned my voice ironic. "You looked like you were in *great pain.*"

"Don't look if you don't like it," she said, probably annoyed by my prying. I doubt she shared the shiver of excitement I felt, and I felt guilty for years about imagining it and even worse about voicing what I imagined. Now when that voice echoes in my head, it sounds exaggerated, even haughty, as though I were making fun of her, when actually I was trying to sneak a taste of something adult, mysterious and sweet.

Shortly thereafter, Mama had a gynecological problem and began going to "the doctor," as she called it, twice a week. She had some minor surgery, and the problem was resolved, but she continued going downtown on Tuesdays and Thursdays, now seeing a psychiatrist, still calling it "the doctor." She didn't tell Daddy, my sister, Sally, or me and paid the bills from her office job. I continued thinking of her absences as mysteriously related to her female parts, and this imagined illness got connected in my mind with her abstracted look and glazed eyes. Apparently it was difficult and dangerous to be a woman. I did not know exactly how, but I'd learned how bad I felt when I spoke out and thought it better not to ask.

One March we went to see the cherry blossoms, the three thousand Japanese cherries that bloom around the Tidal Basin in front of Washington's Jefferson Memorial. This brief time of bloom creates thick clouds of pink and white as soft and light as any of my downy dream worlds. The four of us walked along, enjoying the warm air, Sally and I gathering fallen blossoms. Suddenly Mama walked into an overhanging branch and hit her head, hard. She began to cry, real tears and sobs, and I feared she'd done serious damage. Daddy held and comforted her, as he'd often done for Sally and me. I'd never seen her cry before. Except for one time when she tried to tear the thick D.C. phonebook in half, I'd never seen her angry.

Now I believe that Mama had been shocked and depleted by the demands of first motherhood, something she entered into without ever really choosing it, a prescribed step forward in her life. A photo shows my infant self sprawled across her lap, her arms hanging by her sides. The ill winds of depression have swept the animation from her face, and she stares at the floor. Looking back, I think the bump from the cherry bough cracked open her heart, releasing months of dammed-up melancholy.

Each of my parents had married, in part, to escape the past, and both viewed their marriage as an exercise in creating culture. Wedded, they embarked on a devil-may-care honeymoon road trip, eating oysters and drinking beer all the way to New Orleans, then proceeding to Klamath Falls, Oregon, where Daddy would do fieldwork for his doctoral dissertation. He taught anthropology for a couple of years at the University of Toronto, the city where Sally and I were both born. When the United States entered the Second World War, he moved the family to Falls Church, Virginia, and went to work for the Office of War Information, then continued to apply his knowledge of anthropology to race relations, working first for Roosevelt and then for Truman.

Neither of my parents—like me before 1980—had ever read the Bible, though my father's grandfather had been a minister and my mother's great-grandparents observant. As far back as I can remember, I knew I was Jewish, though I would have said "part Jewish," ignorant of the Jewish law that claims inheritance through the mother. But Judaism played no role in our family life. My parents raised me with books and plays and music, but strictly without religion.

After a year in Falls Church, we moved to a second-floor apartment on Swann Street in Washington, D.C.'s Northwest. It must have been spring when we moved in, because it was only during March and early April that my sister and I were three years apart. I was five and Sally was two, and she liked to invent scenarios that began, "When I was five and Maggie was two..."

I remember the day we moved in, the smell of paint still fresh, and Sally's and my discovery that the undersides of the cabinets had not been painted. Mama was delighted that our short height made us good inspec-

tors, and I experienced the rare advantage of being small. Sally and I celebrated our success by marching up and down the apartment's long hall,
thumbs in mouths, parading our thumb-sucking club. Not long after that
I started seeking power in maturity and persuaded my parents to reward
me for giving up the pleasure of thumb-sucking: a nickel the first day I did
without, four cents the second, and so forth.

The shaded spaces between chairs and walls were my hiding places
and secret playrooms. In one such spot I began a book I called "My Own
Secret Book of Hubba-Hubbas" but never got beyond the title page, ignorant of what should go inside. Soon after we moved in, I met Josie, a
ten-year-old girl who lived several floors above us, and my hiding places
became private clubs to which I might invite her, excluding Sally. Josie's
apartment was dark and mysterious, the hall lined with heavy statues
brought from her native Germany and shrouded with tragedy. The family
had escaped from the Nazis, but shortly after their arrival in D.C., Josie's
father had been murdered on the same front steps where we played each
day, learning to hang by our knees from the railing. Mama speculated
that Josie's father, a violinist, had become enchanted by black jazz before
he'd learned enough about the streets and clubs to distinguish safe from
dangerous. Everything about Josie charmed me: her weight of sorrow,
her German language, her amazing long name: Josefa Teresa Henrietta
Brighetta Simon.

Josie was home alone in the afternoons while her mother worked. One
day she invited me upstairs for hopple-popple, a sort of sweet eggnog she
made from milk and eggs. After we lapped it up with our tongues, pretending to be kittens, she dusted all the statues and then decided to teach me
how to jitterbug. Perhaps "Anniversary Waltz" was popular then, or perhaps
it was a favorite of Josie's mother, but Josie had the record, and we put it on
the phonograph, playing it over and over for our slow-motion Lindy:

> Oh, how we danced
> On the night we were wed.
> We vowed our true love
> Though a word wasn't said.

Soon we knew words and music by heart and took our new accomplishment down to the front steps, singing the accompaniment and eager
to show off. Other children joined us: Shirley from the third floor, who
had introduced me to peanut butter and bacon sandwiches; Boogen from

the first, whose mother talked too much about enemas; Yolanda from my floor, the Chinese girl whose father had taught us to eat with chopsticks at her birthday party. On the steps and sidewalk we danced, singing:

> Dear, as I held you so close in my arms
> Angels were singing a hymn to your charms
> Two hearts gently beating and murmuring low
> My darling I love you so.

Though none of us was over ten or eleven, and I was barely six, the dance gave us an advance view of our teens and made us feel like teenagers in training. We learned to turn under our arms while keeping the step going, beginning to feel the weight of our partners as we pulled together and apart, singing about a commitment as far beyond our understanding as the hemorrhaging tonsillectomy that would take Yolanda's little sister before the year was out.

I attended no funeral and witnessed no reaction to this death, but I heard that the mother had become hysterical, throwing and breaking china, and visions of what I had not seen stayed with me: the mother whose long, bright red fingernails I knew from the birthday party, now heaving plates and glasses, cups and bowls, while the father tried to restrain her, getting scratched in the process, and Yolanda hid under the bed. I thought about Josie's flight from the Nazis, the murderers who'd followed her father home from the jazz club, and Yolanda's mother's grief turned to rage: all evidence of a world beyond my experience, exotic, fascinating, and frightening. But I did not look to this wider world for anything spiritual, for two very different and contradictory reasons.

First, my elementary school, Georgetown Day, gave me much of what church or temple provides. On its first day, when I was seven, the school had just seven students from five families and one teacher, with others coming in part-time to teach dance, painting, and acting. The parents were intimately involved in starting the school and soon formed a board of directors dedicated to cooperative organization and racial integration of students, staff, faculty, and board, the first school of its kind in segregated D.C. As it grew, the school began to celebrate Christmas in the winter and Passover in the spring. Our curriculum continued to include the arts along with math and reading, and the arts invited me to hunt for meaning below or beyond the surface, to wander the crevices of a symbol in search of a way to its depth. I attended the school until I was thirteen, and Dante and Ethel, the teachers of art and dance, became my closest mentors, as well as frequent guests at home for meals and holidays.

Dante took us on trips to galleries and talked about journeys within the picture frame. "See," he'd say, "you enter the picture here," pointing to the foreground. Then he'd usher us through a landscape or among the apples in a Cézanne still life, showing us how color created tension and movement followed. Like any religion worth its salt, this teaching included social justice, and Dante explained Picasso's *Guernica*, introducing us to Franco's revolution and the International Brigade that tried and failed to save the Spanish Republic. Dante directed us in plays as well, telling us the story and letting us improvise the scenes: *Medea* one year, *The Fall of the House of Usher* another. Thus we acted out what we'd seen and heard and learned. Other communities should train their novices so well.

Second, I hadn't noticed I was missing a part of myself. My family lived in a narrow band of acceptable feeling and behavior, above gut-level emotion and below spiritual quest. I grew up as a "perfect" child, polite and respectful, but ignorant of my hungers and angers and unaware of their hidden raging. "If something is a secret, it's probably supposed to stay that way," Daddy used to say. Predictably, this made other people's private lives glow with promise, and my life became a quest to look beyond and through, within or behind, anything that presented me with a surface. Whether it was a filing cabinet with letters my parents wrote while court-ing, a manual on sex, or a drawer with birth control supplies, I would find out what was in there. Around age twelve, when I began babysitting, I'd scan the shelves for medical books and page through them, sugarcoating the chilly mysteries of anatomy with guilty pleasure.

On the other hand, secrets get told, and that was dangerous. I made sure I had nothing to tell, at least not in that spring of words that bubbles just below the surface, waiting to vent. Of course, I had no control over my dreams or fantasies, whether of romantic lovers who swept me off my feet or devilish invaders whose control permitted me to give up my own. These occupied a lower zone, safely insulated from daily life. In reality, I hung around adults as much as I could and imitated their ways, their long words and considered speech, their controlled gestures. Nourishing myself on cool approval, I gave up hopes of impulsive hugs and cuddles. I followed my ambitions but suppressed my wishes, whether for ice cream or kisses. Rejecting appetite itself, I learned not to want what I couldn't have and soon forgot that I had ever wanted it. I could say "please" at the dinner table, but never plead for love or attention. I could say "thank you," but it would be years before I recognized that my entire being had come to me as a gift. Closed off from deep craving and gratitude, and ignorant of desire, I lost the well from which religious feelings spring.

When I was six, I asked every child's first question about sex, essentially the same as religion's basic wonderment: "Where do I come from?" My mother indicated her tummy, then backtracked to outline the facts of conception. I'd seen my father naked and recognized at least one body part in her talk. Her suggestion seemed awful. Could this ever happen to me?

"What's a vagina?" I asked.

"You have one," she said, "right there," and she pointed, hand extended away from her body, willing herself to be direct and unashamed. Had she been born twenty years later, she might have encouraged me to use a mirror, and I can only imagine how stony that would have felt, my private self reflected to me like something in a supermarket meat case. I shrank from the threatened alienation.

My parents were so open to discussions about sex that, in effect, they were closed. Bodies and their processes were as flat and neutral as tables and chairs. The words that named them could be uttered boldly, arranged and rearranged until they lost the power to frighten or arouse. Testicle-intercourse-nipple-menstruation-semen-ejaculate—only   masturbation was too shameful for speech. These words embarrassed me, like Mama's pointing finger or the way she sat, legs apart, as though she had nothing to conceal. Her swirling verbiage promised control over chaotic feelings but sucked away my sense of weight and left my body feeling like an empty shell, floating in space, subject to the panic that would strike in spades in my teens. And it stole the words for speaking of desire.

My parents encouraged Sally and me to visit various churches and temples with our friends, but we never had serious discussions about these experiences. If something ridiculous happened at church, it made a good family joke, like the origin myth of the Ethical Culture Society, which explained dark skin with a story of God baking cookies and forgetting one batch in the oven. Our family viewed religion from the outside, as other people's interesting behavior. We could joke about it, but sex was serious, reduced to the icky-sounding facts. My mother's pointing finger denied both laughter and pleasure and kept us removed from each other and ourselves, while my father's distance from the rituals he studied kept them isolated from questions of faith.

School introduced me to dance, and dance became my religion. At age seven, before I even owned a leotard, I dedicated myself to the technique of Martha Graham and to the person of my teacher, Ethel Butler, who had been a member of Graham's first company.

On the far side of the school's vast assembly room, I see Ethel seated on a low stool, drumstick poised to begin class. She's just taught us the word "torso." I'm sitting on the floor in last summer's two-piece bathing suit, soles of my feet together, back ramrod straight, listening for her "and," the dancer's upbeat. "And . . ." I contract my torso and echo the drum's downbeat, bouncing my head eight times on my feet, then sit up tall, feeling as though I've just arrived inside my skin.

Until now, my body has been nothing but a vague extension of my talking head, dangling somewhere below my eyes. I've been isolated and painfully self-conscious, checking my behavior and ordering myself around. Now that I am moving with intention, I stand on solid ground, and I know where I am without telling myself. Gravity befriends me, challenging me to use it, to make it work for me. I'm in the same boat with everyone else in the class, struggling with memory, weight, strength, and stretch. The space is mine, and I'm moving out, claiming and filling it, as the class progresses from floor work, to pliés in place, to prances across the floor. I've discovered a new, wordless language that reveals feelings I didn't know I had. Trying becomes a way of being, as rhythm, form, and muscular effort wake up each cell in my body and set them conversing, excited, like a happy family reunited at the end of a day.

Ethel set demanding standards, and I fell in love with her angular, opinionated jaw and her upper lip that pursed and flattened, articulate as her feet and hands. I adored the smell of her light and woodsy cologne and the fine, brown hair that flew behind her when she leaped. Several of my schoolmates and I began additional classes on Saturdays at her studio on Florida Avenue. A small, triangular office led from the street into a long, bright studio with one white-painted brick wall facing a wall of mirrors. In back was a dressing area that gave onto a high-walled courtyard, just big enough for an outdoor shower. There we drenched ourselves after sweating through class in the swampy D.C. summers.

When my friends and I were nine or ten, we used to play tag around the studio before class, shouting and running, or sit in a circle, showing off our ability to chew on our toenails. One day, Ethel corralled us, serious. She settled amid her collection of Chinese wood blocks and Native American drums, and we sat cross-legged on the floor.

"When I was in Martha's company," she said, "Martha married Erick Hawkins. He strode into the studio the next day and announced, 'This studio is a sacred space, a temple of dance. From now on, there will be no talking or laughing, only movement and music.' We obeyed. Now you girls," Ethel continued, looking each one of us in the eye, "you can talk, but you have to stop racing around. Erick was right. A dance studio is a sacred space. Think about what that means." I didn't know how to think about it, but I was already awed by Ethel's weighty words, already feeling different from the noisy, careless child I had been a few moments before. And as I grew to my teens and practiced the Graham technique, I absorbed its sense of dance as ritual and the body as sacred vessel. Today I marvel that I entered so fully into the gesture and myth of the Graham technique without ever asking myself whether contractions or falls pointed beyond themselves to something more fundamental, an underlying or overarching object of faith.

Still, part of me always wanted to transcend those limits. At eleven, I sent away for a guide to spiritual practice I'd seen advertised in a magazine and followed its prescriptions for a while. Far too self-involved for any sort of real contemplation, I sat myself down each evening and recited William Ernest Henley's melodramatic poem "Invictus":

> Out of the night that covers me
> Black as the Pit from pole to pole,
> I thank whatever gods may be
> For my unconquerable soul.

I worked hard at the German taught in my school, memorizing proverbs and hearing the foreign phrases slide off my tongue, imagining myself a native speaker. I yearned for anything not me, different from me, beyond me, hoping it would absorb and transform my humdrum self and my flat Midwestern speech. Anything foreign offered spice, but more important, it provided escape from the embarrassing intimacy of my family and my babyish past: the slippery feel of my wet thumb, the callous my teeth had created on its second joint, and the soft fuzz I used to pluck from a blanket to tickle my nose while I sucked.

I grew from a striving child into a thoroughly secular adult, a person who never could have knocked on a parish door and said, as Thomas Merton famously did, "Father, I want to be a Catholic." Such an act would have been entirely outside my frame of reference, beyond the realm of possibility. Yet as I trace the steps that led me to the Church, I discover just as many antecedents hiding in the past, hinting at what was to come. I think of my discovery of the sacred in childhood through Ethel's words and dance itself, and I remember the desire to give I'd felt at childhood Christmastimes, compelling me to bake and make elaborate gifts. Those Christmas projects permitted a time outside of time to erupt into the progression of schooldays and weekends, suffusing the ordinary with the extraordinary. I remember the community of artists in which I grew up, but most of all, and paradoxically, I think of my fiercely secular father.

I remember the bear hugs he gave at night and his friendships with Indians, black people, and anyone in need. I see him walking down the street on a windy, wintry day in cloth coat with frayed collar, approached by a panhandler. Unlike many of my friends today, he does not stop to reflect on the "proper response" to drunks or beggars, but reaches in his pocket for coins or bills without breaking stride or losing the thread of conversation. And though he's seventeen years dead, my mind fills with his music: the violin he played as a young man, the classical records he listened to, and the folk music he played on the guitar and sang: sad ballads like "The Lowland Sea," with its valiant, drowning boy; love songs like "When I Was Apprenticed in London," its sexual meaning a sweet secret that dawned on me slowly as I grew up; and Southern mountain tunes that seemed to twine through treetops on "wings like Noah's dove."

His doctoral dissertation had been on the nineteenth-century Native American Ghost Dance, a religious revival that spread across the country. Starving Native peoples, herded onto reservations and threatened with extinction, found hope in ecstatic, trancelike dancing, anticipating reunion with friends and relatives in the ghost world. The earth would open and swallow the white invaders, and the world would return to its beautiful, natural state. The Ghost Dancers prophesied that the following spring, when the grass was high, the earth would be covered with new soil, burying the white people. All Indians who danced the Ghost Dance would be taken up into the air and suspended there. Then they would be replaced, along with the ghosts of their ancestors, on the new earth.

When I was twelve, I made a dance based on my father's dissertation. One evening in the planning stage, I was trying out various combinations of movement and music in the living room, talking to my father about what might work. I put music on the phonograph, probably one of the Bach concerti Daddy had played as a violin student. While he searched for a book, I improvised a counterpoint to the music, holding dry branches I might use as props. Daddy took a big volume down from the shelf and showed me Muriel Rukeyser's "Dream-Singing Elegy," a poem she'd written about the Ghost Dance, using his dissertation for information and inspiration. I sat down with it, and he went out to the kitchen. Much of it was beyond my understanding, but I shivered with awe when I read, "They are dancing to bring the dead back." I felt privileged and a little frightened to read about this adult experience, as my head filled with the smoke of failed dreams, of "shadows and revelations," and my nose with the perfume of "night-flowering worlds."

> In the summer, dreaming was common to all of us,
> the drumbeat hope, the bursting heart of wish
> music to bind us as the visions streamed
> and midnight brightened to belief.[1]

The concerto's slow movement began in a bittersweet, minor key, and I went to look for Daddy. Suddenly he stood before me in the dining room, eyes shining. His usually solid, reliable form seemed wobbly, as though his tears had become a sheet of water between us. I'd never seen him moved like this; not until Natasha's death would I see his eyes wet again. Taken aback, I ducked behind the door and darted to the living room. A few minutes later, composed, he put a hand on my shoulder.

"It's not that I don't want you to do it," he said.

"I know," I replied, turning back to the music and my branches, certain that he was telling the truth, but nonetheless shaky. The moment passed. He never expressed emotion about the dance or his dissertation again, and we never discussed what had moved him.

At the time, I was just as unwilling to probe the depths as Daddy. Reflected in his shining eyes, I saw my dance as powerful, even dangerous. A new kind of force had entered daily life if I could tip that rock. I was afraid but also wanted to keep my newfound strength, my access to something that touched his heart. Had I asked him what he felt, he would have assured me that ghosts were not real, suppressing whatever had affected him. The moment would have been gone forever. As it is, it's stayed alive in me for more than fifty years.

Now I think Daddy must have been moved by the unlikely connection between the Ghost Dance and me. Here was his twelve-year-old daughter, a child making a dance, picking up on a desperate movement of seventy years earlier, transmitted to her through the passionate research of his own youth. Such a linkage knits the world together.

A month after Daddy's death, I dreamed great string sections blowing like wind through a garden, bending the grass and saturating the flowers with sound, rising to a crescendo and taking on color until the dream was nothing but singing wind, grass, and light. I still sometimes wake to feel my body transparent, each cell floating on the vibrations of those same strings, my whole self filled with music. Looking back, I think the Ghost Dance inhabited the well from which my father's music sprang, and both gave me inklings of religion.

3

Snake Years

Back from Jamaica after the accident, Eric and I wept and hugged, despairing at how little it helped. We looked at each other and marveled at this new emotion, vivid and bleak.

"I don't understand it. I'm not depressed. Are you?" I asked, speaking through tears, struggling to articulate a feeling I hadn't known existed. I'd been mildly depressed before we left, feeling empty of new work for our upcoming performance season.

"No, it's different. Not gray, more like red and black," said Eric, spitting out the words as though he could rid himself of the pain by naming its colors.

"It's hot and sharp, not slack and dull like depression," I said, remembering the sag of my face and the veiled feeling that I always had when depressed.

"Depression's submerged," said Eric. "I'm not submerged."

"Not like depression at all," I said, needing to say or do something, not knowing what that might be.

Grief turned life desolate for Eric and me. The tears that choked our speech ground to empty silence, and it seemed that the smoothly meshed gears of our shared life had filled with grit. In my dance studio I listened to Mahler's "Songs on the Death of Children" and read that he had lost two daughters to influenza and forever blamed himself, convinced that the work had not just prefigured the disaster but actually tempted fate to bring it on. I wondered if my own tentative efforts to make a dance about our loss might court further horrors. We still had three children and knew that things could have been much worse for us, but sometimes it seemed like we'd forgotten how to love each other. We were always either sad or mad.

Fury had filled my chest at the moment when our car hit the embankment and rose, rearing like a horse. In that instant I thought of all the reckless chances Eric had taken in the past, like crossing four lanes of traffic at once, using bravado to mask his chronic fear. I flashed on his other stunts, like walking into a theater without showing a ticket, and in my head I said, "I *told* you to slow down, look out, I *warned* you." But by the end of that day, grief had taken me beyond anger.

In odd moments in the days that followed, I sensed in some remote part of me that I could blame him for Natasha's death, could flail with rage against him. Closer to the surface, I often asked myself what I could have done to change his impulsive, anxious style of driving. In fact, I did a lot to calm his various fears: of children falling, luggage disappearing, and governments dissolving—the latter two he'd actually experienced. But to make him take it easy behind the wheel would have required constant nagging, an annoyance that can wear down the strongest love. Perhaps I should have said, "Whatever it takes," but to my sorrow, I did not. Had I acknowledged the full reach of my anger, it would have torn us apart, and I couldn't risk that. We had each become a part of the other, and I would have lost myself had I lost him.

Neither of us ever asked, "Why me?" Bitterly, I recognized that disaster had struck in the most likely, common way: a car accident. I did not see myself as chosen for tragedy. Eric's escape from Hitler's Eastern Realm was my lucky fluke, and our crash could have taken more than one child. Children everywhere were snatched away daily, and I knew I led a privileged life. Natasha had been the light and center of my life, but the question of "why?" was bigger than one life, one death.

As for Eric, his anger was not directed against me. He became more exasperated than ever with wishy-washy, permissive education, with fathers as pals, with oppression and exploitation of the defenseless, and he developed a new hatred of abortion. Having lost one baby, he needed to save them all.

I don't think Stefan ever knew that Natasha died. At six he was still called Vuggy, nicknamed by Anton sometime during his first year, when he was still the peaceful "Zen baby" we considered unusual but not damaged. He had just learned to walk, with the ingenious help of a red wagon rigged to a tricycle by Tom. Tom rode around the house, Stefan hanging on behind, and soon he was walking without support. He'd developed a rich and fascinating jargon, like normal children have around age one, and was starting to add individual vocabulary words.

One evening shortly before the accident, my parents were visiting, and we all sat crowded around the kitchen table at dinner, Stefan on my left and Natasha in a baby chair on my right. Eric's mother, whom we called Bobo, had recently had a stroke, and lay in a makeshift bed in the dining room, to the left of the kitchen as one entered the house. Eric had been delayed at the hospital and came in the front door. Heading for the kitchen, he called out, "I'm home. Hi everyone," and ducked into the dining room to see his mother. Stefan burst into loud and sudden tears, and we all turned to him.

"What's wrong?" asked Daddy, putting an arm around him.

"Did you hurt yourself?" I asked, checking tongue and fingers for injuries. As he settled down, we realized with excitement and delight that he'd missed his father and cried with disappointment, expecting Eric to greet him and make much of him. Soon Eric returned to the kitchen.

"What happened?" he asked Stefan. "I heard you crying." He turned to us.

"It was you," I said. "He wanted you."

"Me?" said Eric, spreading his arms wide and then wrapping them around Stefan. "Here I am, Stefan, right here," and he stepped back. "Daddy's here; Stefan's there," pointing. Stefan was wordlessly happy. "Look," continued Eric. "Arms up!" and we all raised clasped arms overhead in the game that had started as an exercise for Stefan, now become a celebratory gesture for all of us.

Stefan always had likes—outings, McDonald's, music—and dislikes—pain and the hospitals where he endured so much. But this event at dinner went beyond like and dislike and showed how little he suffered the self-containment of autism, though that word was often included in his diagnosis. Autism's repetitive behaviors were plain to see in him, but he was very social, loving to talk and never wanting to be alone. I thought it only natural that a person as different from others as he would grow to show some signs of autism, if only from his isolation, but his autism was more consequence than cause.

As an adult, he couldn't follow a story, but if he saw a person downcast or weeping on television, he would say, "He sad," and I was often surprised by emotional connections like these, beyond his intelligence.

As I wandered the newly silent house after the accident, my hands reached toward emptiness, and I missed the one I'd cared for, played with, and read to. My attention turned more fully to Stefan, and I took him to weekly swimming classes at the Y, where he floated happily with water wings. I worked with him daily on activity cards designed to foster development, recorded his vocabulary words as they increased, and tried to improve his tooth-brushing and dressing skills. He became fully toilet trained.

My attention also turned in a new way to the two older boys. "Natasha the friend is dead," wrote Tom in his journal. He made a vow to her that he would bury all his money, the nickels he'd earned pulling weeds. He felt that all he'd strived for, like compassion and learning, counted for nothing if Natasha could be taken from him.

I yearned to make up his loss, to give him something to care for. He'd always loved animals, and now he became fascinated by snakes. We bought a boa constrictor about a foot and a half long, gentle and languid, with rectangular dark and light brown markings on its back. Accustomed to the humid tropics, the snake dried out and couldn't shed its brittle skin. I'd never touched a snake, but now my task was clear: run warm water in the sink and massage it until strips of skin softened and peeled away. Gradually I overcame distaste, and snakeskin joined the legion of substances I'd learned to take in stride.

Anton was still yellow-green and swollen from bruises, eyelid stitched and leg in a cast, physical damage somehow insulating him from grief. Eighteen months apart, the boys were the same size and had shared clothes until now. One evening we all sat down in their bedroom and pulled the clothes out of the closet: piles of pants and shirts, sweaters, underwear, socks, jackets, boots. Eric held up a pair of pants. "Who wants these?" he asked, always ready for a game and enjoying competition.

"I do," said both of the boys, jumping up.

"Wait, there's lots to come," said Eric. "Here's a sweater. One gets the sweater, and one gets the pants. You can trade later if you see something you want more."

"You can have those pants," said Tom, "if I can have the gold shirt."

"You can have the gold if I can have the purple one," said Anton.

"One pair of pants and the purple shirt for the gold shirt," said Eric. "Going, going, gone."

"Then I want the plaid shirt too," said Tom. They bounced on the bed as Eric handed out the bounty, each accumulating a stack like poker players sweeping up chips. I sat folding and arranging the clothes into two separate drawers, never engaging in the competitive games played by the household's males. Appalled that we had not divided the clothes before, I wondered: is this what it takes for us to recognize the boys as two separate people? Tom's mourning and Anton's injuries broke my heart almost as much as my own loss of Natasha, to say nothing of her loss of a whole life. I had brought so much grief to all my children, when I'd intended to make them happy. The folded clothes accumulated, shirt on shirt and pants on pants, little piles of hope that we could once again make a good and orderly life for the boys we'd come so close to losing.

At the same time, I continued to work with my dance company at the Body Politic, making *Tropical Juice*, the dance that began at dawn on a mountain. I saw Jamaican women descending, heavy loads of fruit on their heads, necks weaving gracefully from side to side. The women break into a run, pounding, crashing to the floor, and rebounding, in a nine-beat phrase divided *taki-taki-taki-gamala;* then the stage blacks out to reveal spotlit, freeze-framed groups, a series of discontinuous moments. Finally, the women begin a long, slow requiem to sounds of drum, washboard, and triangle, composed by Douglas Ewart. The dance concludes with fading light, that terrible day ending again each time the curtain falls. A singer sang the words I'd written that night in the yellow kitchen to a melody also by Ewart:

> An instant shatters into seeds and pulp
> God's juice has leapt its banks
> Escaped from time.
>
> A fruit is squashed one sultry afternoon
> Time's flow escapes, explodes
> The river dries.
>
> A fragile bird was trapped and now flies free
> Unknown to flesh and juice
> Beyond the leaves.
>
> The tropics bear the fruit and see it fall
> Death slaps the face, confronts
> The living seeds.

I'd never made a piece before without a man in the cast, but Natasha's birth and now death had taught me to love my own kind, and that love took shape in the dance. The piece became a reenactment of that terrible day, starting at dawn with the accumulation of dancers on the mountain and ending with the drawn-out requiem in failing light. Though I did not know it at the time, the original *La Bayadère* ballet takes place in a Kingdom of the Shades. Arlene Croce describes the accumulation as "a crescendo that seems to annihilate all time . . . a ritual . . . a language being learned . . . a ballet that grows heavy with that knowledge."[1]

Perhaps this is how that structure became ritual to me, the closest thing to a real funeral our secular way of life allowed. Liturgists say that every culture has a way to formalize and celebrate the end of life, but our family had no religion at that time, no connection to any ritual community, no way to gather and remember. Memory was too raw for us to share her pictures or tell her stories, and any sort of invented service would have intensified already unbearable grief. Casting about for symbols, we planted an apple tree for her, later built a memorial pool and fountain in the yard.

In April, while I was working on *Tropical Juice*, my friend Francine came to call. I'd met her at "tot lot," a play space for toddlers, ten years earlier. Our first children had been the same age, and we'd provided each other with adult conversation while watching our kids. She sat in a chair in the plant-filled dining room, her voice rambling quietly, while I stood ironing long bias strips in brilliant colors, making head wraps for *Tropical Juice*. The green walls reflected a cool, peaceful light, and the slow, steady task kept me focused as her voice rose and fell: a quarter inch under on one side of the orange, all the way to the end, back on the other side, fold it in half, iron the crease. Coil the strip, lay out the purple. Still, it took all my energy to hold together the edges of the wound inside me, and I could barely keep my mind on what she said. Suddenly her words broke through: "What are you going to do with the remains?" she asked. I stopped and stared at her, fury making my guts boil and outrage rising to pound against my chest. My breath came in jerks. Remains? Is that what she'd just called Natasha?

"You shouldn't have asked that," I said, violating my self-imposed rule against confrontation. How could she reduce this person, just beyond my grasp, to an object?

"I'm sorry...I didn't realize..." she said, flustered, rising. Perhaps she spoke a few more words before she left, but I didn't hear them.

I thought of my baby on the table in Jamaica, how the nurse had pulled a cloth up over her face. I'd lowered it to kiss her forehead, mouth, and belly, then pulled it back up and wished I could tear my blouse like orthodox Jews in grief. That laughing stomach, that thinking brain, the "I" I'd so recently seen behind the eyes—"remains"?

A few minutes after she died, I'd glimpsed through a door in the hospital a stranger fastening a tie around her jaw, and I'd not gone to her, unable to witness the body without the life. Though part of me knew a worker was simply preparing the dead, I could not separate Natasha's body from herself, could not accept that the person was "gone" while the body was "here." It seemed we'd abandoned her in Jamaica; left her in the ditch where life had begun to seep from her body. Indeed we *had* left her in Santa Maria's hospital as we rushed the boys into an ambulance bound for the hospital in Kingston, *life is for the living* repeating in my head like a mantra. When my husband in Chicago said, "They'll send her here by air," I thought for one impossible moment that she'd flown back to life, as though bright bias strips could bear her up like wings.

She did return to us as ashes, but surely the ashes were not her. Ashes, dry as dust and cool, are nothing like the body's heated blood and bowel, its fluid breath. If not contained they'd blow away, drifting like a final exhalation. Only bone, reduced to fragments, comes through the fire with weight enough to fall. Between the living body and its ashes lies the corpse, the body's dark afterimage. But a corpse is not a body, and a body is many things besides a piece of flesh.

Body can divide us into "skin-encapsulated egos," in Alan Watts's words, yet it often joins us to our fellows, as in body politic or the Church as the body of Christ, doing Christ's work in the world. The body of a text reveals its message. A full-bodied wine fills the mouth, its legs running slowly down the glass. Body is the heart or center of anything, but it's also the outward form of the self. By means of my body, I encounter the world. Everything I am or do is expressed through my body, formed and articulated like star-shaped cookies extruded through a press.

My sense of who I am expands and contracts with the balloon of my attention, clinging closely to my skin when I watch it, expanding freely to intersect with others when I forget myself in active engagement. When Eric and I talked, our ideas came to life in the space between us, and parts of each of us flowed in and out of that space. When we made love, our skins were transformed into fluctuating, permeable membranes. Maxine Kumin observes this in her poem "After Love":

> Afterwards, the compromise
> Bodies resume their boundaries.
> These legs, for instance, mine.
> Your arms take you back in.[2]

Small wonder that orgasm is called *le petit mort*. And after *le grand mort*, after the corpse's return to earth, what does in fact remain? In the story "Order of Insects," William Gass's narrator protests the tragedy of human attachment to transitory flesh. "Alas for us, I want to cry," she says, "our bones are secret, showing last, so we must love what perishes: the muscles and the waters and the fats."[3] But the soft parts cooling are not the living body, any more than tooth and bone alone are self. When we return to the dust from which we came, doesn't our voice still echo in the vacant room? Like an abandoned chair that rocks alone, doesn't our breath still stir the air?

A few months after Francine's visit, a cardboard box arrived on our front porch labeled with a customs declaration and Jamaican stamps. Standing in our front hallway, I showed it to Eric, and he turned away. "You can open it," he said. We'd grown accustomed to taking turns bearing the brunt of each new reminder. Vaguely hoping to find something of Natasha inside, I carried the box to the kitchen, cut the tape, and lifted out a flimsy, copper-colored urn, so light as to spite my expectations. A cap lifted off freely, revealing a paper tag with pencil scrawl: baby Natasha Kast. Below that was a cheap seal, a lid like a Mason jar screwed on tight. I shuddered with outrage and disgust at the word "baby," my baby, in proximity to this piece of junk, then cried. I would not look inside, for I could only lose more of her than I already had. What I held was nothing but dust. I carried the urn to the hallway table and found Eric at my side, also in tears.

"She wants light," he said, and I nodded. If she wants light, I thought, then she should have it. Back and forth went my sense of her as a person, now retrieved by Eric's words and allowed to linger on the useless urn, then so obviously absent. But the ashes were all we had. Eric carried them upstairs, and together we put them on a high shelf in the study, where light from three windows flooded the room.

Later, as memory faded, Eric used to say that Natasha had become for him "a depth without a surface." But even when her image seared my brain and the scent of her soft hair and skin lingered milky on her clothes and dolls, her absence signified to me a presence that I can only call her personhood, something more than the corpse we abandoned to flames or the dust that came by air. Her careful sentences—"I bringing book and chair"—her sunshine song, her desire to color within the lines: these were what remained.

By May I was pregnant. I remember driving north to the Body Politic on one of the first warm days, stomach faintly queasy, knowing I wanted to move forward but unwilling to release the old attachment. Suddenly it seemed as though the one depended on the other. Traffic stopped, and I tried deliberately to release Natasha, to let her go, so God could infuse the cells in my belly with a new little soul. I did say "God," though I didn't know what I meant by the word, or by "soul" either. The words sprang up to name experiences I'd never had before. I was humbled, realizing the life inside me could not have been, had the other not been lost, that this new life and Natasha's death were hopelessly intertwined. Her birth had given me the girl I wanted, and four children under seven had been almost more than I could manage. The car moved forward, and I proceeded to teach my dance class, but the old and the new continued their tug of war within me.

I clung to the pregnancy, grateful and fearful, and began to sense realms within myself higher and deeper than the narrow band in which I'd been living. The polite, self-controlled "please" and "thank you" of my old life faded away. Along with gratitude, I was learning to ask, to yearn, to plead, to know my hollow hungers and suspect that there was a well from which I'd sprung, a home I hadn't found. I'd always thought that "real" meant tangible, observable, or subject to proof. Now those ideas seemed simple-minded to me. Who could touch a dream or an atom, observe the subconscious, or prove a moral judgment? Perhaps I'd never known before what "real" might mean.

In June, Tom's boa constrictor died. He sat on the edge of the fountain we were building in Natasha's memory, the cement still wet.

"It's wrong, it's not supposed to be like this," he wept.

"We'll get another one," I said.

"No good," he said, "it's wrong." Three months of misery poured out in a flood of tears. He took a stick and made some marks in the cement. Eric and I placed a rock on top, preserving the inscription, exchanging a glance that meant we knew that love and mourning mingled snake with sister, sister-snake.

At loose ends, we filled the emptiness by painting the house, the most disruptive maintenance chore, then put Stefan into respite care and went to Vienna, where we often revisited scenes of Eric's youth. Four months pregnant, I was uncomfortable standing, and each time we waited for a cab or a train, Tom made a seat for me by dropping to his hands and knees. We traveled by train to New York and stayed overnight at the Plaza, where the boys were thrilled, at tea in the Palm Court, to discover Martin Mull sitting a few tables away. We had all been fans of the absurdist TV show *Mary Hartman, Mary Hartman,* and Mull was now appearing in the successor show, *Fernwood Tonight.* I remember the boys' discovery and delight, how I tried but couldn't quite give myself to their joy because of the grief that tugged at my eyelids and glued me to my seat.

In Vienna, we took the boys to the Zauberklingerl, a store devoted to magic tricks, and the Wurstelprater, an amusement park with cars they could drive themselves. Eric breathed the air and walked the cobblestoned streets, always trying to reconcile his love and hate for the city that had raised him up and then kicked him out. Usually I loved the inventive salads, the new wine, the country hikes, and the theater, but this time I felt bloated, nauseated, sleepy, and sad.

When we returned, I had an amniocentesis, delayed by the trip until well into my second trimester. Doctors recommended it not only because I would be almost forty when the baby was born but because of Stefan. He now fed himself and talked a lot, but he'd need special care and supervision all of his life. We waffled. We would not abort a handicapped baby, yet I did not think I could care for a second disabled child. If I took this peek inside God's kitchen, I might find the promise of another girl.

During the night after the procedure, I tried not to notice the baby's odd stillness. Fetal movement was impossible to predict, I reminded myself. The doctors had assured us of very low risk for the procedure, and we'd examined all the data at length, focusing on the likelihood of Down's syndrome at my age. The next morning, at the hospital, we strained our ears for a heartbeat until hope and fear gave way to painful recognition.

The precious life in my big belly had become a foreign body, and I had to get it out. I'd delivered all my babies using Lamaze breathing and Eric's coaching instead of anesthesia, but now the doctors told me I'd have "monumental" contractions that I couldn't control.

Furious about the amniocentesis and utterly dispirited, Eric went home to the children. Tom, also enraged, later accused the doctor to his face of killing the baby. I was embarrassed to think of my brash ten-year-old accusing the doctor of murder and was glad I had not witnessed it, though I knew Eric was equally angry and had perhaps been equally outspoken. I did not blame the doctor, whose help I still needed, but saved my fury for the medical system that never reported the likelihood of fetal death from amniocentesis or the number of cases like mine where the sampled cells didn't grow, making the test useless.

I made it through that induced labor alone, grim and determined to survive, using my Lamaze training to spite the doctors. I insisted on calling the event an abortion. I did not miscarry; they had aborted. Eighteen hours later, I sat on a bedside commode, and a blue, four-month-old fetus dropped into the bowl. A boy. In part, my physical struggle shielded me from grief, and I did not mourn the pregnancy as deeply as Eric or the boys. But in my heart of hearts, I knew that my unnamed little boy's death made space in my body for the daughter I still needed as much as life itself. Right or wrong, and no matter how selfish, I needed a girl. As soon as possible, I would get pregnant again.

A slim and graceful green snake, native to the Midwest, came that summer. Tom and a friend overturned rotting stumps and harvested worms to feed him. The next year, a king snake: black-and-white banded and strong. Native to California, and almost too big for the three-foot cage, he fed on living mice. The first day, I brought a mouse home from the pet store, lifted the cage's wire screen, and dropped it in. The whole family stood around the cage and watched the snake strike with sharp teeth, then lasso the mouse in an instant coil. Slowly, slowly, the snake's jaw unhinged. For hours we wandered in and out, checking on the progress of the mouse within the snake, shocked, yet knowing that we also kill to eat, that snake and mouse, though enemies, both have roles to play in some larger economy.

One day in the fall, we found the cage empty, the wire-screen lid askew. Tom searched, to no avail. Winter came, and our mouse problem disappeared. One morning in spring, just before dawn, I rose and went into the bathroom. There in the half light, behind the toilet, camouflaged by black tile and still slow from hibernation, lay the snake. I snatched it up, shouting, "Look what I got!" The lazy creature wriggled slowly as I woke the house, holding it overhead and parading from room to room, triumphant.

Shortly thereafter, scrounging the neighborhood for discards, games, and new amusements, Tom found his way with friends to an Episcopal church. The church was seeking young participants, and Tom, unbaptized at ten, became an instant altar boy. Diapers, snakes, mice, church—surely I could rise to this challenge. One Sunday, I drove him to the service, leaving Eric at home with the others. Tom went to change, and I found a seat near the back, tense and embarrassed, hoping to be invisible. I'd get by in this alien land by doing as the natives did.

The organ swelled, and Tom came down the aisle, swinging a censor before him, looking angelic with thick, brown curls above white choir robe. Facing straight ahead, I glanced surreptitiously right and left to know when I should sit or stand, sing or be silent. In front of me and to one side, an African American woman drew a magenta silk shawl about her ample shoulders and flung herself from pew to kneeler. She seemed so generous, so open, as she abandoned herself to prayer. I felt my body stiffen in response, a board from toes to shoulders. I could never do that. Feeling the resistance, I also felt the challenge. Why not? What would it be like, I wondered, to place myself at someone else's mercy? Did the silk-shawl woman know something that let her kneel with so much trust? A spicy cloud of incense spiraled up from Tom, rising and diffusing.

After the service, I patted him on the shoulder; glad to see he was still the same mischievous boy in jeans and sneakers, joking with his friends and eager to jump on his skateboard. When I returned to my familiar world, I put these thoughts out of my mind, but they stayed in my body, a curious temptation: what would it feel like to fall onto my knees?

4

Reconfigured Atoms

EARLY IN 1978, I conceived again. I'd not succeeded in saving either Natasha or the pregnancy that followed, and surely I couldn't take credit for this new life inside me. Events were beyond my control for better or worse, but somehow patterned and fraught with meaning. Unlike pebbles rattling around in space, we were all tied together, the living and the dead, in ways beyond our understanding. The word "God" began to permeate my continuous dialogue with Eric, filling numerous cocktail hours with explorations of what it might mean.

"Maybe 'God' is a word for ultimate reality," I'd say, perched on the wooden radiator cover in the front room, holding my vodka on the rocks.

"That's too intellectual," Eric would respond, stretching his legs in his reading chair and taking a sip of his Campari and soda. "To me, God is the person I address in the elevator going up to my office, the *lieber Herr Gott*."

"Always in German?"

"Of course, God only speaks German." Eric was fluent in both English and German but had lost the ability to speak any language without an accent. We both laughed, enjoying the luxury of uninterrupted conversation now that the boys were ten and twelve and Stefan content to play records on an endless succession of Fisher-Price phonographs, guaranteed to last and thus replaced for free each time his rough handling destroyed a machine.

"Seriously, though, how do things exist?" I asked. "It makes sense to me for God to be a ground of being."

"Not a father?"

"To me God is more child than father, Baby Jesus."

"Baby Jesus at Christmas, yes. But to me, God is the loving Father I never had."

"I think of Jesus more like a child, the person he was to Mary."

"*Fortsetzung fort*," said Eric, "to be continued," as I checked to make sure Stefan hadn't gotten into any of our good records, then went out to the kitchen to finish preparing dinner.

During this period, Eric made some tentative moves toward a Church he'd known from the inside before I met him, the Roman Catholic one. Though Jewish by birth, he'd been baptized Lutheran and converted to Catholicism in his twenties. By the time we met, he was as secular as I. Now I asked him what the Church was all about, and he brought me home an old-fashioned Baltimore Catechism, with its succinct and formulaic questions and answers. I read:

Q. Why did God make you?

A. God made me to know Him, to love Him, and to serve Him in this world, and to be happy with Him forever in heaven.

"This is fine if it works for you, but I can't possibly believe it," I said. He went to see the priest at our local church, St. Thomas the Apostle, and told him about Natasha and about his new and passionate abhorrence of abortion.

"What did the priest say?" I asked.

"He asked me what I considered my greatest sin." I wish I remembered what Eric's answer was or whether he answered at all. I know there was no failing that I recognized. I later understood that the priest had welcomed Eric back into the Church through the sacrament of Reconciliation, Vatican II's reinterpretation of Confession, but I don't think Eric even knew about Reconciliation at the time. He did not begin attending church until later, but he'd sown seeds, the kind that fall into dark and wintry ground, then sprout to yield who knows what fruitful harvest.

Eric's mother, Bobo, died that summer. She had always wanted to be buried in Vienna's Zentralfriedhof, next to her parents and husband, under a stone she had already inscribed with her name and date of birth. Eric packed up her ashes in a suitcase and flew with them to Vienna, taking Anton with him and leaving Tom and Stefan with me.

At home with the two younger boys and used to relying on Eric for orientation in life as well as for driving directions, I was lost. I could cook and care for Stefan, but handling a boy on the brink of adolescence was something else. I could no more balance entertainment and discipline for

Tom than I could figure out how to drive to the North Side, and I felt like I was skittering on the glassy surface of an unknown planet.

We invited Michelle, the ten-year-old daughter of friends, as well as a friend of Tom, to stay for the weekend. She arrived at our door, her straight, slim body dressed in a skimpy halter top and shorts, fresh from a child's version of EST (Erhard Seminar Training), an intensive, sometimes punitive self-development program. I imagine she might have been scared, confused, or disoriented after such an experience, but she didn't say much about it, and her manner was alert, bold, and self-confident. Tom had slicked down his curls in preparation for her arrival, and the two hit it off immediately, running out in the big backyard to play. Together they had an air of precocious sexuality that made me uneasy, but I couldn't think of anything to do but keep an eye on them and let them be.

That night I was ready for sleep soon after the summer's long evening. I put Stefan to bed and told Tom and Michelle to turn out the lights. Two hours later, I awoke and heard them prowling around. "Go to bed now!" I said. They appeared to acquiesce. Two hours later, they were still up. "If you don't go to sleep, we can't go to the air and water show tomorrow." I should have said "we *won't* go," meaning I wouldn't allow it, but I couldn't imagine what we would do if we didn't go, so my threat lacked teeth. They stayed up all night.

The next day I drove them to the near North Side, sat on the rocks beside Lake Michigan, and watched the spectacular formation flying, diving, and swooping of this annual show. Tom's curly hair, gelled for style, and Michelle's straight brown dangled over their drooping eyes as they sat on the rocks just below me, heads nodding, sweating through the long afternoon. I felt them slipping through my fingers, as elusive as the whining planes, already as disaffected as the adolescents they would soon be.

That weekend I got my first hint of how Tom's grief would reconfigure the atoms of his soul, arranging them for angry action. A picture he drew shortly afterward shows a face, half of which is distorted by grief, tears flowing, mouth turned down. The other half bristles with rage, and sparks fly from the eyes. Disaster had disillusioned him, and he would give up on good behavior, good grades, and generosity. None of these could undo the evil of Natasha's death, so he'd decide to go the way of the devil, as he called it, and make his own rules.

Two weeks later, Anton and Eric returned from Europe, jubilant. We sat in the front hallway, finding perches on a suitcase or the stairs, listening to stories that couldn't wait.

"They wouldn't bury Bobo," said Anton, his pretty, almost girlish face animated, shaggy brown hair around his ears. Tom came down and joined me on the stairs, and Anton embraced Cane, the dog we'd gotten him when Tom got his first snake.

"Michelle stayed over," said Tom. "We saw the air and water show."

"How was it with Michelle?" asked Eric, long beard and hippy-style brass chain hanging low on his chest.

"Great," said Tom. "We got along fine." Cane jumped up and licked Anton's face, then ran around in circles.

"They changed the rules," said Eric.

"What do you mean?" I asked. "They buried your father when he died."

"Ashes aren't allowed anymore," said Anton.

"Only uncremated remains," said Eric.

"So what did you do?"

"You tell the story," said Eric to Anton.

"We went to a hardware store," said Anton, articulate beyond his age, scratching Cane behind the ears. "We bought a trowel and took the streetcar way out to the Jewish cemetery." I'd been there many times, for Eric and I used to wander amid the overgrown, sometimes deliberately overturned gravestones of the Jewish cemetery, choosing names for our children from the ranks of the dead. The cemetery's wild beauty stood in stark contrast to the well-manicured Protestant and Catholic sections, a reminder of the millions who had no descendents. "We smuggled the goods past the authorities," said Anton. "No one tried to stop us. At the gravesite only birds and squirrels were around. So we dug a hole big enough for the can, and buried it, and smoothed over the top. Then we put a little rock on top, like people do there."

"What about the inscription on the stone?" I asked. Anton and Tom had started talking to each other, and Eric explained to me that Bobo's date of death would be added to the stone without question.

"Remember 'Wer weiss wo er ist?'" he asked, reminding me of an inscription for someone who had died in the camps. "'Who knows where he is?' They don't need a body to add the date."

With Eric home, I settled into pregnancy's contemplative waiting, intensely hopeful. I watered my herbs in pots on the porch, as late-afternoon sun released the smells of basil, rosemary, and oregano, grateful that this pregnancy was uniquely free of nausea. I snipped them as the long evenings darkened and sprinkled them on rice or salad, making dinner on the old Garland stove, apron protecting my modestly swollen belly.

The air cooled, and the sky grew brilliant blue, yellow leaves bold against it. Anton had applied to several schools for junior high and had turned down the University of Chicago's Lab School, afraid of its reputed snobbishness and competitive atmosphere. Then they sent him a letter asking him to reconsider. This tribute to his qualities as a student was hard to resist, and he succumbed. The school year began, and Anton entered seventh grade at Lab. My due date came and passed, and each day I contemplated the bright leaves fluttering against the brazen sky, a promise of something bold and beautiful.

At two in the morning on October 19, we left all the children asleep and drove to the hospital through air cool and thick with fog. Anton and Tom were old enough to care for Stefan if he awoke, and a sitter would arrive at eight. The delivery suite was almost empty, quiet and sleepy, in contrast to Natasha's delivery, which took place just after Christmas in a suite so full that women in labor were waiting on gurneys in the hall, timing their contractions under dangling paper bells and sleighs. This time my labor progressed rapidly. A resident cupped my stomach with gentle hands.

"This one won't be nine pounds," she said, referring to Tom's birth weight. Soon I was fully dilated; usually an occasion for panic, but my trip to the delivery room seemed to take place in slow motion. I waited.

"Push," said the doctor, looking bored. It was four in the morning, and he'd wanted to induce, to save himself this predawn work.

"I don't have an urge to push," I said, frightened by the absence of that compelling impulse when I was used to urgency both in my body and in the room.

"It's OK," he said. "You will." Soon reflexes took over, and I pushed out a baby so tiny, it seemed as though I viewed it through the wrong end of a telescope. A girl! I laughed and cried, amazed at the good fortune of having Erica, not trusting my luck.

"She's so little," I said. "Is she OK?"

"Five pounds, fifteen ounces," said a nurse. "Anything over five and a half is normal." Later I realized she was small because she was real, a newborn person beginning her life, not a reincarnation of a three-year-old. We went home later that day. Lab School had scheduled an open house that night for parents to visit the rooms and see the students' work. Erica had not yet started to nurse, so I left her at home with a trusted friend and went to the school, triumphant about being up and about after a successful childbirth but humbled by the bounty that had been showered on me: a girl, a second chance.

Stefan was seven when Erica was born. One day when she was two or three months old, I heard her screaming in her crib, sudden, loud screams not preceded by the gentle cries of a waking baby. I dashed from the kitchen upstairs and found Stefan standing on a rung of the crib, reaching over the rails and scratching her face with his nails. Horrified, I scooped her up and assessed the damage: red, crescent-shaped nicks in her cheeks and forehead. I took her into the bathroom, washed her face, and comforted her, and Stefan followed me, watching.

"Stefan, you hurt the baby," I said. "That's bad. You mustn't do it again." He looked blank. "Were you angry, Stefan?" No response. "No matter how angry you are, you mustn't hurt the baby or anyone. Do you understand?" He grunted "Hmn-hmn" but said no more and showed no signs of either anger or regret. Eric reinforced the message when he came home that night, but we did not punish Stefan. Erica was only mildly hurt, and we would make sure in future that her door was always latched when she slept. Though my first concern was for Erica, I was impressed by Stefan's development. Now, apparently, he realized he had a rival and was jealous. Like the day he missed his father, this seemed a milestone. He never hurt anyone again.

Shortly after Erica's birth, the altar boys at the Episcopal church returned to hunting grubs and playing ball, and Tom turned to St. Thomas, the church where his father had talked to the priest. I doubt he even noticed the small denominational differences between Episcopal and Roman Catholic churches, and for me, they were nothing compared to the gap between my upbringing and any form of Christianity. I began to accompany Tom to church for the same reason I bathed his snake or made him birthday cakes.

On Easter Sunday, we entered a packed house of worship. From the back, the assembly looked like a sea of flowers: pink, pale orange, yellow, and light blue. The priest moved through the aisles with water and a sprig of greenery, dipping the branch and showering drops over the crowd. Like wind over a field, the drops created a wave of heads and backs, as each person responded to the shower by bowing and making the sign of the cross. This call and response made one great gesture, reflecting the shared impulse of all the spring flowers.

Knowing I didn't belong there, I still wanted to be part of that joyful, submissive wave. I sat, kneeled, or stood carefully, accepted my neighbors' extended hands for the "Our Father" without meeting their eyes, and worried about the precise moment to let go. Despite discomfort, I accompanied Tom each Sunday after this, and the folk-style music released waves of feeling dammed up for years. I had no idea what was happening to me.

"Lamb of God, you take away the sins of the world," says the congregation three times before receiving Communion. "Agnus Dei, qui tollis peccata mundi." *Peccata*, like peccadilloes. The straight-backed goody-two-shoes I'd always been found it hard to embrace the role of sinner. "Grant us peace." "Dona nobis pacem." Suddenly I wondered: Could Natasha be the Lamb of God? The thought shocked me. What did I mean by that? Was it possible that her death could be right or redemptive in some way? The atoms of my soul were reordering themselves as truly as Tom's.

Soon after Erica was born, I stopped taking Stefan to weekly therapy and swimming classes and began searching for a day school for him. He attended a number of them before we found the perfect fit, and transportation was an ongoing problem. The bus services used by the schools often hired unreliable drivers, and I had to wait each morning with Stefan in the front room, watching out the window, until the bus came. The whole family invented rhythm games to keep him amused:

> Where is Stefan's little yellow bus?
> Is it a red bus? No, No.
> Is it a green bus? No, No.
> We need Stefan's little yellow bus.
> We want Stefan's yucky yellow bus!
> Where oh where is that nasty yellow bus?

We sang and clapped, Stefan joining in on the ends of each line. It could take hours, but he didn't mind. Eventually we found Esperanza, a school that used the Rudolf Steiner method of "curative education," and there Stefan remained. In practice, this meant an emphasis on the arts, attention to beauty in every aspect of the environment, and kind, supportive, respectful teachers. It was perfect for him.

During Erica's first months, I nursed her, cared for her, and watched her grow. If she could grow past three years, two months, and fourteen days, a hole in the world would be filled, a wrong righted, a debt repaid. It wasn't that she could replace Natasha or relieve grief, but that Eric and I could make a new start, doing our best to avoid the wrong choices we'd made in the past. Acting as though we could control the course of events by being careful, we were overprotective of Erica. Without knowing it or meaning to, we taught her to be scared, though we wouldn't notice the effects right away.

She sat up alone at three months, the first of my children to do this so early. I showed the pediatrician how she sat in my lap, and he was dubious.

"Let's see how she does on her own," he said. I plunked her down in the middle of his examining table, and there she sat, back ramrod straight, inclined very slightly forward, the triangle of her chubby legs balancing the weight of her spine and big head. At five months she recognized people and screamed if I handed her to anyone unfamiliar, behavior more common at twelve or fourteen months. She liked the regular sitter we had in the day, while I went to work at the Body Politic, and sometimes we left her at night with her brothers, but we rarely went out in the evening before she was five.

When I picked Erica up and patted her back, she would pat mine too. What a rush of warmth I felt! Maybe she was just imitating me. Maybe, like her first smile, her response acquired meaning from my interpretation, and I did interpret it with amazement and pleasure, but it felt like empathy. What could be more seductive than a baby who reciprocated my care?

I suspect that I withdrew from the older boys' lives in certain ways during Erica's first years. Her growth and development were like showers of rain, like the healing river that "wash[es] the blood from out of the sand," in the words of the traditional hymn. She herself was as much a sign of salvation as anything that happened in church. In part, my withdrawal was a natural division of labor between Eric and me. I was nursing and needed for infant care, and I had the patience to deal with Stefan—getting him to come or go; persuading him to dress or undress; helping him or, harder, refraining from help. Parkinsonism had made diaper changing nearly impossible for Eric, and coaxing Stefan made him feel weak, which he couldn't tolerate.

The boys were becoming teenagers, Tom voracious, impulsive, and rebellious, Anton equally angry but meticulous, compulsive, and filled with self-loathing. Both chafed against the formulaic restrictions of school. Eric had the fortitude to deal with the older boys' extreme emotions of rage, disappointment, and frustration, as well as the insight to help them. I supported all their creative efforts, attending performances and school events, but I was glad to let Eric take over the struggles, whether with him or with school or friends. They scared me.

As I continued to attend Mass after that first Easter, the ritual offered me riches that went far beyond the Baltimore Catechism. Each celebration lifted me out of time's lockstep and drew me into a timeless present, sometimes to weep, sometimes to wonder, and once in a while to reach some understanding of this foreign faith.

"My body is broken for you, and yours for me," said a young East Indian man, a theology student, preaching one Sunday on the meaning of suffering. "We are Christ for one another." His quiet conviction drew me in, while I wondered: then more than one person can be Christ? At least one hymn, "Anthem," said "yes":

> We are called, we are chosen
> We are Christ for one another
> We are promised to tomorrow,
> While we are for him today.
> We are sign, we are wonder
> We are sower, we are seed
> We are harvest, we are hungry
> We are question, we are creed.

Question and creed, yes. This encouraged me to explore, unlike the conclusions of the Baltimore Catechism, and the possibility filled me with joy. Another Sunday an older theologian, presiding, introduced himself: "My field is Christology." It's an "ology," then? A great vista opened before my mind, enticing. I could spend the rest of my life trying to understand what it meant to "be Christ." Later, studying Christology myself, I came to an understanding of Christ as paradigm of what God would like to do for each of us, a model to which I could try to conform my life.

My response to liturgy was mainly emotional. I would weep through the rubrical prayers, the words spoken each Sunday all over the world, then calm down during the more informal, didactic homily, then weep some more. I didn't know what moved me, but I loved the liturgy, and my love literally poured out. Gradually small snippets began to make intellectual sense, and I discovered an inexhaustible world of dialogue among experience, reflection, faith, and understanding.

More and more, I began to hear a call to be all of myself. Transcendence no longer meant becoming not me, but on the contrary, becoming all the contradictory things I was, from the most selfish and self-reliant to the most trusting and grateful. Acknowledging my deepest hunger, I began to feel connections that fed me, little tendrils that linked me to every other human. I faced the choir at St. Thomas, the ceiling a hundred feet above me, and dialogued with the singers, echo-style:

> O healing river, send down your waters
> Send down your waters, upon this land.
> O healing river, send down your waters
> To wash the blood from off the sand.

My voice seemed to rise from my feet in an unimpeded, resonating column and stream from my mouth in a great outpouring. Though I wept, the tears came so freely that no tension strangled my voice. Doors opened inside me, allowing a free exchange among body, mind, feelings, and spirit. No concealment. No pretense. No secrets.

> Let the seeds of freedom awake and flourish
> Let the deep roots nourish, let the tall stalks rise.
> O healing river, from out of the skies.

"Unless a grain of wheat fall on the ground," I thought. I had come across these lines from John's gospel in the earliest days of my grief, and they had stayed with me:

> Truly, truly, I say to you, unless a grain of wheat falls into the ground and dies, it remains alone, but if it dies, it bears much fruit. (John 12:24–25)

There was Natasha, enduring winter in the cold ground, breaking open, "remaining a single grain." The God I sought was one who did break things open, like grains that fall, sprout, and eventually bear fruit; a God like my husband, brash and bold and enjoying confrontation, breaking me open like a black, ripe fig, spreading the thin, green layer to reveal the red, myriad seeds inside, sweet and juicy and ready to go make more figs. Not the God of my fathers or my father playing God, not a God of control or judgment, but a God who plays the world from the inside like a rotating kaleidoscope, creating jewellike patterns that crumble, collapse, and configure all over again. Could I hope that Natasha's death would "yield much fruit"? It already had, with Erica's birth.

By winter of 1979, Tom was having serious conflicts with his teacher at Ancona, the Montessori school where each of the kids except Stefan had started. I don't remember the exact nature of the conflict, but I think it had something to do with a letter he had written and accusations he had made. I do remember a conference with the school's director where she said with a sort of awe, "I've seen kids like him cut quite a swath through a school." After Christmas, he decided he wanted to live with my parents in Wisconsin Rapids and attend sixth grade at Howe, the public elementary school there. I didn't understand why he wanted to leave home, and I saw it as a sign of failure on our part. Eric said, "Go ahead, go," always afraid of appearing seductive to the kids and determined to be the strong father he never had. My parents were willing, and we accepted the arrangement.

Looking back, I think accidents and birth order had made Tom the ultimate middle child, and he needed attention. I remember visiting him at my parents when he was just becoming expert on a skateboard. It was winter, and he rode the board around the tiny furnace room of their split-level home.

"Watch me," he said, and I rose from the living room, where we were having drinks before dinner, and stood in the furnace-room doorway. He turned on a dime in the small space.

"Terrific," I said and turned to go.

"No, watch this," and he repeated the maneuver. "Wait, I've got something else." He went the other way along the little alley around the furnace, coming to a precise stop right in front of me, beaming.

"You're getting really good," I said. His need for affirmation seemed endless, and I returned to look over and over, faintly embarrassed by his

freedom to demand. At Howe he was able to shine, popular and successful, smarter and more advanced than most of the kids, a sophisticated
boy in a small town. He stayed there a year, flirting with girls and playing
alto sax in the band. Eventually he was caught shoplifting fireworks and
came into conflict with my father over rules and authority. After a year,
my parents sent him back.

Eric, Erica, and I returned from grocery shopping one day when she
was two. We stood her on a chair at the kitchen table, where she reached
into the bags and helped unload: a box of spaghetti, a carton of cottage
cheese. I turned my back for a minute, putting a can on a shelf, and she
tipped forward, caught her collarbone on the table's edge, and fell to the
floor, screaming. We took her to the hospital for X-rays, suspecting a
break but not too worried, knowing how minor a broken collarbone can
be. Anton had had this injury at a slightly younger age, and he ran around
freely as soon as he got a simple gauze tie across his chest and under his
arms. Not Erica. Once she had the tie in place, she was calm and peaceful,
but unnaturally immobile. She lay on her back for days while I read to her
or played with her, apparently afraid to move. She sat to eat and showed
no signs of pain, but a stronger force had overcome her typical two-year-
old energy. Somewhere among the subtle details of our tones and touches,
we had destroyed her trust in the world, without meaning to and without
knowing it, and try as we might, we couldn't return to our old careless and
confident ways.

5

Cleave the Wood

ERIC, STEFAN, ERICA, AND I began going to church together, Eric taking Erica out to play when she got restless. Stefan grew to love it, refusing to leave after the service if the slightest bit of music continued to play. After church we would walk home, talking with excitement about the scripture, the homily, or other aspects of the liturgy, me percolating with new ideas, feelings, and energy. At home I would continue the celebration, serving hot soup, maybe chicken and chickpea, with homemade bread and salad. We began to pray before we ate, joining hands and using a prayer designed for Stefan's participation, "Thank you Jesus for this food, amen," pumping our hands up and down in time to the rhythm.

At the same time, my inner experience of conversion was private. While I cooked and played and danced and talked, my developing awareness of God and sense of the Christian story continued on its own track, parallel but separate. In memory, my spiritual experiences exist in a kind of bubble, in but not of my daily life.

Moved by the Mass but unable to say or even think that I wanted to join the Church, I stumbled on an ad for Calvert House, the campus ministry of the University of Chicago. "Investigate Catholicism," it suggested. I considered it OK to *investigate* anything. Thus, I started attending meetings of the catechumenate, the community of people preparing to enter the Church, and learning what the Church was all about.

The Second Vatican Council had replaced private, individual instruction in Catholicism with a group process called the Rite of Christian Initiation for Adults, viewing conversion as a gradual and psychological form of change. The group met one night a week in Calvert's comfortable living room, where we heard a presentation on some aspect of Church teaching or practice: Advent or Lent one week, the sacrament of Marriage or Reconciliation another. Then we moved into a small chapel for a brief prayer service and finally down to the basement for refreshments and talk.

Each session was like a wake-up call to the meaning underlying some part of Catholic teaching: oh, that's what it really means. Our text was a book five times the thickness of the Baltimore Catechism, published in 1966 and intended for adults: the Dutch Catechism. This book revealed the history and significance of feasts, fasts, and other observances. As I read it, I felt myself once again immunized against isolation, much as I'd felt after my first son was born, when I'd realized that this person who was once a part of my body was now another person in the world, yet flesh of my flesh.

The group included a pool of sponsors, from which one could choose. Beth, a young social activist, gave a presentation on social justice in a subdued but humorously subversive way, and I recognized in her a person who shared my critical take on the world but nonetheless had faith. Her voice was soft, with a slight Southern drawl, and her manner accommodating, but her intellect was as sharp and searching as her blue-gray eyes. I'd found a friend.

The liturgy was calling me more and more forcefully to the Church, yet I could not make the move to enter the catechumenate. It did not fit my self-image to call myself a Christian, even a Christian-in-training, and I never told friends where I was going when I went to Mass. I knew my father would not understand. Despite his tolerance, he could not accept real difference from those close to him, and he'd know he'd failed to provide me with an ultimate source of trust.

About the same time, Tom entered seventh grade at St. Thomas, the church school, and his interest in religion reawakened. He began taking instruction in preparation for Baptism, resumed serving at Mass, and chose my parents as godparents. They came to Chicago for a preparatory meeting, and we sat on wooden pews with a few others in the spacious, drafty church as the priest, Father Fitz, explained the responsibilities of godparents: essentially to love and guide the child in faith. My parents sat there in their typically tolerant way, present and unmoved.

Mama's habit was to keep her integrity in church by never bowing her head, and this fit with my image of her unbendable body. Daddy, however, always did as the natives did. Whether bowing in church or exclaiming "How!" at a Native American ceremony, he was always a participant-observer, accepting everything but holding something deep and personal in reserve. Father Fitz was so confident that everyone in the room shared the faith that he never mentioned it. No one asked my parents whether they were Catholic or Christian or even if they believed in God. How could they possibly serve as godparents? I wondered. I was baffled, just in the process of giving up my parents' way of life and moving toward a Christian one. Now I smile when I think of Father Fitz's casual attitude toward identity and belief, a sign of his deeper and less rule-based faith. I tend to agree with the greater value he placed on relationship. Tom wanted my parents as mentors, and perhaps the "God" part was less important. Still, it was hard for me to accept my parents as guides in faith.

Later, as a student at Catholic Theological Union, I would empathize with the discomfort of classmates from Asia and Africa when a professor suggested ways that ancestor worship could be honored within a Christian service. "That's what we turned away from," they said. "That's what we gave up." I'd felt exactly the same way when I saw my parents' names as godparents on Tom's baptismal certificate. And still later, when I joined the liturgy committee at St. Thomas, I would learn to value even more the depth, broadmindedness, and humor of Father Fitz's faith, which reduced the rules for liturgy to two: no human sacrifice, and don't call downtown.

Eric, much more flexible than I, encouraged me to move beyond "investigation" and enter the catechumenate. "If not now, when?" he asked. On Valentine's Day, 1982, he put on his green and gray Austrian suit, and we walked the cold blocks to Calvert House. There, in the middle of Mass, Beth and I stood in the small, carpeted chapel while she blessed each of my senses in the Rite of Entrance.

"Receive the sign of the cross on your ears," said the priest. "May you hear the voice of the Lord." Beth made the sign over each of my ears. "Receive the sign of the cross on your eyes: may you see with the light of God," and she signed my eyes. The blessings continued with lips, breast, and shoulders, "to accept the sweet yoke of Christ," and the words of the rite resonated with my desire to hear and see the word of God, to walk in God's paths and do God's work. I entered the catechumenate with enthusiasm.

Full of excitement, impatient to reconcile every contradiction I found, I began the journey to Baptism at Easter. Beth was always ready to discuss the obstacles.

"What do you think of the Church's views on sex?" I asked.

"Nuts," she said, as we read a simpering passage in the Dutch Catechism that indicated female sex drive was less than male and thus girls could avoid masturbation. "The nuns in school told us that sex was bad. I always thought if it were bad, it would feel bad. But when I discovered it felt so loving, caring, and even healing, I knew it had to be good. God would approve." Similarly we hashed out issues of local autonomy, autocracy, and attitudes toward women and gays. We began talking during the social hour that followed each session and occasionally going out for coffee after Sunday Mass. She was searching for meaning and truth as much as I was and helped me to see Catholicism as a path I could follow, inquiring and discerning, rather than a destination demanding certainty of belief.

A cradle Catholic, Beth came from a local community with a strong sense of social justice. She introduced me to the Religious Task Force on El Salvador, and together we marched in front of the Salvadorian embassy, protesting the massive U.S. aid to that repressive government. For me, this was new: shouting slogans in public and carrying a sign. I'd been home with infants during the Viet Nam protest years and probably would have been too timid to march anyway. My father supported the war, though Eric and I did not. Now I felt new courage, standing up and being seen, opposing my father as much as U.S. policy.

"What's the relationship between faith and justice?" I asked Beth.

"After you've been doing political work for a while, you ask yourself why. It helps to have a fundamental reason," she said. Unfortunately, her upbringing also included a strong element of self-negation. Humility and self-sacrifice were prescribed and meant you could go to bat for the poor, but not for yourself. Once when she had a small business importing handmade *animales* from Mexico, she told me her family was shocked she would use this work for personal profit, to make money.

"What if you enjoy it?" they asked. They understood that a person had to work to live, but going beyond this, with an entrepreneurial venture, threatened seduction by evil, especially if the gain were mixed with pleasure. Thus faith and self-realization were opposed for Beth. Only twenty-three when I met her, she grew to find her own way in marriage, social work, and writing, politically active but more and more distant from the Church.

On Sundays, we catechumens were dismissed before the second half of the liturgy to reflect on the readings. I welcomed this opportunity to study and question and considered it right to defer Communion during this time of preparation. But now I began attending daily mass and stayed for the whole service (without receiving). Each day, just before noon, I walked the six blocks to Calvert House and sat in the L-shaped chapel with transparent, plastic altar and Z-shaped presider's chair. At Communion time, the smell of wine slowly filled the room, and I marveled at the earthy reality of the church's bread and wine, the communion it offered with others and with God.

One inquiry session at Calvert House was devoted to prayer. We gathered in Calvert's carpeted, beige-toned living room, and Rosie, a fellow catechumen, offered her experience.

"If I ask for something or give thanks for something," she said, "it changes my place in the world. I'm not getting through life on my own anymore." I'd resisted the spirit of prayer at the Episcopal church and responded emotionally at St. Thomas, but I'd never connected liturgical prayer with any personal act. Rosie's words made me think, *I can do this.* I began to rise early and go upstairs to my dance studio. Kneeling on a blanket before a low window, I watched the dawn silhouette bare tree branches, then sat cross-legged with my back to the wall, a cup of coffee at my side, a cat draped around my neck. Without my noticing it at first, a space opened inside me, a vast inner space that I could explore. Sometimes it spread out wide like a meadow and sometimes turned back on itself like a cave, with intriguing nooks and crannies. In this space, I could talk to God and, on the better days, shut up and listen.

We did not have a literal dialogue that could be transcribed. But slowly, like rootlets reaching into earth, I began to feel connections to the rest of the world that enmeshed me in a loving reality. Though I sensed myself exploring and discovering, the realms into which I reached were beyond words, as miraculous as the complex maze of blood vessels in the placenta that enable a baby to live and grow. Opening myself to thoughts and feelings soon gave rise to physical desire, and I came down from the studio in time to crawl into bed with Eric and make love before we had to get up and start the day. He was happy to wake up this way. Both sex and prayer touched my deepest center, and each gave meaning to the other, sex lending passion to my hunger for God and prayer infusing sex with holiness. Eric discouraged me from talking about this connection.

"Don't make sex too holy, or I won't be able to do it," he said. I was content to keep my strange thoughts to myself, knowing there are always four people in love's bed. If I wanted God in there, the least I could do was let Eric choose the extra partner that fused his body to his heart.

Sponsors took turns preparing the prayer service in Calvert's chapel each week, and thus each service had a different focus and personality. One might be about Christian unity, showing that the faith was originally one, another about the meaning of dying in Baptism and rising to new life. One evening as I sat there, I noticed that my prayer space had opened in this new location. Participation in group prayer had accessed my private space, and I noticed it suddenly, pleased to discover that it existed outside of the studio at dawn.

Later I learned to laugh at the idea of a "sacred pew," the common feeling that one must sit in the same pew in church in order to have access to the holy. Yet this idea is grounded in the very human, if erroneous, suspicion that God is tied to a specific place. Consider the story of Naaman, the leper, in the fifth chapter of the second book of Kings. The prophet Elisha cures him of leprosy. Naaman wants to offer sacrifice to Elisha's God, Yahweh, and asks if he might bring "two mules' burden of earth" back to his native country. Naaman assumes the God of Israel to be bound to Israeli earth and plans to import it, mule load by mule load. I love the way this story shows how the concept of God evolves slowly from a god of my place and people toward one of all. Still, I had to make my own discovery that my prayer space could traverse the six blocks from my house to Calvert, without transporting earth.

While I was still in the catechumenate, I danced for the first time in a church. A Disciples of Christ church in a neo-Gothic building offered me space for *Dies Irae* (Days of Rage), an extended solo with a short trio section. Like *Tropical Juice,* this dance was a sort of personal funeral, but it gathered together several deaths. Lynn Masover, Eric's young research assistant, had died suddenly in the South Pacific, writing poems about another young friend dying of cancer. I began reading the work of Anne Sexton, who courted death like a lover and finally killed herself, and I listened to the music of Anton Webern, shot accidentally just after the end of the Second World War. I fantasized a "death collection," a sort of big bucket into which I put each death I encountered, stirred them together, then added the music Lynn had always said she would want for her funeral, Verdi's triumphant, dramatic *Requiem*.

Though *Dies Irae* was a dance of death, it was equally about discovery of the holy. Where *Tropical Juice* blinded with brilliant, stark colors, emphasizing absence, *Dies Irae*, gray and purple, enriched the stone sanctuary with multiple presences, released from my collection. Verdi's music swept me into a whirlwind of rage and triumph, the reality of death yielding to one greater. I danced Verdi's "Sanctus" with ardent joy and conviction, the church's stone gargoyles like Isaiah's six-winged seraphs inviting me to join their cry, "Holy, holy, holy!"

Somewhere between *Tropical Juice* and *Dies Irae*, a change had crept into my dance-making process. I had often used words with movement, but now the words gained ascendance, and I couldn't focus on the intricacies of movement as I had before. I couldn't go inside the envelope to find the detailed gesture, because my gaze was fixed outside the gesture on an external purpose. The dance was merely a vehicle to serve something beyond itself, and all I could think about was that something.

I noticed this at the time on the fringe of my awareness, but much later, as I wrote about dancing in sacred space, I discovered the essential rivalry between art and liturgy. Bishop Albert Rouet, who writes about liturgy and the arts, discusses competition for the sacred. The arts community wants to symbolize the sacred on its own terms, while liturgy sees the sacred as "channeled, modified and shaped by the person of Christ."[1] Within my own body, liturgy was edging out art, and the two continued to compete within me as long as I was dancing, me standing in the middle and wishing I could have both.

Inevitably, the Roman Catholic Church attracts some people who like structure and want authority, and sometimes that means personal authority. Cardinal Cody was still archbishop of Chicago when I came into the Church, and he set an autocratic tone. My relationship with Father Barnes, the pastor of Calvert House, was never an easy one. Though I saw myself as a submissive inquirer, he saw me as a threat, and my son Tom, now a teenager, even more so.

The former Episcopalian altar servers were still on some sort of mission from God, though the direction could change with the wind. Shortly before Easter, Tom and his friend Philip, a Haitian American, decided to check out Calvert House, maybe attend daily mass or go to Confession.

Like many at the University of Chicago, the staff at Calvert House was highly wary of crime, and neighborhood kids, especially black and white teenagers, were doubly suspect.

As far as I remember, they did attend Mass, and perhaps they asked for Confession, giggling, or took a few steps up the stairs toward the priest's living quarters, or poked around the living room too much. I know their bodies always seemed to claim every space they entered, as they shoved a chair to one side or sprawled on a sofa. In any case, the priest asked them to leave, and they brought the story home.

Eric was furious. Father Barnes suddenly became a medieval crusader, Cardinal Innitzer and Pope Pius XII all in one. He became the perpetrator of every hurt that Eric had received from those who viewed him with suspicion, while Eric became the defender of everyone on whom the Church had trampled. He turned on me. "How can you go along with that man's actions? How can you accept what he's done to your son without protest?"

I was only a few days from Baptism, deep in a process to which I was fully committed. I knew I had to be reconciled in some way with Father Barnes before Easter, and I searched for the impossible: some way to justify my entrance into the Church both to Eric and to myself without antagonizing the priest. Confession, of course. I would confess my fear that the Church would not stand up for the underdog, for that was precisely what had offended Eric so much. Only partially aware of my strategy, I dressed in pastel colors, wore no makeup, and rolled my hair in a bun, all devices to make me seem as demure as possible. Father Barnes did not fall for this subterfuge and reacted defensively to the criticism that was inherent in my raising the issue at all.

"I can't have kids coming in and out of here whenever they feel like it," he said, "and you have no business telling me how to run this place." The issue of the Church and the underdog had flown out the window, and now my humility was real. He'd rejected my effort at peace, and I was devastated. Eric would say, correctly, that I'd been trying to win his sympathy with a nonaggression pact, a tactic bound to fail. Yet what else could I have done? Expressing my anger openly would have gotten me nowhere. Father Barnes was the gatekeeper, and I wanted in. I could not continue the journey without taking this step, and I credit Father Barnes with accepting me. A few days later, at the Easter Vigil, 1982, I became a Catholic.

Spring was late and Easter early that year, and I'd taken scrupulously the injunction to fast on Good Friday and Holy Saturday. The ancient Easter fire had been lit outdoors, and the congregation assembled around it, stamping feet. The priest lit the Easter candle from the fire and blessed it with words dense with meaning, thickened by centuries of use:

> Christ yesterday and today,
> the beginning and the end,
> Alpha and Omega,
> all time belongs to him,
> and all ages;
> By his holy and glorious wounds
> may Christ our Lord guard and keep us.
> May the light of Christ, rising in glory,
> Dispel the darkness of our hearts and minds.[2]

"Light of Christ," chanted the priest, while we each kindled tapers from the big candle. We followed him into the University of Chicago's neo-Gothic Bond Chapel, singing "Thanks be to God" and squeezing into pews. Next to Beth, in flickering shadow, I listened as a cantor intoned the lengthy Easter proclamation. He sang praise of Adam's *felix culpa*, the "happy sin" that made possible the story we now heard: Creation, slavery in Egypt, Moses's triumphant Exodus through the Red Sea, Abraham's offer of his son to God, Isaiah's prophecy of a servant who will suffer.

Then the organ started to rumble, lights blazed, and a great processions of flags waved down the central aisle: pink shading to red, purple, and blue. The organ shook my bones, and we stood to sing "Alleluia!" Beth turned to me: "Happy Easter," she said, and her face glowed in the light. The priest dipped the Easter candle into the font to begin the liturgy of Baptism. It's easy to miss this symbolic act of fertilization, in which the font becomes a womb. From this womb, the Church—that's us—is born. With others, I was doused and spawned.

The shock of first Communion: bread in my mouth, dry and crumbly, then a soggy lump. Did I think that the presence of divinity would eliminate bread's grain and yeast and nourishment? "Fruit of the earth and work of human hands," says the liturgy—of course it tastes like its humble self. If left uneaten, this bread would be buried in the ground, returned to earth. I ate the blessed and broken bread and laid it to rest in the grave of my stomach, where it shared its divinity with me, reaching into my most obscure corners and suffusing them with light, the transformed bread beginning to transform me. "Be what you see," says Augustine of the Eucharist, "and receive what you are." Swallowing food for a lifelong journey and born from the fertilized font, I became part of the body of Christ in the world, warmed by those around me and illuminated by the Easter candle burning in the dark, spring night.

Shortly thereafter, Beth and I and another new Catholic proposed a social justice committee at Calvert House. One evening we met with Father Barnes, who greeted us at the door and led us up the stairs to his study. "Oh," said Beth, her voice pitching upward to tease, "he's wearing his blacks."

"Well," said Father Barnes, hearty, "what are we going to overthrow today?"

"Just the U.S. government," said Beth.

"As long as you don't overthrow me," said Father Barnes.

Our committee floundered at Calvert, but this interchange has stayed with me as I try to understand my relationship to the Church. Despite her leftist politics and upbringing in a family and parish that did support the underdog, Beth was not threatening to Father Barnes. Apparently he was satisfied that she would not overthrow him.

I said nothing that I remember at that meeting, but I'd been reading allegations of fraud against Cardinal Cody, and I knew Father Barnes had cancelled his subscription to the *Chicago Sun-Times* because of its investigation into the cardinal's finances. Perhaps Father Barnes sensed skepticism or a hardness of heart somewhere below my submissive surface, something that would prevent me from teasing him about his clothes.

In fall of that year, I started classes at Catholic Theological Union, a graduate school of ministry located near where I lived, in Chicago's Hyde Park. My faith, to quote St. Anselm, sought understanding. I studied the liturgy that had drawn me so irresistibly and began integrating faith and movement in liturgical dance. At the autumn equinox, the school celebrated the Feast of All Saints, and the homilist at this Mass talked about the Celtic New Year's festival called Samhain, the origin of our All Hallow's Eve, or Hallowe'en. The Celts believed that at the equinox, a crack developed between the worlds, allowing one brief glimpses of eternity. This image stayed with me: the world of passing days and weeks existing parallel to a world that does not happen but simply is, outside of time.

Occasionally I get a peek. I might be driving on an ordinary day when suddenly I see some dusty leaves or a barren tree crack, as though struck by lightning, its true nature suddenly shining with blinding light before it dims and returns to blowing dirt or naked branch. "Cleave the wood," says Jesus in the gnostic gospel of Thomas, "and I am there."

PART TWO

6

Opportune Moments

"Cleave the wood," yes, but that is not as simple, direct, or definitive as the blow of an ax. A crack that had developed as I sat alone in a yellow kitchen led me both forward, toward the Church, and backward, to discover antecedents of faith. Just as Daddy's Ghost Dance and his music gave me inklings of religion, so a chance encounter with the Sistine Chapel frescoes gave me an early sign of hope, warming a chilly world.

When I was about thirteen, in a place I no longer remember, I glanced up at the night sky and was seized by panic. Perhaps I caught a glimpse of moon or stars from the window of my third-floor bedroom in our Washington, D.C., house. Maybe I was at summer dance camp in Massachusetts and stood outside my cabin in an open field, the Milky Way a broad swath undimmed by city lights. Terror of the vast and empty sky took root and grew, so that wherever I was, I only needed to think of stars to realize that I too was hurtling through space, unattached. What I'd seen in the sky was *all there was,* anywhere, stones and space and more space, stretching to infinity. How could I live without a "where" beyond or around the universe, something to hold all of it, something to make human sense out of matter, motion, and cold atomic facts? These words, *that's all there is,* slammed back and forth in my head, held me in their teeth, and shook me.

I had recently moved from my third-floor bedroom, next to Sally's, to the piano room in the English basement of our Georgetown house. When panic struck, I'd leave my bedroom and race up and down the stairs, seeking a way out of my mind, ashamed of the disorder in there and afraid to tell anyone what I felt. If I moved fast enough, the sensations of churning legs and rapid breath would take over from the thoughts. I'd invoke names from the past, people who'd lived in this same universe and called it home: Plato, Shakespeare, Pavlova. The world was crowded with warm, jostling bodies, more than I could ever know or see. I tried to hang on to this sense of belonging, but the terror kept shoving it aside, claiming for itself the privilege of fact.

No night skies invaded my nestlike basement bedroom, carpeted and a little dark even in daytime. The window showed only the street and passersby. My parents and I brought the wooden desk I'd waxed myself from upstairs and placed it facing floor-to-ceiling bookshelves. The drawers of that desk made perfect hiding places for the elegant but unusual lunch items Mama packed, making my conformist self squirm in the high school cafeteria. Ashamed of my shame and afraid to hurt Mama, I couldn't tell her I preferred a regulation square sandwich, and so my stash accumulated, foil-wrapped chicken legs turning green and plastic containers of salad mushrooming into balls of gray wool.

I did homework at the desk late at night, after school and rehearsals, eyes drifting up to the multivolume *Century Dictionary-Encyclopedia* on the bookshelf. Always trying to avoid thoughts of stars in space, I memorized the headings on those volumes, and now, more than fifty years later, they rise up, carrying the damp, slightly mildewed smell and private solace of that room: AB—Celt., Celt.–Drool, Drool—EFG, and so on. Long hours of dancing at the studio where I took class had the same reassuring effect as my race up the stairs. When I strove against gravity or succumbed in a choreographed fall, I felt rooted and related. Floor was hard, muscles ached, and others moved in unison with me, our bodies sharing space with an intimacy greater than talk or touch could yield. But if I stayed too late or worked too long alone, scary thoughts would start to bounce off the studio's bright walls and mirrors, and even the discipline of practice couldn't crowd them out.

Panic came and went as I lived an outwardly normal life at school and home, and my disconnection was countered by my warm relationship with the adult teachers I loved and emulated. Dante, our art teacher, could explode with sudden anger, something we kids both feared and admired. His face would grow red as he marched with flat-footed gait to your table, buttons threatening to pop over his fat stomach. God help you if you were drawing careful outlines with a pencil or, worse yet, erasing. His hand slammed down on the table. "Use color!" he'd say, snatching the pencil. "Fill the page!" We'd exchange glances, giggle, pick up a big brush, and swirl paint across the paper.

Though neither of my parents would have connected festivity to faith, I learned ritual at home. We celebrated everything: not just Christmas Eve, Christmas, and New Year's, but also St. Patrick's Day, birthdays with homemade cakes, picnics even in winter, clam roasts on the beach in summer, an all-day cookout with a haunch of venison on a wood fire for the Fourth of July. The minute Thanksgiving was over, we started on fruitcake, cutting up whole candied fruit with knives dipped in water, then dousing the baked cakes with brandy and nurturing them until Christmas. The same sharp knives served to cut delicate deer and trees and angels from cookie dough, each one an individual creation to be pierced, painted with colored glaze, and hung on the tree. On my own I made equally elaborate gifts: model houses; hand-painted cards; bizarre glasses of layered, colored liquids instead of stockings for the adults; a deck of cards I shellacked one by one for Sally, working all night in a walk-in closet until the fumes threatened to suffocate me.

One unusually warm night before Christmas in 1950, the doors stayed open as my father brought the Christmas tree inside. Sally and I ran in and out, pleased by the winter freedom, while Daddy engineered the tree stand, then sent us to the basement for ornament boxes. Sally began to decorate the tree, following a carefully prescribed order: first lights, then ornaments, then tinfoil icicles, each one precisely vertical, and finally weighted holders for real candles. We would light them when the sun went down on Christmas Eve and Day, watching and singing carols as they burned, reserving the electric lights for more casual times during the season's twelve days.

The usual progression of minutes and hours seemed to stop as the house filled with the mentholated, woodsy smell of pine, and furniture shoved aside to make room for the tree made the familiar suddenly strange. Suspended in the present, I waited for vision. Dante and Robert arrived, laden with aluminum foil, red ribbon, and double-sided tape. Daddy fixed drinks, and Mama put a big pot of water on the stove for spaghetti, while I stepped outside to fetch the mistletoe we'd bought. Suddenly, in the quiet and solitude of outdoors, my awareness shrink-wrapped itself around my puny, sticklike self, and my spirits sank. Was Christmas losing its power to transport me? I passed Mama in the hall as I came back.

"Do you lose the magic of Christmas when you grow up?" I asked. She paused, looking up from the box she was unpacking.

"Christmas," she said, in her slightly detached way, as though quoting someone or making a speech, "is the time when we celebrate the miracle of birth." I moved on down the hall, holding what she'd given me close to my heart, saving it for nourishment but afraid of looking at it too closely or spoiling it with sticky fingers. I could have asked her what she meant. "What's a miracle?" I might have asked, and "Why birth?" I ended the discussion, fearing the power of words both to evoke feeling and to suppress it. I would not speak of the unspeakable, lest I imprison it. Instead, I went on making things in a search for meaning that remained obscure, no matter how many cookies I baked, cards I painted, or mittens I knitted.

After supper, my father got out the guitar and practiced Christmas music, carols of every country and age. From the Trapp family book he'd learned "Es ist ein Ros entsprungen," about a rose blooming in the snow at Jesus's birth. He sang the sweet, modal song the Virgin sang, "When she to Bethlehem was come," from a medieval collection. Stories that he couldn't and wouldn't tell were fine when set to music.

Thus, long before I encountered Christianity, I had an inkling of a present that could break into the flow of time, a time without anticipation or regret, a time to simply be, though it would be years before I even thought about why I made so many gifts and decorations and what purpose these rituals served. The rhythm of gathering and celebration was hard-wired into me, body and soul, long before I encountered the Church.

Dante's open heart exemplified for me a life of feeling, color, and taste, and a dinner party at his house has stayed with me for over fifty years. I was close to thirteen the night my family and I left the damp of a D.C. winter evening to enter his warm hallway, then clamber out of slushy boots and coats. Dante mixed the adults glasses of whiskey and soda and made me my favorite, Coke-and-milk, a sort of modernist root beer float.

"Come out to the kitchen," Dante said to me, taking my arm and guiding me past a table set for twelve with candles, wine glasses, and two sets of plates. "This is my mother, Gabriella," and he gestured toward a round-bellied, gray-haired woman encased in white apron. She indicated with upraised arms that her hands were too full of flour to hug me, and I saw with amazement that the board before her was full of noodles she'd made by hand.

"Here," she said, "put these on the table." I carried out some small plates of mozzarella dressed with olive oil and black pepper, garnished with black olives, and put one at each place. We returned to the living room, and Dante sat with one foot under him, arm over the back of his chair, lit a cigarette, and addressed the group.

"What did you think of the play?" We'd performed *The Fall of the House of Usher* the week before, and I'd played Lady Usher, buried alive in that dark and gloomy house.

"Great," said my father. "Scared me!" I looked down, self-conscious, then up at my father's approving face above his fat middle, paisley-patterned tie, and double chin. His affection shone on me, and I permitted myself a brief slouch.

"The moment when you step through the door and reveal your half-dead face—that was dramatic," said Ethel, the dance teacher I adored, her bright red lips curved around the words with precise articulation.

"Good work," growled Verne, Ethel's lanky, reticent lover. Memory makes me the focus of this discussion, yet Sally must have been there too. I don't remember what role she played.

"So well rehearsed," added my mother from across the room, holding a cigarette as though it were a flower, ribbons of smoke streaming from her nostrils. My mother's praise was easy to win but cool, like a checkmark on homework or a grade in school. In fact, she never disapproved or punished. A withdrawal of attention or a raised eyebrow carried the threat of what was left unsaid and easily kept Sally and me in line, as though the air itself were the enforcer. No one ever shouted or slammed a door in our house, and I'd almost never seen my parents angry. Dante and Ethel could argue loudly at parties and hug each other the next day, and I loved to listen to them debate art or politics.

"You see kids acting from the gut like that, it gives you a good feeling—here," said Dante, indicating his crotch. I saw my mother's eyes go glassy; then I looked away. Dante was gay, as Mama had told me, speaking openly as usual about the facts of life, but never about the feelings. My friends and I whispered "homosexual," and the fact hung in the air, a piquant variation on which I might hitch a ride to some variations of my own.

"Verbal kids don't really act 'from the gut,'" said Robert, Dante's partner, "until you take the words away." His slanted black eyebrows attracted and intrigued me, with their hint of menace. He always seemed to know more than he was letting on. We moved to the dining room and continued talking as Robert poured wine, giving me a little and filling the glass with water. Within a year, barely fourteen, I'd be sharing cocktails, coolly requesting, "Scotch and soda, please," letting the alcohol release my self-consciously straight upper back but still playing the part of a little grown-up, never wobbly or loud.

"That's why I let the kids improvise," said Dante, picking up where Robert left off. "So they express the feeling before they kill it with words. Remember, Maggie," and he turned to me, "how I made you scare yourself before you started talking? Sometimes you let your mind play games, like a toy wound up to spin along the floor, and then the words come out without the sense." I heard the criticism and cringed.

Silverware clattered as we began to eat. After the antipasto, Gabriella served the noodles I'd seen in the kitchen, the *plato primero* now tucked with little nuggets of meat and coated lightly with tomato. How different from my mother's bright red spaghetti sauce! I heard my father's deep voice begin a long story, "In nineteen hundred and forty . . ." and I explored the way the noodles hid the bits of beef within their folds and filled my mouth with winy sauce.

Next came the *plato segundo,* roast turkey, in modest slices. I'd only had turkey at Thanksgiving, surrounded by its cornucopia of trimmings, and this one seemed so understated, like the clean lines of modern art or the stark gestures of my idol, Martha Graham. Then spotless leaves of nearly naked lettuce, grapes in a bowl of water, and homemade *amaretti.* The nutty crumble dissolved in my mouth, and I went on nibbling as we sat late in the table's circle of light. Cold, night skies had never seemed so far away.

Well into my young-adult years, appetite seemed fraught with danger to me, whether it was for food, sex, comfort, or attention. I sought satisfaction in order to eliminate desire, always afraid I would want too much and never get enough. Without realizing it, I turned my back on friendships I might not be able to have, rejecting before I was rejected. Longing itself shamed me as weak and needy, so I learned to push away my wishes. To me the good state was one of stasis, where I could feel whole, complete, and at peace, perfected and essentially dead.

I never knew when panic would spring to life. I suppose my moving to the basement did nothing to help, for I surely needed human contact then more than ever. Often, when I was frightened, I'd ask myself if it were death I feared. I'd try out the fantasy: suppose you could live forever. What then about the moon? The answer came back on a fresh wave of terror: without death, no end to the infinity of space.

When I talked like a machine, Dante's partner, Robert, was quick to pick up the metallic clang. His summer place was the site of an art camp, where four girlfriends and I painted mornings, explored Connecticut's rocky hills and waterfalls afternoons, and rehearsed Greek tragedies nights. One evening we plotted a trick, gleeful, bouncing on the beds in our sleeping loft. Robert sat on the floor, a willing accomplice. He smiled and scowled at once, light and dark and laughing.

"I can catch frogs," said one of the girls. "I'll get a bunch of them."

"Are they sacred animals too?" asked another.

"No," I said, "just snakes. But frogs have power too." The week before, we'd found an intact snakeskin in the woods, and now it rested on the mantelpiece in the loft. It had to be a god, or else the remnants of a god. The snake was unknowable and, above all, missing, the remains uncorrupted and beautiful. The snakeskin pointed beyond itself to something evanescent, something holy.

We'd consulted Robert, who knew Japanese, a sufficiently esoteric language, we thought, for worship. With a black brush on a small square of white paper, Robert wrote for us "Hebi," the word for snake, and its ideogram. From these we invented a pantheon of gods and a heaven called "Kazan." Looking back at our made-up religion, one might say that we were hungry for faith, but I don't think we ever missed what we didn't have. Rather, we were exercising the muscle of religious imagination, reading the mystery of animal skin, and inferring presence from absence, the unseen from the seen. We were following a sort of childish Via Negativa, in which one searches for God by exploring all the things that God is not. Our snake religion, like our dramatic and dance productions and art classes, was an exercise in discovering symbols and joining them in actions. All of these prepared me, remotely, for the great imaginative leap of faith.

Our ceremonies quickly became a means of outwitting the adults. We already had one of them on our side.

"So what are we going to do with the frogs?" asked Robert.

"You'll be the priest," said a girl, "with a frog in your pocket."

"At breakfast," I said, jumping up, "wait for an opportune moment and . . ."

"Then stand up," said another, "and chant or something . . ."

"OK," said Robert, "then what?" We all began to talk at once.

"You take out the frog . . ."

"At the perfect opportune moment . . ."

"And hold him up . . . solemn!"

"Then dip him, real slowly . . ."

". . . Opportune moment . . ." I repeated.

"Just cut that!" Robert's deep voice drove through the chatter, like a punch in the gut. "Just cut that stuff about 'opportune moment'!" The room hushed as I sat, isolated, stripped of my garland of fancy words, the pretense that concealed my buried self exposed. Slowly, the ripple of chatter returned to fill the silence with plans for a froggy ritual, while I sat wordless, ashamed of what my friends had seen.

Though Robert's reaction seems mean to me today, I still feel grateful to both him and Dante for being on to my game, for trusting there was more to me than the monkey who aped grown-ups. Beneath my showy words, they must have heard a resonant voice, and they probed fearlessly for it, demanding and reprimanding, seeking the person that only my husband would fully bring to life.   And though we all agreed the frogs were just a joke, I'd thank the empty snakeskin, my first intimation of the holy, for calling me to escape the neutral zone, to risk deep feeling and imagine a world beyond my limits.

Shortly after I moved to the basement, I came upon a recording of *Lost in the Stars*. This musical tragedy by Maxwell Anderson and Kurt Weill was based on Alan Paton's novel *Cry the Beloved Country*, set in South Africa during apartheid.[1] In the novel, Steven Kumalo, an aging black minister in the tribal village of Ndotsheni, travels to Johannesburg in search of his son, Absalom. By the time Kumalo finds him, Absalom has shot and killed Arthur Jarvis, son of the owner of High Place, a plantation above Ndotsheni, and an advocate of black and white equality.

Paton describes his book as "a song of love for one's far distant country" and thinks of his beloved land as approaching Isaiah's vision of a just Kingdom: "that land where they shall not hurt or destroy in all that holy mountain." Like Isaiah, the book points out injustice and envisions an idealized order. After Absalom has been condemned to death, Kumalo returns to his church in Ndotsheni and speaks to his people. "If I stay here now," he says, "I become a hindrance to you instead of a help." James Jarvis, white settler and father of the murdered man, urges him to stay. "If I stay, do you know what I would preach?" Kumalo asks. "That good can come from evil and evil from good. That we are all lost here on this rock that goes around the sun without meaning." The choir sings:

> Sometimes it seems maybe God's gone away,
> Forgetting his promise that we heard him say,
> And we're lost out here in the stars. . . .

For the first time, I'd found another who voiced my private fear. I listened to the recording over and over, letting the music draw me into a snug but fleeting fit in the world. The opera spoke to me in the way it brought together opposites, not so much black and white as faith and doubt. When Kumalo loses his faith in an ordered universe and plans to leave Ndotsheni, the chorus sings "Bird of Passage" about the unknown darkness before birth and after death. At this point his flock urges him to stay, and Jarvis, overhearing, turns to forgiveness. Anderson and Weill once planned to write a funeral service for unbelievers and considered including this song from the opera:

> A bird of passage out of night
> Flies in at a lighted door,
> Flies through and on in its darkened flight,
> And then is seen no more.
> This is the life of men on earth:
> Out of darkness we come at birth
> Into a lamplit room, and then—
> Go forward into dark again.[2]

How strange it is that this parable, which speaks entirely of absence, carries with it a feeling of hope as much as of despair! The last four lines were engraved on Weill's tombstone. Though I knew nothing in my teens of Isaiah's dreams of a holy mountain or a great banquet, I think I was touched by the opera's hope in despair, its discovery of meaning in the heart of chaos.

Then, sometime in 1951, *Life* magazine ran a story on the Sistine Chapel. Working on this chapter, I opened up my book of reproductions of Michelangelo's frescoes, and to my amazement, out tumbled the flaking, brown-edged pages of the original *Life* story. How objects testify to what's important! These pages must have followed me from childhood in D.C. through college dorms and apartments to my old house, then escaped the piles of detritus I discarded when I moved. I unfolded the pages and found pictures both strange and familiar.

Powerful, sensuous bodies crowd the ceiling and wall of the Sistine Chapel, each one as detailed in expression and pose as a character in a novel. A God more motion than form spirals within pale pink fabric, as he divides light from darkness. He spins and hurls sun, moon, sky, and water from his generous being into the world, commanding their existence with outstretched arms, the gesture so forceful it turns him, and his back races away from us. Here space is not empty but active, filled with vibrant and essential force, utter potential. In a center panel, life streams from God's hand into Adam's against the bowl of the sky, imbuing all life with meaning. A thick serpent twines around a tree in Eden, dividing a panel in half. On one side Eve takes the apple, and on the other the avenging angel strikes Adam with a sword and sends the pair out to make their way in the world. Surviving the deluge, a child in floodwaters clings to its mother's leg. A man carries a woman on his back, while others reach to those still in the water. The entire ceiling is crowded with figures in action, struggling with primal forces, impinging on, climbing over, or reaching for each other. All of the characters are nude and full-fleshed (despite loincloths overpainted later), utterly human and caught in medias res. Absence plays no part in this vision; presence layers upon presence, filling every interstice with a new image, as prolix and varied and swarming as life on earth, a sort of Via Affirmativa that sees God present and revealed in all creation.

Life accompanied the images with an explanatory text, so I received a crash course in Christian tradition. On the huge wall behind the altar is Michelangelo's fresco of the Last Judgment. A condemned man covers half his terrified face with one hand as demons circle his legs and hang on his feet, dragging him down. An oarsman with horns and mean red eyes threatens his human cargo as he ferries them to hell. Four hefty angels nearly burst their cheeks as they aim their long trumpets at the underworld and blow to wake the dead. The dead respond, skeletal or draped in shrouds, awestruck by the heavenly host.

Heaven and hell share space on the chapel's great wall, from the heights to the depths, and no space is devoid of meaning. The pictures drew me into a frame that could hold the infinity of space, the ages, and also me. They assured me of a meaningful place in the world, a place among others, right or wrong, good or bad. This comforted me, despite the severity of judgment. Neither judgment nor death, apparently, was the source of my terror.

The wall's scenes were the absolute opposite of my mother's frequent assurance, "Everything's going to be all right," and I found the chapel infinitely reassuring, where my mother's words made me suspect exactly the opposite. Anything that made me feel deeply, physically or emotionally, was welcome.

I did not name the experience of the Sistine Chapel at all or connect it with any sort of faith or community, but I must have sensed the source from which Michelangelo drew his images, or perhaps the faith of the artist himself, embodied in paint. In any case, panic simply left me, and the world became my home.

One spring afternoon, a friend and I took a walk in the woods behind her house in a Maryland suburb, and my new sense of belonging made the pine needles underfoot soft and supportive, like clouds. Even the air seemed thick enough to hold me, and budding trees appeared to bend protectively over my head. I braved a thought about rocks in space, and the Sistine images rose to shield me from chaos. For days or weeks or maybe months, I moved more easily through a populated world, not quite as dense as the Sistine ceiling, perhaps, but rich, vivid, and safe.

7

With My Body I Thee Worship

JUST AS BREAD, MUSIC, word, and community can communicate God, so can human love. In some ways my journey to the Church began with my embrace of an "other," a person very different from me. Born in 1916, Eric grew up in the contentious world of Vienna between the wars, where Christian Socialists fought with Social Democrats, and both were opposed by Communists; where Catholic despised Protestants, and pan-German parties preached hatred of Catholics, Jews, and Slavs.

In that socially stratified and racially charged environment, he couldn't help but discover his Jewishness as he grew, despite his Lutheran upbringing. I still have his baby book, "Merkbuch Unseres Kindes," the title stamped in gold on the book's brown, leather cover. His mother's entries begin in careful, feathery script, then race and tumble along the page with the speed of a child's growth. The section titled "Die Taufe," baptism, has been crossed out and replaced with a handwritten "Bermerkungen," observations. The crossed-out "baptism" is followed by "took place 16 October 1919," and the last digit is overwritten with a "6." Thus, his Lutheran baptism at the age of three is made to look like it happened at his birth. Eric took the middle name "Christian" at his confirmation, and the family converted to Catholicism following his mother's accidental meeting with a charismatic priest.

My own background reflected denial of Judaism as much as Eric's, but the turbulence had been concealed beneath a smooth surface. All four of my mother's grandparents were German Jews who immigrated to the United States in the nineteenth century. By the time I was born and grew to know her, my mama's mother was a committed Unitarian. Grandma had met her husband at All Soul's Church in Chicago, where they worshipped and studied with the Unitarian preacher Jenkin Lloyd Jones. She was active all her life at Abraham Lincoln Center, the interracial outreach program of All Soul's, and black people were frequent guests in her home. In those years before "diversity," religious and racial tolerance was essential to her worldview, but she never admitted to Jewish heritage.

Like body parts in the house where I grew up, all people and all faiths were equal. Though D.C.'s downtown movies denied entrance to my black schoolmates, I knew from Daddy that the only real race was human. Thus, Judaism was a religion, and religion was a matter of choice. When I met Eric, I didn't understand his negative feelings about Judaism. I winced when his mother said, "Let's go to 'the Jew' for lunch," referring to a delicatessen, but I still didn't get it. Though we shared assimilation and denial, Eric had nearly been killed for an identity he neither chose nor wanted. What difference did it make, I asked, if you were Jewish or not?

In 1938, shortly after Hitler marched into Austria, Eric fled Vienna. At twenty-two, he had just finished the first Rigorosum, the exam that culls more than half of the students admitted to medical school at the University of Vienna. After a year in Switzerland, he crossed the ocean on the last boat allowed to land in Cuba, before the S.S. *St. Louis* was infamously denied permission. The story of that voyage is told in the novel and movie *The Voyage of the Damned*. In the movie, two men escaped from a concentration camp are beaten up by marauding Nazi thugs to the triumphant sound of the fascist "Horst Wessel Lied"; passengers on the boat dance to "Blue Moon," then become silent and tearful as a solo performer sings the nostalgic "Wien, Wien, Nur Du Allein" (Vienna, Only You). The film shifts to documentary mode at its end to report that 600 of the 937 passengers died in concentration camps after the boat was sent back, and each historically based character steps forward to report his or her fate. That movie showed me the terror that Eric had barely escaped and helped me to feel his fury at exclusion and his intense longing for embrace by Vienna. These contradictory emotions dominated his life.

The movie also gave me the biblical gesture of grief. When a man dies during the crossing, his wife rips the shoulder of her blouse, weeps briefly, and then talks to him with the same warmth that colored her voice when he was alive. Her gesture stayed with me, embodying the full, spontaneous, and heartfelt expression I admired in Eric. That gesture rose in my imagination but remained just out of reach at the moment when Natasha died.

Eric invited me to share not only his past but also his enthusiastic, critical worldview, informed by Freud, Marx, and his practice of medicine and psychiatry. Everything was interesting, and everything mattered, from the libido in art to the ownership of the means of production. At the grocery store, he always suggested we buy champagne, "in case a celebration should break out."

I was near the end of college when we met, dating guys most of whom I didn't like and mourning separations where there had never been much connection. Eric was in the process of a second divorce, living with his parents, when we went separately to see a performance of original one-act plays in the small, third-floor theater of the Reynolds Club at the University of Chicago. I'd been living with roommates in a third-floor walk-up for two years, finding my love life more and more hopeless. My roommates would lie with their lovers in the front bedroom while I slept alone in the back, fantasizing a man coming from the fire escape through my window, a man whose strength would overcome my reluctance and make possible the intimacy that seemed to come so easily to everyone else. Hyperrational, my mind skated on the surface of things, even as my inaccessible insides became more tumultuous. In the months before I met Eric, my life had broken into disconnected fragments, each one sliding toward failure. I had gotten my first D, taken some incompletes, and stopped dancing altogether. A frightening edge loomed, and I don't know what I would have faced had I not gone alone to that theater the night we met.

As I walked through the door, I passed him smoking a cigarette in the hall, and later he told me he knew at once that he'd finally found his true mate. Holding the program, he took a seat one removed from mine. I heard the paper shaking noisily in his Parkinsonism-affected right hand and wondered why he didn't move it to the left. As the theater filled, someone approached to take the seat between us, and Eric moved over next to me. I found this startling, but interesting. We talked during intermission and went out for coffee afterward.

"My son calls this place the 'Troc-i-pal Hut,'" he said. Son? I'd never dated anyone with children before, or anyone divorced. I observed his sensual, sensitive mouth, big chest, and well-muscled limbs, while he told me about his lifelong sympathy with the underdog and work with Socialist groups in Austria, before the Nazis marched in and kicked him out. Despite a priggish objection to divorce, I felt a deep attraction from the beginning to his dark complexion, strong emotions, and partisan politics.

The day after we met, he called me up repeatedly, and the conversation flowed. He told me about his infatuation with the paintings of Mondrian and other abstractions, including the logo for "Phillips 66," with its juxta-position of rigid frame and playful script. To him the logo, like Mondrian's works, was an analogue for the psyche, the internalized parent struggling to control unruly impulses. I found this view of art reductive but was struck by the existential immediacy of his views about infantile develop-ment. "Maybe the reason babies cry so hard," he said, "is because it really is that bad. It's best to face the truth with ruthless honesty." Reasons, for my family, had always been ways of explaining things away, of avoiding extremes in favor of the safer center. Now I was thrilled to hear a "reason" that recognized a hard reality. This sort of realism implied a deeper trust in the way things are and began for me a lifelong process of stepping back, seeing more, and realizing I'd been failing to notice parts of my own experience: pain and pleasure, hope and despair.

My life until then had made me ripe for attachment to a powerful man. In the household where I grew up, Daddy had all the fun, and I hoped I'd grow up to be like him. He gave bear hugs, drank whiskey, played the guitar, and sang. Mama found me "uncuddly" at birth, whereas Sally, born two years later, seemed like a part of Mama herself, clinging and adapting to her curves. Whether too close or too distant, Mama had a hard time engaging with us as real and separate people. Apparently my parents had hoped I'd be a boy: a mock-up of my birth certificate names me "Thomas." The inevitable corollary to the hope my parents and I shared was fear that I'd always lack something essential to womanhood.

In my first weeks with Eric, it felt like spring had come, little green tendrils reaching out from myself to connect with another, even though it was a frigid February. I felt myself return to a golden age, a primal, sun-drenched time before a fall into darkness and confusion. Eric generated heat, and I basked in the warmth, feeling that I'd never be cold again. When Mama met Eric, several weeks after we'd moved in together, she said that I seemed as though I'd been let out of jail, a rare acknowledg-ment that she and I had both lived in a cage with transparent bars, that the apparent freedom of our shared home concealed unspoken prohibitions.

Three weeks after Eric and I met, we moved into a spacious second-floor apartment in Chicago's Hyde Park, in a building Eric called "castrate's castle" for our fussy upstairs neighbors, who complained when we played

Beethoven symphonies and asked if the footfalls of their cat disturbed us. Eric's sobriquet emphasized the virility of which he was proud but strikes me now as revealing insecurities not so different from my own. The landlady refused to put my name on the mailbox, and the boss at my part-time job asked me not to tell anyone that my roommate was a man.

I brought along a red ceramic frying pan and a wok from my student apartment, and Eric came home the day after we moved with everything we lacked: spatulas, big spoons, and flatware, all purchased on impulse in an afternoon. That night I made baked chicken, bending over the small broiler to turn each piece, Eric looking over my shoulder.

"I see the piece I want," he said.

"You're not supposed to say that," I said, straightening. How could I tell him to think of me first, when he was supposed to know that without being told?

"I only like the breast, and my mother always takes the skin off."

"Your mother! She treats you like a child."

"It's true; she acts like I'm playing doctor." Eric still made house calls, and his mother used to ride along with him, keeping him company while demeaning his ability.

"You said you can't trust her."

"That's right, I can't, but I still want the breast. I don't like chicken skin." From childhood I'd been afraid to ask outright for anything I wanted, from fear not of punishment but of disapproval, and simple pleasures always felt guilty to me. I'd assumed my years of self-restraint would guarantee the same abstention on the part of the other. How could this guy just come out and demand what he wanted? Hadn't he ever heard of the command to share, to offer to the other first?

"You're scared of a little bit of chicken skin?"

"I'm not scared. I just don't like it." Now he was breaking a second rule. Try everything and learn to like it.

"I can't cook for a picky eater," I said and threw the spatula, hard, in the sink, then stalked out of the kitchen.

"Whoa!" he said, coming after me. "We have a problem, we talk. You don't throw things."

"I didn't."

"You did. You threw the spatula in the sink."

"I didn't throw it at you."

"You threw it. That's dangerous. That's what I'm divorcing."

"But you know I'm really not the throwing kind."

"Don't say 'but you,' blaming the other guy. I put myself on the block—I know violence from the streets of Vienna and from marriage, and I'm scared of it—now your turn. You did throw the spatula."

"I didn't mean it. Really, I didn't."

"OK," he said and put his arms around me. "I believe you, but you upset me just the same." We stood there for several moments. "*Carthago delenda est,*" he said. I'd gotten used to his quirky changes of subject, but I'd never studied Latin and had no idea what he meant. "It means 'Carthage must be destroyed,'" he continued. "The Roman censor Cato once announced that every speech he would make in the Roman Senate would finish with those words, to ensure that it would happen. When I say it, I mean you're going to dance again." His confidence made dancing seem natural and opened a door for me to the possibility of discipline without compulsive scheduling, without too much self-denial, and most of all without forgoing sex. I could let my native impulses carry me.

We lived in that apartment for a year. In its kitchen I baked my first Thanksgiving turkey, and I still have the roasting pan with the handle we hammered sideways to fit the small oven. In the apartment's narrow shower stall, Eric wrapped his arms around me and announced, "*Carthago delenda est.*" On the balcony we ate watermelon naked on summer nights, shielded by darkness and spitting seeds over the edge. "*Carthago delenda est,*" said Eric, between bites. And in that bedroom I learned a language of touch as articulate as talk, connecting my core to his more deeply and firmly than I had ever thought possible. "There's more ways than one to skin a cat," he said, making me wince with his unlikely metaphor for sexual variety. Still, I rejoiced to discover that pleasure didn't have to be guilty; that my body was more than an errant child to be disciplined and molded into a dancer's instrument. "You are eminently satisfactory," he said. "*Carthago delenda est.*"

I'd known Eric two months when the university's spring vacation came, and we decided to fly to Mexico. Not yet twenty-one, I had to get a copy of my Canadian birth certificate and a letter of permission from my parents in order to enter the country. Wearing a new navy blue dress with white cuffs, I called myself Eric's "wife" for the first time as I got on the plane, thrilled by the deception. We spent one night in Mexico City, ate an omelet packed with vegetables, then rented a car and drove to Vera Cruz. The next day we took a long walk on the beach, holding hands. The sun was hot, the breeze cool, and we hadn't seen another human being for an hour. As we entered a protected area between two dunes, we began to kiss. We had already gotten to a certain stage of undress, lying in the sand, when I looked up and saw three little boys peering over the edge of the dune. Unspeakably embarrassed, I jumped up, pulled on clothing, and saw the boys disappear over the dune's edge. Eric was concerned mainly for the boys' psychological well-being.

"It won't hurt them to see sex," he said, "if they get along with their father. They'll just see something they'd like to do one day. But if they're scared of their father, the sight of an erection might be threatening." It probably didn't hurt me to be seen, either, but all I could think of was punishment, the downhill course from frowns to jail. I took in Eric's response, acutely attuned to his words, but still full of shame. A crucial difference between us had come to light: Eric took pride in his mind, body, and feelings, whereas I feared that any exposure of my self was bound to reveal a shameful inner emptiness or lack, worthy of punishment.

One night in Vera Cruz after dinner, we walked in moonlight, his arm around my shoulder, mine around his waist, as he taught me about Marx and the need for force to achieve justice.

"I'd rather lose ten men than one factory," he said.

"What!" I exclaimed. "I can't believe you mean that." Our arms dropped to held hands and then separated. He not only frightened me; he offended my faith in negotiation, the subtle means by which I won my place in the world. Eric hated my indirect approach, my assumption that my self-restraint would guarantee the same on his part, and came to call it "the contract."

"Loss of a factory means the livelihood of hundreds," said Eric. I dropped to a stone bench and sat, feeling like my man had become a stranger. The moon on the paving stones shone silvery gray, making the small park look like a graveyard. But I wasn't ready for a funeral. Eric strengthened me for combat, and we continued arguing about ten men and one factory for years, until the phrase became a catchword for his black-and-white vision and my gray one. "Oh yeah," we'd say, smiling with recognition at a certain point in a discussion, "that's 'ten men and one factory.'"

Back at the hotel, in the faint light from the street, I got to know another Eric.

"I hope you don't mind," he said, "if I turn the mirror to the wall. I don't like to see myself." I was puzzled. In bed he explained, "I'm a poet at heart, a delicate fellow. I hate the image of myself as a bull."

"What do you mean?" I asked, raising myself on one elbow and peering at his face, eyes like dark hollows in the half light. "Right now to me you look deep and half hidden, a handsome poet but a little scary. You're different in the day, with your glasses on. Here." I turned on the light. "Put them on. Now I see your pink, protective daytime self." He turned off the light and removed his glasses.

"What do you see now?"

"A poet and a lover."

"But never a bull, please. No charging, no stampeding." I never quite understood why he didn't want to see himself as one who fucks, an aggressive male, especially since he placed great value on his sexuality. His male self seemed to coexist easily with his feminine side, expressed in a love for rose-patterned china and childhood desserts eaten with tiny spoons. More conflictual for him was his desire for passivity, something he feared and combated by assertion all his life. But for me the poet was charming, more masculine and sexual than any brute.

"Never a bull," I promised, not sure what that meant but already learning to prefer the hidden face of my radical poet to his safer, sensible self. I turned to him.

On our first trip to Europe, the summer after we met, we visited St. Peter's in the Vatican. The imposing, pillared Basilica, with its myriad arches and frescoes, side altars and balconies, spoke of pomp and power. We walked past Michelangelo's *Pieta,* the sorrowful mother holding the body of her son, then statue after statue in blazing white marble, all larger than life. A small crowd had assembled at one of the side altars, and we approached, seeing nothing but backs until we got close. People had lined up to pay homage to a black, life-sized St. Peter with frightened gaze, two fingers barely raised in a humble gesture of blessing, toe worn away by kissing. Eric took one look at this image of Peter, the flawed and vacillating leader who'd denied Jesus three times, and burst into uncontrollable tears. I put my arms around him and held him until the flood abated.

"The little guy," Eric explained, "trying so hard, all alone in here among these marble giants." We kept walking, arm in arm, looking at the altars. "Did you see how he's trying to raise his arm, those two fingers just making it?" I did, though I didn't get what made it so pitiful. "It's like the coal shovelers," said Eric, referring to the exploited workers about whom he'd written in his youth. "Or a Jew, running for his life." He raised his right arm in imitation of St. Peter's gesture and released a fresh flood of tears. I tightened my hold on his arm and thought of my own failure to attend to the poor, the oppressed, or the injured.

"What makes him so sad?" I asked.

"He's not sad, he's valiant," said Eric. "Like a little kid that faces down a bully."

"Is it something to do with your father?" I asked.

"Probably," he said. "I always wanted a strong, supportive father. Mine resented the way my mother indulged me, so we could never be close."

"Is St. Peter like that, defeated from the start?"

"Maybe. He looks scared." We'd reached the back of the church and reversed direction, heading for the street, and continued to discuss the dynamics of Eric's reaction in psychological terms, without recognizing his overflowing well of religious feeling. As we passed St. Peter again, Eric took a last, tearful look at the life-sized man among the massive, white statues, Peter doing his resolute best and continuing to offer himself, even as his very body was diminished by devotion. I had rarely seen anyone moved so profoundly by religious symbols, and I sensed that I was approaching a deep center of meaning, once missing in my life and now slowly revealing itself to me.

Two years later, we decided to get married, and a friend of Eric's, a Unitarian minister, agreed to preside at our ceremony.

"Weddings and funerals," said the minister, "I love them! But I'm not sure what marriage means to you—you're already living together."

"To me it means commitment to the future," I said, "and a link to the past—carrying on a tradition." I tended to speak glibly, but in fact it was true. When I asked myself why I wanted to marry, all I could think of was ancestors, peering over my shoulder. In *Our Town,* Thornton Wilder writes of "all the other witnesses at this wedding—the ancestors. Millions of them." I wanted to join with them, to carry them forward, to do my part in the shared project of marriage. At twenty-one, I had no interest in children, but now I wonder if that sense of forward motion was not at root a drive to procreate.

"Making a family," said Eric. Then, looking at me, "Not yet, of course." He already had two sons from two previous marriages and knew better than to rush me. The minister pulled out Thomas Cranmer's sixteenth-century Book of Common Prayer. Entranced by the time-honored words, we chose the traditional promise to marry, originally used in advance of marriage: "To have and to hold, for better or worse, for richer or poorer, in sickness and in health, from this day forward, 'til death do us part, and thereto I plight thee my troth."

The last phrase contained the most difficult of sound combinations for a native speaker of German, with its three hard *t*'s, two voiced and one unvoiced *th* in the space of six words, but Eric bravely pledged his "throth." The ring ceremony we also took from this book:

> With this ring, I thee wed;
> This gold and silver I thee give
> With my body I thee worship
> And with all my worldly goods I thee endow.

But when it came to the ratification, at the end of the ceremony, I had trouble.

"What God has put together, let no man put asunder," said the Book. "No 'God," I said. In 1960, I didn't question "man."

"How would you put it?" asked Eric. "It sounds all right to me."

"What has been put together . . ." I suggested.

"'God' might make it richer for Eric," said the minister, "though it doesn't feel right to you." I ignored the conflict. I almost remember forgetting it, and my preference prevailed. Now I am ashamed of choosing to be married in the evasive passive voice, but it didn't dampen our spirits at the time as we prepared the celebration.

We wanted everything about the wedding to be stripped of pretense and claims of status, to represent us as our true selves. Later, I picked out flat white shoes to anchor my white velvet wedding dress. With my heels firmly on the ground, I could be simply me. A college friend made my bouquet and provided flowers to decorate the cake, which I made myself, storing the layers in the freezers of friends until the day. Eric wore an embroidered Mexican shirt, no tie.

A Renaissance cupid graced the front of the announcement we'd de-signed with the help of Misch Kohn, an artist friend. Inside, my parents, Philleo and Edith Nash, announced the marriage of Maggie and Eric. I'd always considered my parents as unconcerned about status as I, but this time I'd gotten them wrong. They supplemented our announcement with a formal, engraved version, in which the lieutenant governor of Wisconsin and his wife announced the marriage of his daughter, "Margaret," to Eric C. Kast, titled M.D.

My sister came from Washington to be my maid of honor in mustard velvet, and my old friends and art teachers, Dante and Robert, brought decorations. They hung our apartment with white ribbons, blue-and-green porcelain birds and butterflies, and gold-paper roses, making a fairytale arbor of our long hallway and re-creating the spirit of my child-hood Christmastimes. Empty rooms in our rooming house provided accommodations for the guests. At the reception, my father presided over a punchbowl, offering toasts, then cooked lobsters flown in from Damariscotta, Maine. Sitting on the floor and couches, bibbed, we cracked and extracted and dipped with friends and family, knowing our ritual contained a truth about ourselves.

Though I'd thrown my bouquet in the air with glee as I left the chapel, I could not look at the new gold band on my left hand and kept it covered with the other. I'd finally stepped over a chasm into the adulthood I'd always sought, and suddenly I regretted all I'd left behind. I'd never let myself feel the pull of childhood before, but now, as I faced this huge transition, it broke through. I thought of falling asleep with my head in my mother's lap, laugh-ing until it hurt when Daddy read us *Cheaper by the Dozen* on Sunday af-ternoons, the clear sound of a bell in late afternoon at art camp, reminding me further of the poignant, minor tune of a song about a broken bell that rang, miraculously, so a couple could wed. If I didn't get away now, I might stay here with my parents for good. Pulled two ways, I bolted. We changed clothes and left for our motel. "It's for real!" said the card accompanying flowers that Eric had ordered for our room.

Over time, our perception of the significance of the "real" widened and deepened until it included realms we would have considered unthink-able before. Eric's experience at St. Peter's was like a harbinger of things to come, somewhat like my moment of doubt just after we were mar-ried. At the time I merely paused, then charged ahead. Today that crack in my single-minded self-confidence seems an appropriate acknowledgment of uncertainty, but also a sign of the false self-sufficiency that my daughter's death would one day force me to surrender. I caught my breath momentarily on my wedding day, but that was not enough to make me acknowledge that our marriage, with its origin in accidental meeting and the miracle of our unlikely fit, could hardly be an act without an author.

8

Dancing in New York

WHEN I WAS FOURTEEN, a new dancer came to Ethel's studio, soon joined the company, and became my friend. Jo was tall but not skinny, just round enough to be womanly with soft brown hair in a short ponytail, about ten years older than I. She treated me like an adult, including me in her jokes but also taking me seriously, and I adored her and her delicately arched feet. Soon I got to know her roommate, Charlotte, whose blond curls circled an impish face with close-set features.

A clutter of furniture, some brightly striped Madras cotton, and an air of improvisation rise from memory of my first visit to their crowded apartment. They offer me wine in a short, plain glass, the first time I've had more than a sip of someone else's, and we listen to songs of the Spanish Civil War, played on a phonograph in the corner. Jo and Charlotte sing along, "Viva la quinté brigada," and I tap my feet and nod my head, connecting the music to Dante's explanation of Picasso's *Guernica*. Soon Jo gets up and starts clapping and dancing, and Charlotte pulls back a crate to make space. "Manuela, ay Manuela, ay, Manuela," goes the song, and I want to join the cry for a lost and noble cause. Jo sweeps around as best she can in the small space and pulls me to my feet. We trim the reach of our arms and legs, avoiding the phonograph and chairs, but the music calls for more. "Solo es nuestro deseo, rumbala, rumbala, rum-ba-la / acabar con el fascismo, rumbala, rumbala, rum-ba-la." I don't understand the words, but I get the message, and my fondness for Jo and Charlotte blends with the music's dedication. The moment demands drama, and I go for one of the Graham falls, throwing my head back and my pelvis under, imagining myself suspended by a thread from the top of my head to the ceiling. The thread gives way, and the floor slams up to meet me.

"Are you all right?" asks Charlotte, laughing. I am, but I'm embarrassed, knowing the wine caught me off guard, hating my loss of control. They help me up, and we go on dancing and singing late into the night, joining the bleak longing for home of "Die Moorsoldaten," the peatbog soldiers, delighted by songs with verses in French, English, German, and Spanish—words from people all over the world who came to fight in Spain. Before the night is over, I've learned some of the English words and can join in:

> And just because he's human
> He doesn't want a pistol to his head.
> He wants no servants under him and
> No boss over his head.

They invite me to stay overnight, and I call my parents, then curl up on the couch.

After that I visit them frequently, learning to play cribbage from Charlotte and loving her intelligence and ironic humor. Jo and I talk dancing when we're not doing it. The three of us listen to Mabel Mercer sing about the first warm day in May, and they promise to take me one day to hear her live in New York. I meet others in their building, which comes to feel like an adventure palace: an attractive young man who works as a translator and tells me the sound of his typewriter is the clink of dimes paid for the words he cranks out; a man over eighty whose birthday we celebrate by bringing him a cake. It is almost as if they give me the childhood I've never had, one that allows me to play at being adult, flirting with the translator or drinking wine, but does not demand adult self-control or maturity. And the music plays on—"Los Cuatro Generales," about Franco and his cronies trying and failing to seize Madrid; "Venga, jaleo, jaleo" the echoing cry that Franco will be defeated; "Wir kämpfen und siegen für dich"—we fight and win for you—"Freiheit"—freedom. The songs etch a groove of teenaged pleasure, rebellion, and devotion in my mind and heart, taking over the path created by my father's guitar and moving it in a new, defiant direction.

The next summer, the three of us go to New York together, renting a one-bedroom walk-up in Greenwich Village. Jo and Charlotte have the bedroom, and I sleep on the living room couch, where Jo brings me an English muffin each morning. She and I take classes daily at the Martha

Graham School of Contemporary Dance, peeling oranges during the sweaty break, while Charlotte stays home, mostly sleeping, I think, but trying to write. In the hot evenings I step out the window onto the fire escape and look down on passing pushcarts selling Italian lemonade, mothers with strollers, and teenagers gathering. I try to notice everything, to drink it all in: the warm, orange light of late day, illuminating brick and brownstone; the cries of vendors; the lonely young men walking with hands in pockets, heads down, who are surely looking for someone like me. Much as I remind myself to be aware of the outside world, I try to suppress the churning life within.

We go to a small nightclub to hear Mabel Mercer. By now I know many of her songs by heart, and I like her subtle, sexy humor, her coy promise to "show the birds and bees a thing or two." At the club, I am surprised to see her sitting at a table, as though she were a customer. The light in the room is soft and rosy, and her light brown skin seems to glow in harmony with the shiny fabric of her dress. All is enclosed and intimate. We order drinks: Coke for me and Johnny Walker Red Label for Jo and Charlotte. Just a few feet from us, without getting up, Mercer begins to sing. She seems as comfortable performing as she would having an ordinary conversation, and I see how art can be open to life, not framed by technique or walled off by a proscenium. The next morning, Jo and Charlotte complain of hangovers.

"I guess you must be Coke-logged," says Charlotte, including me as always. I smile and shrug but privately long to experience the mysterious adult condition of which Daddy often complained.

It was obvious to others, but not to me, that Jo and Charlotte were lovers. In the course of the month in New York, knowledge of that fact inched its way from a totally obscured part of my mind toward the surface. When Charlotte finally said, "I assume you know . . ." the revelation exploded my world.

"Of course I know," I said. I loved both of them and wanted what they had, but I couldn't let myself think of what they did behind their closed bedroom door.

"Are you jealous?" asked Charlotte. I couldn't begin to form an answer out of the tumult in my head. I was angry that their love existed at all, excluding me, but I wouldn't admit it to anyone, least of all myself. Reason was my anchor, and anything unreasonable had to be vanquished. How could I fault Charlotte for "telling" me what I supposedly already knew? I cursed my naiveté.

In the middle of June, I went for a weekend to visit my cousins in Westport, where I'd lived the previous summer. One evening, as I walked from kitchen to picnic table, their father grabbed me, pulled me behind an arbor, and stuck his tongue in my mouth. Another bombshell, unbelievable: this fat-lipped, bald man, my father's age and married! What was he doing with me? Shock at his betrayal of both wife and children, just a year younger than I, competed with the fearful realization that this must be how grown-ups kiss, what lay in store for me. I pushed him away and ran, then continued the picnic supper with the family as though nothing had happened. Later I looked at myself in the mirror, searching for the attractive person he must have seen, but found only my plain green shirt, flat chest, big head, and scared eyes.

The next day, he and I shared a cab from the train as he went to his office and I to our apartment in the Village. He took my hand, smiled his greasy smile, and said, "Yesterday was nice. Maybe I could come visit you sometime." Petrified, utterly embarrassed, and ignorant of how to extricate myself, I slid away and counted the seconds until I could jump out of the cab. I never told my apartment mates what had happened, for putting the unspeakable into words would have made my nightmare real. Instead I played hooky from dance class and drank Seagram's Seven Crown until I threw up.

Back home that fall I told Mama about the cousin, raising the subject as we moved through our sunny dining room on the way to the kitchen, busy with some task.

"Last summer," I said, "the cousins' dad made a pass at me." I couldn't say "tongue" or describe my horror in the cab, but "pass" was vague enough. She didn't ask any questions but paused and leaned a hand on the table. I sat down.

"That's not unusual," she said, seeming undisturbed. "Many men with strong, intellectual wives, like the cousins' mother, turn to young women like you." I was surprised at her calm but relieved the subject could be discussed as easily as the weather. Later, her replication of my dumb acceptance outraged me, but at the time I merely added her interpretation to my store of information, perhaps proud to know something new about men, unaware that she had helped me reinforce the barrier between the talky part of myself and the deeper place where desire and disgust continued to compete.

Only twenty years later, when Mama began writing about her childhood, did I discover that her own mother was the "strong, intellectual wife" to whom she'd referred obliquely, and she, herself, was the victim, a young girl, eating an apple and reading on a couch after school, feeling "pinned like a butterfly," as she wrote, while her father attempted to arouse her.

I returned to class at the Graham School the day after I came back from Westport, eager to lose my complicated adolescent self in a sea of purpose, and Martha provided the way. Her feet barely touched the floor as she swept into the classroom, her entrance itself a dramatic gesture. She moved as though on wheels, slender body outlined in tight-fitting, delicately ribbed fabric, gnarled bare feet as articulate as her face. We students leaped to our feet like metal filings to a magnet. She was both queen and priestess of dance, and we were pilgrims to Mecca who had arrived at the source. We waited for her signal. She sat; we sat. The class began with the same bounces Ethel had taught us, each series initiated by a contraction of the pelvis. The technique demanded not only strength and flexibility but also honesty and awareness of the body and all of its potentials. We could not fake it; all movement had to originate in the center.

The Graham technique's emphasis on the pelvis was not explicitly erotic, but it opened dancing to a full awareness of the body and its potential for feeling and action. Both Ethel and Martha stressed animal sensuality and held up the MGM lion as a model of passionate movement with full presence. No part of the body was to be excluded or ignored. This emphasis dissolved barriers for me, opening up a world accessible through physical expression.

Martha saw mythic significance in every gesture. Everything about the body was suffused with a sense of the sacred. "Pleadings" from the floor were contractions with arms outstretched, hands bent at the knuckle into little triangular houses. A contraction was never just a shape, but a cry from the vital center, life force reaching out. Spirals around the spine created whiplike extensions of arms and legs, always motivated from the core. Becoming a disciple, I surrendered to the vocation of modern dance with ecstasy. Dancing enabled me to have it both ways: at the same time as I yielded my will, I gained control of my unpredictable body.

One day I sat on the floor in class, both legs bent to the left, preparing to initiate a fall with a deep pelvic contraction that would throw me down and to the left, the small of my back pressing into the floor. I could not bring enough power to the movement; I had failed to connect with the source. Martha crouched in front of me, hair drawn sharply back from her skull's planes, rectangular red mouth full and sensual, eyes black and focused on me. "I'm going to slap your face," she said. The right side of my face exploded, and I fell away from it, spiral and contraction doing their work for real this time. If there were ever a perfectly unified action, an action that brings together an idea and a bit of physical reality, this was it. Of course, I was surprised and shaken, a little embarrassed, and gratified to be singled out. But the important thing was that she had given me her movement, transferred some knowledge directly from her body to mine. The slap gave me Martha unmediated and transcended my warring desires to be aware and dedicated at the same time. Her hand spoke wordlessly to me, and my body responded instantaneously, without reflection. I now possessed Martha's physical impulse, a tiny bit of her sacred self.

Every June, the Graham School gave a garden party on the patio of the school, and Martha spoke graciously to each student. "Tell Ethel I think you're working very well," she said to me. Jo, Charlotte, and I headed for the subway arm in arm, me a little tipsy from both praise and punch.

"You're going to dance hard and drink hard," said Charlotte, and I felt a new self-image taking shape from her words. I would no longer be a "perfect child," but an imperfect, rough-edged person dedicated to dance and ready to celebrate. Though still confused and upset about what she had "told" me, I loved her for affirming my intensity, looking into my future, and thinking about how I would turn out.

9

Necessary Reflection

I N THE EARLY '60s, when Eric and I were newly married, I'd take ballet
downtown after work, then walk to Eric's office. I'd wait anonymously
until the last patient was gone, then burst into his inner sanctum for an
embrace. On Fridays, we'd head up to a bar on the near North Side, where
we soon became regulars, drinking martinis on the rocks in a soft-cush-
ioned, dark corner.

"Hi, Doc," the bartender would say as we came in, then nod at me,
"Miss Maggie." The jukebox often welcomed us with a song we considered "ours": "Gee, Officer Krupke," from *West Side Story*.[1] It made us feel
like bona fide rebels, with its send-up of social workers, judges, cops, and
psychiatrists, all impersonated by teenaged delinquents. The corner where
we sat was "ours" too, and it was almost always empty when we arrived. I
remember vaguely a few well-dressed people sitting quietly at the bar and
a couple rising occasionally to dance, silk dress swishing past our table,
but otherwise, the visual world retreated, leaving us to listen to each other
and the jukebox. Eric would order, then turn to me, often continuing a
discussion about psychosexual development.

"A boy has to fight a strong father to become a man," he might say. "A
cuckold won't do, and neither will a chum, like the typical American Dad,
or a 'constipated volcano,' like your father, afraid to express feelings." He
applied his theories to child rearing, advocating a hierarchical relationship among siblings, with the father giving orders and the sons obeying,
older brother coming first and younger brother second. I protested the
Prussian-sounding idea of "orders," so different from my home, where all

1. "Gee, Officer Krupke," West Side Story. © 1956, 1957, 1958, 1959 by Amberson
Holdings LLC and Stephen Sondheim. Copyright renewed. Leonard Bernstein Music
Publishing Company LLC, publisher. Boosey & Hawkes, Inc., sole agent. International
copyright secured.

rules and requirements were subtle, if strict, but mostly I just listened. Estranged from my sister at the time, I welcomed any child-rearing method that might reduce sibling rivalry.

I was a good student, and Eric enjoyed teaching me his version of Freud's theories about the dangers of "castrating mothers," identified with the "clip-clip" gesture and a knowing glance. His mother, Bobo, personified this stereotype. She adored her only child but belittled both him and his father, admiring a more sophisticated man, a colleague at the newspaper where she worked. The three of them met every day at the *Kaffeehaus* after work, a regular ménage à trois, and I expressed surprise that she could have an affair in the open. Eric wasn't sure whether she did or not, but he remembered his mother in a fit of hysteria shouting that his father was impotent. "In any case," he said, "I never got to fight him on my own. She'd already castrated him."

My mama's mother was also dominant, but more straightforward. She ruled the home so strictly that her husband, who once expressed a preference for rye bread, had to sneak downstairs at night to eat white. Eric's upbringing and two failed marriages had left him highly suspicious of women, and he considered "seductive" a negative term, meaning not "appealing" but "threatening" and especially "two-faced." My straightforward manner and lack of wiles were precisely what attracted him to me.

Eric also held the then-common view that homosexuality in men was caused by failure to identify with the father, and he used this theory to explain Mama's gay twin brothers. Having grown up with gay teachers and lived with lesbian roommates, I accepted them as friends without thinking about causes, and it didn't occur to me that Eric's theory was prejudicial. Eric recognized that his own upbringing matched the dominant-mother scenario. I'd seen him panic when he stumbled into a gay bar on our honeymoon in New Orleans, and he knew that he feared his own homosexual impulses. In the middle of one such discussion, I signaled the waiter.

"You don't realize it," said Eric, "but you're competitive with men."

"How?" I asked, taken aback at the criticism but not questioning the concept. Eric explained that giving orders to a waiter meant assuming a male prerogative, a consequence of competition. Recognition washed over me. I saw my urge to "take over," to compete, and now I could suppress it. Whenever I think of that moment of charged awareness, I hear "Gee, Officer Krupke" playing in the background, partly because it did, and partly because it placed us so squarely in the age of irony. Here we sat, discussing psychological dynamics while the song made fun of kids pleading with a shrink: "my sister wears a mustache, my brother wears a dress, goodness gracious, that's why I'm a mess."

Thomas Szasz's *The Myth of Mental Illness* had been recently published, and we were both interested in its subversive idea that mental illness was a social construct and psychiatry a system of social control, as the song suggested, though we didn't really believe it. Szasz's theory added spice to our delight when the chorus of gang members sang: "we are sick, we are sick, we are sick, sick, sick." We believed the rebellious kids "never had the love that every child ought to get," even when they didn't believe it themselves, and we delighted in making fun of our own way of thinking. At the same time, we questioned the authorities as much as the kids did and considered ourselves squarely on their side.

Eric ordered our second round, and I brushed my cheek against his rough wool jacket, fingers tingling and whole body glowing with new self-knowledge. His affirmation of my femininity gave me a safe and loving haven, where I could grow. We would be a team like the gang in the song, thumbing our noses at convention and authority, reading Beat poetry and experimenting with LSD, studying Freud and Marx, and hopeful that revolution could create a just world. Proudly, we replaced the euphemism at the end of the song and sang along with its final line: "Gee, Officer Krupke, fuck you!"

At the time, it didn't occur to me to question his views or defend myself. I wanted so much to be a real woman, the kind of good woman men liked, and I had so little faith that I could be. What I lacked in feminine attraction I could make up for with compliance. Acceptance, love, and above all respect from men were my deep need and main goal for a long time, though later I would deride even the concept of competition "with men," not to mention the idea of "castrating women." I was quite willing to sacrifice my autonomy to participate in Eric's larger-than-life sense of self, and I sought, almost literally, to absorb him.

I'd loved to cook ever since I'd learned to make packaged pudding and tuna fish sandwiches at age eight, and now, newly wed, I abandoned myself to the foods of Eric's Vienna. I researched ways of combining eggs, sugar, and air to make *Salzburger Nockerl;* studied the mysteries of *Tafelspitz,* a special cut of beef, boiled with an array of accompanying vegetables and sauces; and rose at four in the morning to make *Kaiserschmarren,* a torn pancake, when a research project demanded his early presence. I covered the kitchen table with a floured sheet and attempted to pull out strudel dough until I could read the newspaper through it and molded heavy potato dough around plums for the dumplings he loved, served with sweet buttered bread crumbs. I cooked and ate Vienna until its lean, white wines ran in my veins, its paprika-scented *gulyas* beefed up my bones, and its raspberry-jam-filled *Linzertorte* sweetened my breath, chewing and swallowing culture and attitude. I liked to read and hear about the vibrant and troubled culture of Vienna between the wars, where even the menu was subject to argument, for a person had to be properly *eingestellt*, adjusted, to what he or she was going to eat, and it couldn't be beef if fish had been planned. I took in the world where everything mattered, bite by bite.

And in between bites, I learned how Eric's self-confidence had both threatened and saved his life. By 1938 he'd finished two years as a medical student at the University of Vienna and participated frequently in coffeehouse debates and street demonstrations. Inflation was out of control, unemployment was massive, and a Christian Fascist government had outlawed both Socialist and Nazi parties. At night in the cabarets, satirists turned the constant clash between hope and encroaching doom into laughter, calling Vienna "a laboratory for the destruction of the world."

Early in March of that year, Eric made a trip to Italy to visit his cousin Kurt. His parents had arranged a signal: if it were unsafe for him to return to Austria, they would send him a postcard with a picture of the Stephansdom, Vienna's cathedral. The card arrived. He was so convinced he was Austrian, a citizen and patriot, that he marched into the German consulate in Venice, said "Heil Hitler," and got a German passport, without the stamped *J* for Jew. Thus he returned to Austria after the Anschluss, risking his life, with the same enfant terrible confidence that later enabled him to walk into a theater without showing his ticket or talk his way out of a speeding fine.

Shortly after his return, he was followed by storm troopers, their boots pounding behind him on the street, then beside him, and then, thank God, passing beyond him to grab some other Jew and force him to his knees to scrub the street, then vanish into the camps. Eric fled for his life, compelled to leave the Austria he considered his own. He made a drawing of the family's apartment, showing the placement of each piece of furniture, knowing that strangers would steal everything. He showed me this drawing, and I longed to feel that attachment to a place and its language, to curtains and couches, to the names of cobblestoned streets.

Despite Eric's bare survival, he spoke almost with nostalgia of the day Hitler had ordered everyone in the country to stop work and other activities to sing "Deutschland über Alles," in unison. He'd wanted to join in, thrilled by the show of unified enthusiasm, even though he knew they'd kill him if they could. Later, to my embarrassment, he refused to stand for the "Alleluia" chorus of Handel's Messiah, remembering the seductive but dangerous appeal of mob action set to music.

Six years after we were married, I got pregnant. Hoping to avoid Mama's experience of helpless fear and pain in childbirth, I learned as much about options as I could. We both mistrusted the delivery practices of our own time as well: drugs that dampened perception but could not conquer pain, exclusion of the father, domination of the event by medical procedure.

Eric was studying Pavlov and steered me to a book based on conditioned reflexes: *The Psychoprophylactic Method of Painless Childbirth.* This Soviet publication had recently been translated into English, and Dr. Fernand Lamaze would soon import the method into France. I did the breathing exercises with a dancer's discipline, practicing them daily with Eric during the last six weeks of pregnancy, determined to be awake, aware, and in control. We would have opted for home delivery, but Eric knew how sudden and serious obstetric emergencies could be, and I readily agreed to the hospital, as long as we could be in charge. We met with our obstetrician to arrange the conditions of delivery: no drugs, no anesthetic, no IV, no fetal monitor, no shaving. "I can live with that," the doc said. "Just don't ask me to read anything." On our prelabor visit to the delivery suite, the head nurse told us it was "against Board of Health regulations" for a father to be present in the delivery room. Quite sure such rules were an invention, we determined to chain ourselves together if need be.

At six in the morning of August 20, a couple of weeks after my due date, I stood before the mirror in the bathroom and said to Eric, "I think this is it." Though Eric had already had two children, he'd never participated in labor and delivery, and now he seemed more scared than I. But labor progressed slowly, and we strolled around the neighborhood, taking our dog to a friend, then made our way to the hospital. I settled into bed in a wood-paneled room on an upper floor of the hospital, with open windows and no air conditioning. In midafternoon, hard labor began, and the environment receded, leaving only my body and mind, the clock on the wall, and Eric's voice.

The Lamaze method worked by conditioning me to relax and breathe in a structured way at Eric's signal: "Take a deep breath." Any grimace or clutching was forbidden. Eric was a perfect labor coach, counting off the seconds by fives as I panted, watching my hands and face for any signs of tension. Thus we got through one contraction at a time. As I approached the difficult transition to the expulsive phase of labor, I got scared. "I don't think I can stay on top of it," I said.

"You don't have to be very far on top to be on top," Eric said. I've never forgotten that reassurance, no false confidence or denial of my feelings, but an acceptance of what was happening that reinterpreted its meaning by a hair—a hair that made all the difference. Suddenly a shudder, and I felt an overwhelming need to push, an urge greater than anything I'd felt in my life. In no way comparable to the usual urge to defecate, this demand was beyond control and volition, undiluted by the epidural anesthesia now in common use. Rushed from labor to delivery room, I panicked.

"I don't know how to push," I said. I remember the doctor saying, "I'll tell you how to push," and I thought no, not you, you don't know what we're doing. Soon Eric resumed the Pavlovian signals, "Inhale, exhale, inhale, hold, push, push, push, push," and my body followed them, responding automatically, the way a dancer leaps without thinking. Three or four of these intense pushes, a burning sensation, and my baby was born. I was ecstatic. Already wired for speed, my first son began to nurse, right there on the table. After a local anesthetic and repair of a midline tear, essentially the same as an episiotomy, I walked to the recovery room, carrying my baby. Eric and I shared a picnic I'd made in advance, an expression of my faith that there'd be a time after the birth, a faith that carried me through a passage as narrow for me as for my baby.

Before giving birth, I hadn't realized it was possible for me to suffer that much pain, so I was shaken by discovery of my own vulnerability. The pain would be repeated in subsequent deliveries, but never again the shock. Accompanying that shock was exhilaration: all that pain, and I hadn't been harmed. When it was over, it was over. Free of drugs, I had full use of all my mental and physical faculties. The next day I went home. And in a day or two, the magnetic little ball of energy would lie on my stomach, fists clenched, and love beyond anything I'd imagined would course out of every pore of my body in wave after wave.

A few days later, I was sitting in the bathtub, basking in warm water. My baby was asleep, and Eric faced me, sitting on the toilet lid, while we talked. Summer sunlight filtered onto the bathroom's black and gold tiles and gaudy pink fixtures, by now so familiar we hardly noticed how they evoked a '40s movie house. I felt the solid tub beneath me, supported by the floor and planet Earth, and knew I'd arrived at a place where I belonged. Another human being had been part of my body and was now outside me; I could never again be alone on a rock in space. "Now we are a family," I said, and Eric smiled agreement. Held by the firm, elastic bands of connection, I swirled my hands in the water, and the old enemy drifted away. Sixteen years later, in the catechumenate at Calvert House, when we were asked to list the five most important events in our lives, that first birth was among them for me, as well as the first death, twelve years later.

I was so enraptured by my first baby that I got pregnant again as soon as I could. I loved the idea of having a big family for the faith it expressed in the abundance and goodness of life, and I liked to see myself as a big-lapped, generous mother. It never occurred to either of us to question whether it was good for children to be born so close together, but the minute Tom was born, eighteen months after Anton, I realized I had set the stage for conflict, both between them and in myself.

During Tom's first months, I held him and talked to Anton, perhaps stimulating Anton's verbal and intellectual tendencies and Tom's emotional ones. As soon as they were old enough to play together, they began to fight as well as polarize, Anton worried and self-controlled, Tom impulsive and messy. Three years later, I was ready for another, hoping that three would dilute sibling rivalry. Stefan seemed normal at birth, and my third child, the "Zen baby," felt like an ultimate affirmation of life. But I often wished for an empty lap, and sometimes squabbling children were more than I could stand.

One Christmas Eve, when Anton and Tom were four and five, Stefan one and called Vuggy, the older boys' excitement and anticipation grew to impatience as we waited for dusk. Our celebration would begin with a walk on which we searched for the first star. Like many things in our household, this had become a competition, and each boy strove to be the one that found the star. I'd already dressed Anton and Tom in festive clothes: matching vests I'd made with brass buttons. Looking angelic with curly hair, they tried to occupy themselves, playing on the living room rug below the tall tree we'd trimmed the day before. As usual, they began to fight. I don't know if it was a toy they couldn't share or some other insult, but they went at each other, punching, accusing, and crying, and suddenly I'd had enough. I'd put a huge effort into Christmas preparations, making cookies and presents, and the one thing I couldn't stand was fighting. I exploded.

"Eric," I called up the stairs in a strident, panicky voice, as though calling could summon his power to squelch the battling boys. "Come down—I'm going out." I heard his steps on the stairs and his booming voice, "*Sapperlot noch einmal!*" This was his father's curse, a contraction of "Yahweh Sabaoth"—in other words, "Good God! Again!" I walked out the front door into mild December air.

In the peace of approaching evening, I walked two blocks to a nearby park and sat on a bench, feeling relief, emptiness, the absence of demands and even of thought. The sky slowly turned from blue-gray to a yellowish color, signaling a winter sunset. After fifteen or twenty minutes, I got up and walked home. I found the boys quiet and Eric angry.

"What's the idea?" he asked. "Where were you? We didn't know where you were."

"I went to the park," I said, calm. "You should have known I wouldn't go far. I just needed a break." I proceeded to get the boys into their coats and Vuggy into his stroller. "I'm sorry," I said. I recognized Eric's truth: they had no way of knowing I was just around the corner and could have been frightened. I also knew I couldn't have told them where I was going, because I didn't know.

Still, looking back, it doesn't feel to me like such a bad thing, that escape into air and sky. I suspect the competitive furor was taken down a peg by my exit. That evening, as we searched for the star, read the Christmas story from the giant book Eric had made, opened presents, and ate Christmas cookies, the boys may well have been a bit more forgiving.

In contrast to Christmas, a demanding holiday long before we became Christian, Hallowe'en was always carefree, with no weight of meaning and no expectations. The boys invented and made their own costumes, with my help, starting with simple capes and masks. Eric and I would take them trick-or-treating soon after dark, when misty air and leaf-filled streets would veil the scuffling feet of midget ghosts and princesses and pirates. Vuggy wore a cape too, in his stroller, and we tried to teach him to say the magic words that brought forth goodies. At home, Anton and Tom would sort their haul, Anton arranging his neatly in a box, intending to save the best for last but prepared to negotiate trades. Tom ate and arranged and traded all at once, while Vuggy liked to unwrap candies—all of them—and keep them stashed in a sticky jumble.

I made dinners that, I hoped, were antidotes to candy: big pots of soup or hot dogs baked in rolls with cheese and mustard. One year, recalling my childhood stunts with food dye, I made blue mashed potatoes and green baked chicken. As the boys got older, their costumes became more complex and ghoulish, and we went out later at night. My father had rightly pointed out that Vuggy needed a grown-up name, and we began to call him Stefan. At six, he walked, carried his own treat bag, and said "thank you," even if he couldn't manage "trick-or-treat," and Tom especially encouraged him.

Eric had developed a ritual sharing of chocolate as a treat for himself and the kids. Everyone had to sit down, butt on the floor, and take turns dusting off a box. Then each chose just one chocolate. Anton and Tom looked forward to this and enjoyed it, but as Stefan grew, his excitement soon turned into frenzy. He wanted the whole box. Unsure what to do, we consulted a psychologist at the Pritzker Institute, a place where we sometimes left Stefan for respite care, and they made a video of us interacting with Stefan around a box of candy. A week later, we returned for the results.

"The video showed so much," said the psych, looking grave and portentous behind his mustache. "You wouldn't believe what we saw."

"So what did it show?" I asked.

"You respond to him too much, you both do. You reinforce the undesirable behavior by paying him attention."

"What would you do?" asked Eric. Requesting advice was rare from Eric, but Stefan had us stymied. The psych turned around, demonstrating the blank back.

"Stefan does something you don't like, you turn around and shut up." I found the session simplistic and humiliating, with its implication of errors revealed by a spying camera, but I was intrigued by the utter finality of the blank back: absence and silence. For a while we tried it, together and separately, and it probably helped at times. In truth, it was one of many ways of relating to Stefan that we developed over time, modifying in response to his growth and change. And contrary to some expectations, he did both grow and change.

Unfortunately, the term "developmental delay" implies normal development on a slow time line. With a child's early milestones, it's appropriate, for Stefan learned to walk at six rather than one, and his walk was more or less normal. He was somewhat like an average three-year-old at nine, but nothing like a normal ten-year-old at thirty. He found his own track for development, and it kept on going, never normal and never coming to a halt.

Stefan was three when I arranged my dance-touring schedule to allow for another baby. It hadn't occurred to me that I wanted a girl, but Natasha's birth focused my love in a new way: on one like me. New feelings and ideas about being a woman poured in, challenging and affirming me. Though her birth meant two in diapers again, and this time for nearly three years, it gave me a self-respect I'd never had before.

"Bad for business," said the obstetrician when she was born, and he was right. Both the family and I were now complete.

During the mid-'70s, Eric and I belonged to a study group that read Marx's *Das Kapital*. After that, we needed another equally massive project and settled on the Book of Genesis. For the first time, I read beyond the creation stories and learned about Abraham and Isaac, Jacob and Esau, Joseph and Benjamin and all their brothers. As far as I remember, we read without benefit of scriptural guide or historical interpretation, certainly without faith perspective. I suppose we read it as literature, though without specific attention to plot or character, surely without attention to the interweaving of myth and history.

The epic extremes of good and evil in the stories surprised me; I had expected simple morality tales. The day we came to the end I felt a powerful forward surge, as though an engine had built up steam behind me and were charging into a future, carrying me and the twelve tribes along with it. The steam was generated by the stories themselves: by Abram's willingness to leave home, family, and land; by Sarai's asking "Is pleasure to come my way again?" as she laughs in her tent; by the tragic abandonment of Hagar and Ishmael in the wilderness of Beersheba; by Jacob's tricky deception of Esau; by the rivalry that caused Joseph's brothers to sell him to the Ishmaelites. I had expected the Bible to impose some sort of unrealistic order from above, but instead I found it revealing the great disorder of the world I knew, and this disorder, churning and roiling, itself issued in a powerful drive forward. I had tumult inside me and a full head of steam, but no place to go.

Like many lapsed Catholics after Vatican II (and long before the accident), Eric liked to talk about how the Mass had been "ruined" by the priest turning to face the people and speaking in the vernacular. One night we sat on the floor in the living room in front of the fire with our friend Joe, a young ex-Dominican who had recently started a workers' training program with Eric, the Lawndale Association for Social Health. The program was addressed to unemployed African American men and combined vocational rehabilitation and group counseling with political education. Joe was no longer practicing as a Catholic, but he had been privy to liturgical reform as it developed over the time he'd been in the order. French Dominicans had produced the Jerusalem Bible, one of the first direct translations from the Hebrew and Greek into a modern vernacular, and liturgical reform had been pioneered in this and other religious communities long before it culminated in Vatican II.

"The Church has lost the sense of awe and mystery," said Eric. "Nothing's hidden anymore. The priest is just like a speaker at a meeting, facing you and addressing you in English." He threw a log on the fire, and sparks arced up, then showered down. Firelight reflected red and yellow from Joe's face.

"There's a reason," Joe said, speaking slowly, "for turning the Mass around. It's not modernization. It's a return to origins, eliminating a lot of medieval accretions. It makes it more like it was in the beginning, a shared meal, with people facing each other around a table." It had never occurred to me that a church service could be a meal. The Protestant services I'd attended were more like a lecture plus sing-along, the Catholic ones some mumbo-jumbo I watched but could not understand. Joe explained that the disciples had dispersed when Jesus died a shameful death. When they experienced his presence still among them, they began to meet in each other's houses for prayer and the breaking of bread, like it says in Acts. The liturgical reform aimed to recall these times and to help the whole community participate in celebrating the Mass. As Joe went on talking, I felt a foundation of meaning spreading under me as solid as the gray rug, as interesting as the dancing fire. I knew shared meals.

Memories of all the makings of my childhood joined with the pleasure I'd taken in teaching my children to cook and sharing late-night suppers in bed with Eric. So that's what Catholics were doing. I understood content where before I'd seen only form. Only "they," of course, not me. I hadn't the least knowledge of the Catholic Mass facing in any direction, but I found meaning replacing suspected sorcery in my imagination.

By 1977, we had four children under twelve, and family life was cacophonous. After starting dinner each evening, I'd join Eric for a drink in our front room, settling on the wood-covered radiator next to his easy chair, while Natasha and Stefan played on the floor. I'd try to tell him everything I'd said or done that day, and his big chest and rooted presence would anchor my flights of thought and doubt, while his fierce convictions gave mine a point of departure. Most important, his listening gave me a self as substantial and coherent as his body, the way a mother's pleasure reflects and thus gives meaning to an infant's incidental smile. I sat down with him one evening just months before the accident, worried about my dance company's upcoming performance season.

"I have a vague idea for a piece," I said. "But I don't see how—"

"Can you help me with German?" Anton came in with his books. I joined Natasha on the floor, and Anton took my seat on the radiator, opening his homework. Natasha and I stacked blocks as she counted under her breath. Stefan spoke in jargon on his stomach, propped up by his hands. Eric took a sip of his drink, then tried to make sense of German grammar rules as taught to English speakers.

"*Wer* or *was*," he said. "That's what you have to figure out." Then, to me: "Michael Reese agreed to take our patients for nothing—we'll have hospital backup for the clinic." Eric was currently directing the second of two free clinics he'd founded.

"Great—how'd you do it?"

"I told them it's a privilege for them to help out. They should thank me for giving them the opportunity."

I began again: "The season's coming up, and I'm afraid . . ."

"One, two . . ." said Natasha, standing up by Eric's chair.

"Take me up," said Eric to her. "But not too high." Natasha's eyes gleamed, and she bounced on her toes.

"One, two, three . . ."

"It's so high, I'm getting scared," said Eric, hand over mouth.

"Four, five, six," continued Natasha, face growing red with excitement.

"I can't look down," said Eric, peering over the side of the chair.

"Seven, eight, nine, eleven. I tried to get to eleven but I could!" sang Natasha. Tom, nine, wandered in and sat on the couch facing us.

"When can we go to the pet store?" he asked. "The snake's hungry."

"Saturday," I said. Eric began a train of blocks with Natasha on the floor. "Choo-choo-choo," said Eric.

"The snake can't wait," said Tom.

"Snakes digest for days," said Eric.

"I saw Phil today and talked to him about music, but . . ."

"I don't get it!" said Anton, stabbing his paper with the pencil and marching out of the room.

"My armed patient was in today, weapons strapped . . ."

"Weapons?" asked Tom. "What weapons?"

"The dates are set—they can't be changed. That guy scares me."

I left for the kitchen to put the children's supper on the table, unfinished thoughts clamoring inside my head. Except for "family dinner" nights, when the kids planned the menu and helped cook, I fed them early. After their supper, we got them ready for bed, and then we all settled on the floor of Natasha's room. She climbed the side of her crib and threw all the animals out, then joined us on the floor.

"Bedtime," Eric told the animals, preparing to impersonate each one.

"Not yet," said the cat. He tossed it into the crib.

"I'm staying up," said the lamb.

"Too late," said Eric and tossed him in. Last of all came Natasha, nesting among her animals, delighted but not a bit fooled. I took the boys to their room to read them a story. If I was working on a dance that required gymnastic skills, I'd practice standing on my head while the boys fell asleep.

Finally, settling into peace and leisure, Eric and I would climb into bed and talk about my search for a theater or designer or his plans for his free clinic, the exchange filling my emptiness and calming my fears, until speech gave way to the language of touch. Afterward, I'd go downstairs and make us a fried-egg supper, completing the meal with whatever was in the fridge. "Pig's ear for dinner," I'd say, because I wouldn't claim I'd cooked up a silk purse. We'd eat in bed, then prepare for sleep, my head quieting his Parkinsonism-affected arm.

When I was pregnant, fetal feet and elbows would choose that moment to wake up, stretching and poking, and I needed a sounding board for sensation as much as I'd needed one earlier for thought.

"Can I give you the baby?" I'd ask.

"Here," he'd say, offering his side. I'd map the tense skin of my stomach into the curve of his waist, so the baby poked us both. Now he'd feel what I felt, and, with that necessary reflection, I'd drift into sleep, both sides of skin in balance.

PART THREE

10

Return to Paradise

EVERY SUMMER, WHEN THE kids were little, we went car camping in Michigan, pitching our tents in a county campground on Lake Charlevoix. We bathed and washed clothes in the lake; cooked breakfast on a propane stove and dinner on a wood fire; ate local corn, green tomatoes, and cherries by candlelight; and went to sleep just after the sun. These trips were a special kind of paradise to me, freeing me from all need for success and achievement, filling life to the brim with here-and-now, daily necessities. Cooking on the fire by the lake as the sun went down, I stood on a threshold, looking beyond the transforming fire to water and sky, each reflecting the other's beauty. My family, often scattered at home in our city house, gathered around the fire. No shouting from room to room or up and down stairs. Busy but free from worry or distraction, I became as collected as the family.

In the summer of 1976, in our zipped-together sleeping bags, I read *The Book: On the Taboo against Knowing Who You Are,* by Alan Watts. An Anglican priest, Watts became a major interpreter of Eastern philosophy and religion to the West. *The Book* is an explanation of the Vedanta philosophy of Hinduism, which contrasts the illusion of oneself as a skin-encapsulated ego with a sense of continuity between self and other, organic and inorganic, living and dead.

In *The Book* I encountered for the first time an idea of God that was not a king, a technocrat, or a supervisor, but Being itself, assuming the innumerable forms of people and things and just as quickly dissolving them. Rocks had produced people in the history of the earth; thus all of existence shared the sacred quality of life. Reading the book again recently, I was struck by two things: how much it reflects its decade, with its contempt for "squares" and "standard brand religions," and how deeply it has influenced my thinking about God and self. Though much of the book seems irrelevant to my own journey today, it laid the groundwork for me to open to a wider horizon. Nine months after I first read it, life forced that opening upon me.

One night on Lake Charlevoix, Natasha woke at the foot of our tent, screaming, "There's a cow in my bed!" I could almost feel that cow, limpid-eyed and mooing, threatening to crush her with its terrible weight. Eric cured such visions by treating them as real and fighting back, and I'd learned from him. "We'll twist that cow's nose and poke his eyes, and he'll be *so* scared," I said. Natasha slept, soothed, and had forgotten the cow by morning, but I wanted to re-create her experience in dance.

I began to observe her with choreographic eyes, studying her expressions and gestures, trying to get her movement into my body, like painting a portrait in flesh: a new way of loving her. I tried to mimic the easy way she crouched to look at something on the ground, then jumped up and ran. I tried to get her tuneless rendition of "You Are My Sunshine" and the pure terror of her nightmare. A short solo resulted with her cry as title, *There's a Cow in My Bed*.

That fall she started nursery school, and Micky was her excellent teacher, warm but firm, with black curly hair and a precise way of talking. She and Natasha seemed to have a bond of understanding, stronger than usual between teacher and student. One night she came to dinner at our house with the man Tasha referred to as "Micky's wife." After the meal, Tasha invited Micky upstairs, showed her the yellow, flowered curtains in her room, and introduced her to the owl that lived there, maybe also the monkey and others from her nighttime menagerie.

The year before, my company had premiered a children's show, *Hop, Skip, Run, and Dance*. Successful, it helped keep the company afloat, and we kept on doing it for a couple of years in schools, at our home theater in the Body Politic, and on tour. The core of it was participatory sequences about body parts—"Where's your hand?" Shake your hand. "Where's your foot?" Kick your foot—and exercises adapted from *Sesame Street* for distinguishing same from different gestures. At the end, we performed various dances and used this opportunity to try out *Cow*.

The dance begins with a three-year-old happily exploring the world. Then lights dim, and she goes to sleep. She wakes up screaming, "There's a cow in my bed!" and dances the nightmare, her terror emphasized by flashing lights. Day breaks, and she realizes she's in her bed. The cow was just a dream. The first time we tried it, the young audience was not entertained but terrified. The second time, we warned them ahead that the dream wasn't real, but they were still scared. By January 12, 1977, when Natasha's class came with others from Ancona to see the show, the piece had been reserved for adult performances.

I don't remember Natasha's reaction to the show, but she was very familiar with me dancing, and the "Boly Poditic," as she called it, was a second home. I do remember the sense of wholeness I felt with Tasha in the audience, Micky taking good care of her charges, and myself doing my work. Micky came up to me afterward and handed me a barrette that must have fallen off during the show.

"You really take care of the stuff," I said.

"No," she said, "Reenee takes care of *the stuff*," referring to a classmate of Tasha's who'd found the barrette on the floor. It seemed like nothing, even the most trivial, need be lost.

Two months and a week or so after that performance, back from Jamaica, I went to Ancona to pick up the boys, and there in the hall stood Micky, blanching at the sight of me, neither of us willing to acknowledge the chasm made vivid by seeing the other. Tears came, and we embraced.

"I'm just glad I saw you," she said. "That you're all right." I know she meant she imagined me physically disintegrated, grief seeping through my pores to corrode my skin, and I was glad to reassure her, even though I wasn't all right. But her relief didn't help me. I was in a barren place known only to those who have been there. I think I taught *Cow* to another company member and retained it briefly in the repertory, but after Natasha's death it seemed more travesty than tribute. I never danced it again.

That summer, on our mournful trip to Vienna, I saw a movie marquee that advertised *Natascha: Todesgrüsse aus Moskau*: "Natasha: Death Greetings from Moscow." The words gave me dreams of Russia, a country I knew only from reading Tolstoy, Dostoyevsky, and the Soviet writer Mikhail Sholokhov. Russia for me was wondrous and remote, a land of onion-domed churches and troikas, and now my dream seemed an invitation to explore the most foreign mystery of all.

The whole family went camping on Lake Charlevoix again the summers Erica was one and two, and the sun was still warm, the fire enticing, the cherries almost falling from the trees. I had a little girl, healthy and laughing. The two girls were clearly different people. Natasha had Eric's long, thin head and brothers so close in age she imitated them, serious, trying to play their boy games. Erica had the round head and face that would make her beautiful, brothers more like older cousins, and a sunny, playful disposition.

Those summers, the boys were old enough to make friends with local kids their own age, but not so old as to take off on teenaged escapades. I remember rising before the others at dawn and taking a volume of Anne Sexton's poetry to the lakeshore, where I sat on a rock and read the poems in which she mourned the year's madness that had separated her from her child. I read her *Death Notebooks,* poems that courted death, and I explored the mythic image of a White Goddess, an influence on the poet Sylvia Plath, whose work I'd used as basis for a dance before. These images joined with dreams of Russia, perhaps all death greetings from Moscow, suggesting meaning in loss.

When we returned, I began to have my dancers improvise around related dream images: a group standing on shore, waving, viewed from the perspective of a departing ship; children enacting a funeral; a group discovering a vessel precious beyond measure, then dropping it; a family struggling to escape but constantly dropping shoes and clothes. In the finished dance, *Travels and Farewells,* I became an old woman, dressed in black, first rocking in a chair and observing the action, then a sort of witch, holding a backyard religious revival, beating on pots and pans, while another dancer, my counterpart, was a White Goddess, a figure of strength and purity. We shared female power: one a dark mama, casting circular spells, the other bright, light, and linear.

Summers on Lake Charlevoix with Erica were truly experiences of restitution, rare and blessed. Like the exiled people of Israel who sat by the rivers of Babylon and wept, I never thought I could return to paradise, and at first it did seem like a dream. I had left that campground weeping, carrying a seed I wasn't even sure I had, and now I was there again, reaping the harvest.

Part Four

11

Conflicting Hungers

AFTER BAPTISM, IN 1982, I was filled with desire for the God who comes "leaping on the mountains, bounding over the hills," in the words of the bride in the Song of Songs. "Let him kiss me with the kisses of his mouth," she says, "for your love is more delightful than wine" (Song 1:2). Now fully awake to my need for the unattainable, I felt compelled to "rise and go through the City [to] seek him whom my heart loves" (Song 3:2). That summer, without direction for my quest, I resonated with the bride abandoned: "I sought him but I did not find him. I called to him but he did not answer. . . . I am sick with love" (Song 5:6–8). Like Mary, the sister of Lazarus, who pours perfumed ointment on the feet of Jesus and wipes them with her hair, I wanted to pour myself out, this time not in grief but in gratitude. My Baptism had opened a yawning hunger for God, a compelling need for prayer, practice, and understanding. This hunger made Eric jealous.

"What's the rush?" he asked one Sunday as I stood in our front hall, coat on, one hand on the doorknob, while he dragged his feet getting ready to go to Mass. By now Erica was three, and I had gotten her and Stefan dressed and fed. Stefan, ten, had put on his own coat by laying it upside down on the floor, inserting his arms in the sleeves, and flipping it over his head, and he was eager to go. The two children were the closest developmentally they would ever be. They were nearly the same size and looked like siblings two or three years apart. Once out the door, I took their hands and practically ran, driven to be on time or even early. "What's this all about?" asked Eric. "Is there someone you want to see?"

"No," I said. "Of course not. I just want to be there." I couldn't explain what drew me. It wasn't anyone in particular, though the feelings could coalesce around a person who offered me a glimpse of holiness, whether it was Beth's friendship or a minister of Communion cradling my hand as I took the cup and responded "Amen" to "Body of Christ."

Stefan sat through the whole Mass happily, sometimes echoing the last words of the priest's prayer or singing along with the hymns. When Erica got restless, Eric took her out to play, respecting my need to stay put and focused. After Mass, I stopped to thank the priest and comment on the homily. "Why were you smiling so much?" asked Eric on the way home. Again I had no good answer.

"Mass just makes me feel 'zingy,'" I said, looking forward to making lunch, continuing the celebration at home. "Excited and happy."

"I understand 'zingy,'" he said. "But I'm afraid you're turning into one of those old ladies in babushkas who spends all her time in church. You don't see men going to church every day. Those ladies who go to daily mass are secretly in love with the priest." I resented his suspicions but knew I was going through as much change as our teenaged sons, and it was bound to disturb him. Trying to reassure him, I told him I was still the same person and loved him more than God. I meant what I said, but I did sometimes feel like a lamp had been lit inside me, and I'm sure it shone through my eyes, looking like illicit excitement.

On our camping trip in July, I attended church in small towns. For the first time, I heard the "Hail Mary" chanted over and over at the end of Mass, as was common before Vatican II, "for the conversion of Russia, the defeat of Godless communism." I felt alienated. It wasn't that I had anything against the "Hail Mary." This beautiful prayer first greets Mary with the announcing angel's words and then asks her to pray for us at the hour of our death. I say it often in stressful situations and even chant it to myself. But at that time, I needed to ask questions, engage in dialogue, and listen. I had no resource to balance rural Michigan's old-fashioned liturgy. I had faith, hope, and love, or maybe it was only a desire for these things, but I needed understanding. Where was the Church of social justice, the Church where, according to Acts, "all who believed were together and had all things in common; and they sold their possessions and goods and distributed them to all, as any had need" (Acts 2:44–46)?

It would be a few years before Eric and I discovered Marxist interpretations of the Bible or liberation theology, with its emphasis on redistribution of wealth and attention to people on the margins. I'd not yet heard of the "preferential option for the poor," articulated by the Latin American Bishops' Conference at Medellin in 1968, and I could not accept the idea of polar opposition between Catholicism and communism. I was dying of thirst, and I didn't know where to turn.

I think it was Beth who suggested I take a course at Catholic Theological Union, and I signed up for "Introduction to Theology." There I joined men studying for the priesthood, women in religious communities, and laymen and -women in all forms of ministry, some just out of college and some returning to seminary to update their theology. My first day began with a student-led morning prayer. Though glad to be there, I was nervous and stared straight ahead, as I had so often done in church. The leaders asked us to bless each other with a sign of the cross on the forehead, and I held back, hesitant. Next to me was Dianne Bergant, a brilliant scripture scholar and former schoolteacher whom I did not yet know. "Oh, is that what we're doing now?" she asked in her bright, good-morning-class voice and turned to me for the sign. The simplicity of her tone and question—like the everyday grain of consecrated bread—told me even I could perform the sacred gesture, and I touched my thumb to her forehead. I plunged into the sea of faith trusting I could learn to swim, a happy fish in water.

Eric had welcomed my joining him in a love of God he had really never lost, but he didn't welcome my passionate involvement with the theology I was learning at CTU. Before Vatican II, the Church had deposited its theology in manuals of conclusions, and these dogmatic propositions had informed the Church Eric knew. Now I was learning that every tradition had a history, that church teachings had evolved and were evolving, that the Bible had been written by people in and for communities, that the revelation of God was not fixed and final but the personal communication of God to human freedom, making different demands on the Church at different times. Each one of these ideas attacked a belief Eric cherished.

Tom graduated from eighth grade at St. Thomas that June and was admitted to St. Ignatius, a conservative Jesuit high school. Proud of getting in, he talked about becoming a priest or a neurosurgeon, but the school year was only three-quarters over when his complicated reaction to Natasha's death erupted in the form of a Mohawk, head shaved on either side, central spikes sticking up. It seemed that my curly-headed, generous lover of sister and snakes had turned against himself, and I regretted more deeply than ever that I'd been unable to save him from Natasha's loss. After a brief struggle with the school's authorities, in which Eric supported Tom, he was expelled. To me the expulsion was inevitable. Tom had already begun to grow marijuana for a school biology experiment, and I knew that the moment the teacher read his paper, he'd be out anyway.

The garage in our backyard was a former carriage house, and Tom discovered an unused second floor, swept it out, and moved in, creating a gathering place for all the disaffected teens in the neighborhood. They called it the Horse, for its previous use. The arrangement was tenuous and potentially dangerous, but the teens were doing nothing criminal, and it kept Tom off the streets. Both Eric and I were trying to balance communication with enforcement, letting him live in the Horse but insisting that he go to either school or work, and he joined a crew painting apartments in a rental property we owned.

Shortly thereafter, he and his friends formed a band, Mind Release, which practiced in our basement. Eric heard echoes of his own rebellion in Tom's and wanted to support Tom's creative efforts. However, the music was amplified, and that heavy sound pounded Eric's authority in a personal way. Occasionally, a visiting male friend would hear the band start up and ask Eric, "How can you allow that?" Eric saw his weakness revealed, and he struggled with his desire to crack down. Somehow he managed to find a balance, forbidding practice after ten and enforcing rules against smoking and sleeping in the living room.

For me, it was much easier; the music was loud, but it didn't threaten me. For Stefan, the band was a godsend. The guys always welcomed him to rehearsals, and he could stand down there for hours, hands jerking happily to the music. And when the band took a beak, doing rhythm jams with hands and feet on the front porch, Stefan was there too, having the time of his life.

One evening during my first months at CTU, Eric and I sat in the front room side by side at cocktail time. Erica played on the floor, Anton and Tom were busy elsewhere, and Stefan was occupied with a tape recorder.

"Jesus didn't come to found a church," I said, repeating what I had learned in a New Testament class that day. "Much less a hierarchy. He came to proclaim the Kingdom and to rescue 'the lost sheep of the house of Israel.'" Being Catholic was giving me my first experience of the riches of Judaism, as I learned the Jewish origins of Christian fasts and feasts and came to know the sad, celebratory Ladino songs of Sephardic Spain. Eric was particularly disturbed by my emphasis on the Jewishness of Jesus.

His negative feelings coincided with everything he'd been taught in the Lutheran and Catholic churches of Austria before the Second World War, and his family had tried to escape Jewish identity for at least two generations. I'd been deeply moved by Moses's discovery of monotheism and the effect of this discovery: that no person could now claim to be God, and people would have to treat each other as equals, as sisters and brothers.

"But Jesus rejected Judaism," said Eric. "He internalized the Law." I agreed with the latter, but not the former. Eric found it hard to accept the Jewish cocoon in which Christianity was spawned, while I was thrilled to think of Jesus as a person, a Jewish person, feeling close enough to God to call him "Abba," discovering through his human experience what God wanted of him.

"Jesus didn't think he was God," I said, warming to my subject and to my newfound role with Eric. "You can see that would be delusional."

"Sounds like you're dismembering the Trinity," said Eric.

"Jesus didn't teach the Trinity," I said. "That's a matter of later interpretation. Scholars and theologians try to understand Jesus's experience of becoming Christ from his own human point of view. It's called 'Christology from below.'" I'm sure I was an obnoxious teacher, but my pleasure was keen.

"Next you're going to be telling me that bread and wine don't really become the body and blood of Christ." Eric was growing agitated, and that always made his tremor worse. He tucked his right hand under his seat to hold it still. I attempted to summarize my teachers.

"In the medieval worldview, objects consisted of substance and accident. Thus, the substance could change—bread become the body of Christ—while the accidents, taste and texture, remained the same. Modern people don't conceive of objects in this way, so we have to find new ways to talk about the reality of the symbol."

"Heresy!" said Eric. I smiled, shrugged, and shut up, for we studied many movements and trains of thought at CTU, and yesterday's heresy might be today's orthodoxy, though the Church would be loath to admit it. In any case, we didn't throw the word around as an accusation.

Around this time, we had several meetings with Father Nelson, a progressive priest in an inner city parish, as Eric was searching for a site for a free clinic. As we departed, Father Nelson would say, "Shalom."

"Why does he say that to me?" asked Eric, taken aback. "How does he know I'm Jewish?"

"It's not you," I explained. "Everyone says it. It's a reminder of the Church's Jewish roots: 'Peace,' the way Jesus might have said it." Eric remained skeptical, marked by his upbringing and his narrow escape from the Nazis, though he knew that times had changed. And I didn't get it. I still thought of religion as an individual choice among diverse offerings, like produce at the supermarket, logically separate from nationality. On a trip to Austria, I'd been puzzled by the concentration camp memorial at Ebensee, where one section of graves was labeled "Jews" and another "Czechs." The idea that a person could not be a Jew and an Austrian or a Pole at the same time offended my persistent sense of equality. If a Catholic could be an Austrian, why not a Jew? Not until much later would I begin to understand this.

Every time I discovered the sense behind a theological concept, I was deeply gratified, while the experience of life in a faith-based community gave me a new way of being at home in the world. Thus, at CTU I found the kind of crack that widens and deepens with time, not a flash of the "other," but a fountain of wisdom, learning, support, and faith that would sustain me for five years and beyond.

After finishing eighth grade at Lab, Anton enrolled in our local public high school. He stayed for an impatient year and a half and then dropped out, furious at incompetent or unconcerned teachers, but not before writing "fuck you" on the blackboard in a music class and not before being held at knifepoint just outside the school by a student who stole his watch. Anton's rebellion was opposite in character from Tom's. He wanted intellectual purity uncompromised by the desire for good grades, success, or money. Everything had to be perfect, from the right-angled intersection of baseboard and floor (always off-kilter in our old house) to the list of tasks in his datebook. I still have a sheet of paper he designed and posted on the fridge headed "Sodidy-Bop Ledger," using Eric's playful variation on "soda pop." We had made a rule that no one could take more than three in a day, and this was Anton's attempt to regulate consumption. The sheet has columns for initials, the date, and the flavor taken, with entries that run a couple of weeks. At the bottom it says, "Limit of three (3) per person. *No* exceptions," and along the side, "Note all withdrawals, even for guests. *Be honest.* Remember—Jesus gave it to you." The reference to Jesus must have been satiric, as he felt nothing but hostility toward our involvement in the Church. Despite its humor, the sheet seems to me today a cry for order in the face of chaos. Tom's freedom to take whatever he wanted drove Anton crazy, and Anton's haughty disdain pushed Tom to further feats of extravagance.

After a few months working and without a high school diploma, Anton was admitted to Roosevelt University. Much happier academically, he felt incompetent socially and busied himself with electronic inventions and an early Radio Shack computer. While Tom had had girlfriends since he was six, Anton was shy and unable to connect with the girls he now desired. He began neglecting his clothes and failing to bathe.

One night about seven, Eric, Erica, Stefan, and I sat down to dinner. I lit the candles and turned off the overhead light before we joined hands for our prayer. Soon the darker reaches of the kitchen filled with hulking shapes.

"Say, Dad," said Tom. "Can you loan me ten dollars?"

"It's dinnertime," said Eric. "Sit down and join us, all of you." Friends were always welcome at meals. "Sit down or leave."

"Have some minestrone," I said to Tom's friends. "It's vegetable soup." Bodies shifted beyond the circle of light, taking up space, disturbing the air.

"Thanks, but we've got to go," from a voice behind me.

"I'll be back for some of that homemade bread another time, though," said another voice.

"Tom, are you ready?"

"Sit down or go!" said Eric. "Go! Now!"

"Look Dad, we're going, but we just need ten dollars," said Tom.

"Go!" said Eric.

The shapes drifted out as Anton came in the front door, home from Roosevelt, and greeted us.

"Sit down," said Eric. "Join us. Don't stand around." Anton sat, and I served him some minestrone, indicated bread and salad on the table.

"That's gross," said Anton, an aggrieved snarl in his voice. "I came home to eat, but I can't eat this stuff. Why can't you make regular food for once?" Skinny and on the verge of tears, he seemed like a reiteration of his tantrumming eighteen-month-old self, the child my mama used to the call the "sick poet" for the Weltschmerz in his face.

"To me this *is* regular," I said, hurt and angry.

"You're always trying to make something *interesting*," he said, "from some exotic country." It was true. I loved to cook, and meals varied from

Chinese-style stir fries to Indian curries to French stews and soups to spicy salsas and tortillas.

"What would be regular to you?" I asked, sneering. "Supper in a bag?" referring to a recipe Anton had found in a newspaper, a Sloppy Joe mix served over a bag of Fritos.

"Yeah," he said, ignoring my sarcasm, "that's OK. Or three things on a plate, separate. And nothing weird." I hated causing him pain, but I also feared being a weak and overindulgent mother. I'd always adored this kid, even when he screamed about a broken gingerbread person or some other loss of virginal perfection. He'd been brilliant but brittle from the moment of birth. He pushed his plate away and sat back.

"Is it true that you guys are planning to baptize Stefan?" he asked, nearly spitting the words with disgust. "How can you think of doing that, of imposing your dogma on my poor little retarded brother?"

"Let's talk about it," said Eric. "He really likes church. We thought it might be one more way for him to participate in life."

"He likes all kinds of ritual," I said. "Remember how he learned to clink glasses and say '*Prosit*'?"

"That's different," said Anton. "Baptizing him would be terrible. He has no idea what you're doing. Please don't." He rose and went up to his room.

"What do you think we should do?" I asked Eric. "He really seems to care about this."

"We can wait with baptizing Stefan," said Eric. "Anton will get over it." This was fine with me. I liked the idea of deferring Baptism until children had some idea what it meant and didn't plan to baptize Erica for a few years. She and Stefan could do this together. "He's so upset about the food, as though it were a personal affront," I said. "What can I do about that?"

"You could just do what he wants for a while," he said. I was surprised and relieved. It was actually OK to give in? I had no desire to resist; I could cook whatever I wanted some other time. Making good food from the American lexicon in three separate units was a nice challenge, and I probably started with my childhood favorite: chicken, peas, and rice, then moved on to meatloaf and mash. Despite my love of restaurants and innovation, I liked food that reflected place and culture, food that spoke, and I was happy to use this channel to communicate with Anton.

Later that year, Anton began to develop some strange ideas about what he called "network people," people connected with what he saw on

TV, sort of like "illuminati." These people had special power or privilege, able to function in the world in a way that he couldn't. His ideas seemed to have a paranoid tinge, but I left the worrying to Eric. One night Eric found him curled on the floor in our upstairs hallway closet, lying in the fetal position. Eric took almost all deviant behavior in stride, but this time he looked truly alarmed and proceeded to find Anton a psychiatrist.

Anton saw the psychiatrist for a couple of years, until he entered the University of Chicago. Eric and I met with the doc just once, sitting on the far side of his big, forbidding desk. Anton was studying physics at the time and expert at making things, and the doctor was concerned about Anton's invention of a listening device that enabled him to hear our neighbor's private conversations.

"I tried to explain to Anton," said the doc, "that people have secrets. They get angry if someone else discovers them." We nodded, but I was proud of Anton's inventive ability, and I doubt Eric was very concerned about Anton's invasion of privacy. "Which of you is closer to Anton?" asked the doc.

"I am," said Eric. I was taken aback at this. I would have said we were both close, but thought better of it. Prejudice against mothers and their supposedly harmful influence was still rife in those years, and I felt suspicion directed at me like a draft.

"Where does Anton sleep?" asked the doc.

"In the study," I said. "Where Eric and I have desks."

"But I spend my days in the office," said Eric. "Maggie works in the study when she's not in the studio upstairs." We always had one fewer bedroom than children, and rooms rotated frequently as shifting ages and births made new demands on the space. Anton had inhabited the baby room, the back room, and the study, and he would move to the basement before he left home.

"How close to your desk is his bed?" asked the doc.

"Four feet, six feet, something like that," I said. What was he imagining? I never found out.

"Parents usually resent the therapist," said the doc. "When the child begins to get better, they pull him out of therapy." I resolved that this would not be true of me; there was nothing I wanted more than to see Anton happy, despite his transient anger at me. I always shared his intellectual, subversive humor and continued to do so, even while mourning his absence, when he entered the University of Chicago and moved to a dorm down the street.

One night I was awakened by a clanging doorbell and pounding. Firemen wanted the key to the padlocked first-floor door of the Horse; it was burning, and they feared for people inside. We didn't have the key; the boys climbed up or jumped down from a second-floor hinged window that faced the alley. A quick phone call found Tom at the house of a friend, and no one was hurt, but the Horse was gone. Eric and I decided to rebuild it without the second floor.

Workmen were nearly through shingling the roof when I looked out and saw Tom and a friend climbing on it. I literally couldn't believe what I saw, and I tried not to. Later, I had to admit the truth: they had gotten drunk and were ripping the shingles off, enraged at the loss of their living space. Faced with such an extreme of anger and uncensored action in my own son, I could only deny it. I may never understand it.

After the Horse burned, Tom moved back into the house and shortly thereafter started a series of neighborhood performances called the Satisfaction Reaction. Anyone could sign up to read poetry, play music, give a talk, show a painting, or dance, and he encouraged parents as well as friends to participate. One time Eric gave a talk on free medical care, and another, I did a performance piece about making things: babies, bread, and dances. Mind Release played, and Tom developed what he called his "philosophies," slogans about fear of failure and the importance of overcoming taboos, about self-interest and altruism. "Altruistic action = egoistic satisfaction" read a poster for one of the shows, and he preached his philosophies with religious fervor. On one occasion, he acted out taboo violation by walking naked with a pal around the block at midday, but Satisfaction Reactions were usually creative and constructive affairs, and I attended whenever possible.

Then one summer, while Eric and I were in Europe with Erica and Stefan was in respite care, Tom got a license as a street entertainer, made some money playing music, and used it to take the G.E.D. He passed and entered Roosevelt in the fall, registering his name as Raef fo Ruliaf, or "fear of failure" spelled backward. With Tom studying music at Chicago Music College, a part of Roosevelt, and Anton studying physics at the University of Chicago, it seemed that we were out of the adolescent woods.

Stefan had found an excellent school placement at Esperanza Community Services, marred only by the frequent delays of his "little yellow bus." He'd become enthralled by illustrated cookbooks and could spend hours pulling down volumes from shelves above the kitchen sink, poring over photos of glowing yeast breads and gooey chocolate mud cakes. Occasionally he got into our good vinyl records or Eric's fine turntable, and once he overturned a few boxes of sorted photos, but most of the time, his behavior was under control and acceptable. I was free to devote myself at CTU to courses on God language, on liturgy and liturgical seasons, and on the structure of religious experience. Each of these became a part of my own religious experience, broadening and deepening my feelings of love and gratitude, but never satisfying my hunger for more.

12

All Roads Converge

ERIC AND I HAD fruitful dialogue even when we disagreed, but he drew the line at my desire for spiritual direction, one-on-one conversations about the spiritual life. This time-honored sort of "companioning" or "soul friendship" on the spiritual journey was taught at an Institute for Spiritual Leadership, located near us, where fifteen or so men and women came each year, from all over the world, for a year of training in spiritual direction. They had classes in psychology and Jungian active imagination, their own spiritual direction, and supervision. For the latter, my parish recruited directees who would consent to have their sessions taped and reviewed by the supervisor. This opportunity opened for me a tempting vista: I'd be able to talk to someone about my search, ask questions, and get guidance on the way. I crossed Eric's line.

His objection? "All my patients are in love with me," he said. He was as aware of the mysteries of transference as I was ignorant, though I'd heard the term. No one can really know until they've been there how the meeting of two people in a contained and isolated time and place elicits every forbidden and repressed emotion, especially sexual ones, and the feelings cling to the director or therapist. That person becomes a symbol around which cluster parents, lovers, sisters, brothers: every person with whom the directee has had a relationship of desire, resentment, or jealousy. Add to this discussions about God, and you have a seething cauldron of emotion.

Even without the special situation of transference, love of God and human love have always been thoroughly intertwined. Father Zossima, in Dostoyevsky's *The Brothers Karamazov*, exhorts his fellow monks to "love all God's creation, the whole and every grain of sand of it. Love every leaf, every ray of God's light. Love the animals, love the plants, love everything. If you love everything, you will perceive the divine mystery in things."[1]

"A new commandment I give to you, that you love one another, even as I have loved you," says Jesus (John 13:34). Though the biblical tradition differentiates among *agape,* the unconditional, overpowering love of God, *philia,* brotherly or sisterly love, and *eros,* erotic love, life rarely separates them so neatly. The mix of God and sex can be fatal, as in hero-worshipping or death-dealing cults, and it's essential to differentiate sane from crazy, abusive from kind, and idolatrous from reverent in religion, where desire can so easily be aroused and perverted, and so much is at stake.

Once I started spiritual direction with Father Bill, our weekly meetings became a drug. I waited all week for the precious hour that permitted me to connect parts of myself with church teachings I'd learned from the outside, to personalize the connection between "dogmatic" and "existential" I was studying in my theology class. At first, I asked about concepts like the Trinity and marveled at Father Bill's interpretation. "If an 'I' gives itself to a 'thou,'" he said, holding up two fingers, "completely and utterly, and the 'thou' in turn gives itself to the 'I,' so that they are intertwined"—the fingers twisted around each other—"then their love proceeds from them into the world"—one hand now drawing downward from the twisted fingers—"and that's the Spirit." I was transfixed, inspired to see how an intellectual, theological concept could be understood so directly. Like a greedy child, I craved mystical experience and understanding all at once. "Take it easy," said Father Bill.

"Down, Fido," I said. "I think that's what you're telling me." He laughed and agreed, advocating quiet scripture reading and a listening sort of prayer. His selfless receptivity was altogether new to me. As wife and mother, I'd always taken care of everyone in my family, managing household, schools, and meals and keeping the peace. Anton had gotten therapy when he needed it, and Eric had completed years of analysis as part of his psychiatric training, but I had common sense and supposedly needed nothing more. Thus, spiritual direction was my first experience of that personal encounter where I became the exclusive center of attention, invited to reveal myself to another. I found the weekly hours utterly compelling.

Eric hated what I was doing. When Father Bill was through with the tapes of our sessions, I'd bring them home and offer to let Eric listen to their very ordinary contents. He'd wave them aside, then later object if I turned to walk down the street where Father Bill lived, one of the direct paths from our house to church. "Why do you want to go that way?" he'd ask, so much more aware than I of the devious ways attraction expresses itself. But Eric was always flexible. He could see how important the meetings were to me, and he put up with them for the nine months Father Bill was in Chicago.

One Thursday, Father Bill called with a bad cold, to cancel. At first I felt like I'd stepped off the edge of a cliff, cut loose and falling. Then I became obsessed with the need to do something for him, to take care of him, to make him grateful. But I had to hide my need, mask it with something that looked reasonable. Chicken soup. I'd make him chicken soup. I dropped everything and rushed to the store, bought chicken and vegetables, and set them simmering.

I knew I was acting crazy, and Eric wouldn't like it. I didn't know whether I would tell him at the end of the day or whether he would notice the gap if I left it out of the daily account, the hour when we told each other everything. I threw the soup into the freezer to chill, removed the fat, and carried it the one block to Father Bill's apartment, where he greeted me with mild surprise. Gratified to have done what I could but embarrassed by my obsession, I handed over the broth, hoping that soup was thicker than water. I don't remember whether I told Eric or not, but if I did, I surely rationalized the event as a casual favor and omitted my overwhelming need.

Except for soup, I did not cross any barriers with Father Bill. As time went on, Father Bill's first question to me, "Who or what is God to you right now?" gradually segued into "Who is God and therefore who are you, as word or breath of God?" The topics of direction gradually moved from theological discussions to more personal ones, as I got in touch with buried feelings. I began to integrate the various parts of my Christian self: nonrational with rational, selfish with generous, evil with good.

Eric had always talked about feelings, unlike my parents, but his words came quickly to contain the dangerous impulse. It worked for him, for words could only slightly stifle his strong and sudden desires, angers, and fears, which sometimes contradicted each other. He felt no need to be consistent. My feelings were much more hidden, and the words he asked from me could arrive too soon, before I knew what I felt. If he said, "You're angry; admit it," he was probably right, but if I said, "OK, I'm angry," my words were just words. Father Bill encouraged me to let myself feel before interpreting or explaining what I felt, and this opened up for me a new dimension of self-awareness.

Gradually, talking to Father Bill, I discerned what I wanted to do with the ferment in my life. I loved the liturgy, and I knew how to dance, so perhaps I could join these things in ministry. I began dancing in CTU's liturgies, elaborate, art-filled celebrations for feast or fast days, prepared by the students. Soon I began offering classes in "embodied prayer," calling on Sally for a crash course in methods of teaching improvisation. Dance could not function as prayer unless it were linked to the dancer's own feeling and experience, and improvisation could access these. Embodied prayer, a spontaneous, personal expression, led to liturgical dance, which aimed to serve the needs of an assembly gathered for the public work of worship. Liturgical dance required embodied prayer as antecedent, to keep it sincere and avoid formalism.

The faculty in liturgy at CTU was extremely knowledgeable and sophisticated, and I studied the meaning and history of seasons, feasts, fasts, and the Eucharist itself, the mystery of Christ's life, death, and resurrection celebrated each Sunday. Gradually I began to research the relationship between liturgy and performance. At the same time, I was developing a dance-theater piece called *Word in Motion* with two dance colleagues, one Episcopalian, one Presbyterian. This hodgepodge piece tried to make choreography out of gestures of worship, then moved on to mourn the disappeared in Chile. A bit of dialogue made fun of high-church pretense and low-church disorder, exploiting the joke that communion wafers "take more faith to believe they're bread than to believe they're Jesus." The piece ended with participatory bread sharing that continued my long-standing interest in integrating audience and performers, moving a show toward ritual. I was testing the waters, searching for forums where dance and religion could interact. *Word in Motion* was more like a collision than an intersection, perhaps because I hadn't resolved the conflict in myself. Later, when I attended a dance conference in Hong Kong, I discovered that the split between sacred and secular is unknown in many Eastern cultures. "Your problem," said attendees from India, China, and Japan.

During the five years that I studied part-time at CTU, I responded to requests for dance from churches of all denominations, temples, nursing homes, and schools. My greatest ambition was to wed liturgy and dance in a great, group ritual without the isolation of church. I used to fantasize a Mass celebrated over several hours in my backyard with all parts danced by all present, a sort of sacred improvisation party. The movement would unpack the emotions of gathering, repenting, storytelling, blessing, breaking, sharing, and sending: all the actions of the Mass. Fortunately this never happened, and it never could, for we Anglo-Americans are not a dancing people, and a Sunday service would lose focus and dissolve into chaos before it evolved into a ritual performance in a backyard. Unlike some in African or Latin cultures, we do not dance in markets or in the streets, never in the halls of finance or government. Anything beyond pre-scribed gesture meets resistance.

As I taught and practiced liturgical dance, I tried to root movement in the rocky soil of everyday life, to connect it to the liturgical actions of praising, offering, and petitioning. I discovered that people's reluctance to move has two very different effects. First, movement observed or executed releases emotion. When dancing at a funeral, I was often told, "I couldn't cry until I saw you dance." In a workshop once, I asked people to imagine a weight on their shoulders and respond physically. As their shoulders sank, old griefs welled up. Something about nonverbal, physical expres-sion touched people in a direct way, whether they were releasing grief or breaking the bounds of words with joy. When I danced at a wedding, people felt the promise and challenge of two bodies bound together for life. Possibly these effects are dependent on the usual repression of gesture in our culture, so that movement opens an escape valve. Many churches try to hide bodies, perhaps precisely because of the way they tap feeling. We sit in wooden pews, read from behind solid lecterns (ambos), or sing behind "modesty rails," a choir of heads. The history of Christianity is full of attempts to suppress dance both in and out of church, for fear of its sexual connotations.

The second effect of our reluctance to move is almost the opposite. Dance in church can irritate. It often looks awkward and self-conscious if it's not professional, or narcissistic and self-centered if the dancer is well trained. Training produces a dancer graceful and pleasant to watch, but set apart from the community. No one watching will think, "I could do that, and I will." Readers can lead reading, and singers can lead singing, but it's much harder for a dancer to lead dancing. It can be beautiful to see people performing simple movements to which they seem born, and many mod-ern choreographers have found ways to use untrained dancers, but it takes years of artistic experiment to find the tone that will feel authentic, that will speak to the needs of the assembly while still being part of it.

I began to teach Sunday school when Erica was kindergarten age, and both she and Stefan attended my class, with Eric as assistant. We tried to help the children see God's love in their parents' care, bright fall leaves, sun and rain, and to manifest that love in things they made and in respect for one another. Stefan's presence was, in itself, a lesson in acceptance and respect for difference. Thus, both Stefan and Erica were prepared for Initiation at the Easter Vigil, 1985, when she was seven and Stefan fourteen. By this time Anton was occupied with his own life and work at the university and made no objection. The Church offered Baptism, Communion, and Confirmation all together, but we opted to defer Confirmation for Erica to her teens, so it could be a more mature choice. For Stefan, Communion itself would require a special preparation. Though he sometimes licked walls or swiped a bit of someone's cake as he walked through a restaurant, he was very particular about what he put in his mouth. He had no trouble accepting bread as Jesus, but you couldn't persuade him that communion wafers were bread. We never did surmount the wafer obstacle, but fortunately, our regular mass used homemade altar bread, so I cooked up a batch, and we practiced.

"Stefan, would you like to go to Communion at church?" I asked, breaking off a piece of the slightly sweet, brown bread.

"Yeah." Stefan was already nervous, looking suspiciously at my hand.

"At church we have special bread, like this."

"OK, Ma."

"Try it, it's good." He took a piece but did not eat it.

"Next time we go to church, you can have the special bread, but you have to eat it. It means God loves you very much. Let's pretend now. Hold out your hand, and I'll say 'Body of Christ.'"

"Body Christ." Stefan's breathing grew heavy, and he bit the back of his hand where a callous had formed, moaning with agitation. I could see he wanted to do right.

"You say 'Amen,'" I said, "and then you eat the bread. Can you do that?"

"Amen," he said. He knew that from our dinner prayer, but he was through. No eating the bread. Enough for one day.

"It's good, Stefan, you can eat it," I said and ate a piece. "Yum." After several days' practice, he ate the bread.

The next Sunday I asked him if he wanted to go to Communion, and he said yes. I guided him into the line but couldn't get him to cup his hands to receive or to say "Amen." He did take the bread, and I followed him back to the pew, hovering and saying "Put it in your mouth," afraid he would stash it in his pocket, as he liked to do with candy. He did eat it, and from then on, he always participated. I was never in a Catholic church that failed to accept him and all handicapped people, regarding them as blessed children of God and worthy of respect. If I had "chosen" a church, rather than having it choose me, I would have chosen the Catholic one if only for this reason.

My father was diagnosed with kidney cancer in 1987 and died that year, ten years after Natasha's death. I lost one pole of the secular-sacred conflict and began, ever so slightly, to assume my father's position. I felt an increased sympathy for his folk music and his rationalist views, antagonizing Eric greatly. The conflict between the two men dated from the day they met. Eric had never deferred to Daddy and never asked for my hand in marriage, and Daddy neither confronted him nor ever forgave him for that. Eric hated Daddy's tact and politeness, all the qualities of compromise that enabled him to succeed in public life, where he'd moved on after working for Truman to serve as the lieutenant governor of Wisconsin and the U.S. commissioner of Indian affairs. Daddy hated Eric's revolutionary zeal, the uncompromising boldness that enabled him to found and run two free all-volunteer clinics, first with the Black Panther Party and later at St. Basil's Catholic Church. When we became Catholic, the conflict escalated. Daddy's anthropological approach to religion seemed wishy-washy to Eric, allowing everything and touching nothing. Sometimes I tried to explain that Daddy had faith in community and viewed religion as an aspect of culture, like politics.

"Dammit it," Eric would say. "I hate that cold, liberal perspective." I don't know why he added an extra syllable to "damn it," but he always did. "And damn tolerance. A thing's either right or wrong. Sticks in my craw." Most disturbing to Daddy, Eric probed the psyche with his "ruthless honesty."

"What are you angry about?" he asked Mama one afternoon in the early '70s, as she stood in the middle of the living room, eyes flat and body as frozen as a startled deer. Eric, my children, Daddy, and I sat on couches around her. I don't remember what the issue was, but the air had grown thick with unspoken irritation.

"I'm not," said Mama.

"Yes you are. Look at you!" said Eric. Mama said nothing. "Try again," said Eric. "Aren't you annoyed by what's happening?"

"I don't know what you're talking about."

"I'm making you angry right now, by insisting you talk about your feelings."

"Shut up!" exploded Daddy, shocking us all, his smooth surface breaking like crazed ceramic, his body trembling. "Just shut up!" I stared into space, avoiding eyes, insides roiling. We dispersed in tense silence, unsure just what had pushed Daddy over the edge.

Now I think that Eric threatened the protective cocoon Daddy had long since woven around Mama, treating her like the fragile and disturbed person she'd been when he met her and in some ways still was. I didn't realize how fully he protected her until much later, when she planned to take a car trip across the country with a woman friend, and he confessed to me he feared she couldn't make it alone. She couldn't? Mama, who'd raised Sally and me, who'd directed the Georgetown Day School for fifteen years? She'd always seemed capable to me, if subject to depression. But how much do children really know about their parents? Gradually I concluded that this was how they'd worked out the fit between them: he stood guard at her door with a club in his hand, and she was safe from prying questions, confrontation, and anger. I was used to Eric's ways, and I was unprepared when my usually self-controlled father wielded the club: "Shut up!" And I was equally unprepared when I found Eric in tears at the end of Daddy's memorial service.

"I hated the bastard," he said. "Then why am I crying?"

As I grew up, Mama used to quote Daddy as complaining that a father worked hard and cared for his daughters for years, only to have "some son-of-a-bitch come and take them away." I'm sure he meant it as a joke, but there was truth behind it, and this truth we never discussed. If I were to have a full and satisfying adult life, I would have to find a son-of-a-bitch with power equal to Daddy's: physical, intellectual, and spiritual. Of course, I could have found Eric's power in myself, but I was too overwhelmed by my inhibited, threatening daddy to fight my own battles. I let the two of them fight it out, always putting my marriage in first place and keeping peace with my parents as best I could.

Daddy's death disturbed a fundamental dynamic between Eric and me, and our compatibility was challenged again. If he noticed me angling my shopping cart to make way for others, he would say, "Let them move over for you. You're acting like your father." Eric liked to step right out in front of moving cars, "giving them the privilege," he said, "of looking out for me." I hated the accusation and did not want to be like Daddy, but sometimes I'd hear myself taking on his ideas.

"It seems to me," I might say, "that marriage is a part of social structure, as well as a personal, romantic attachment."

"Two people either love each other or they don't," Eric would say. "You can't put it under a magnifying glass, like some kind of interesting native custom. I hate your father's distancing, anthropological point of view, and now you're talking like him. Makes a fellow mad." Without Daddy as ballast, the very brashness that had attracted me to Eric seemed more abrasive than brave. Eric's bad-boy antics and bold self-assertion antagonized me, as I slid back along the polarized line that distinguished the two men, leaning toward the liberal, the tactful, the relativistic, and the secular. I'm not surprised that Eric didn't like it.

At the same time, I began sliding back from liturgy to art, symbolizing the sacred in my own terms rather than "modified by the person of Christ," to quote Bishop Rouet again. With no father to fight, my heart turned toward songs of "secular faith," folk songs that expressed faith in meeting after death without using overtly religious language, and I listened repeatedly to Anita Silvert's "All Roads Converge," which I'd heard on Rich Warren's radio program, *The Midnight Special.* "I do not know what runs my life," sings Silvert, "or if it runs alone, / I do not know if travel waits or if I'm headed home. / I do not know which stories in my life will have an end, / but I know I'm sure to see each one of you again." A traditional song expresses a similar faith: "Fathers now our meeting is over, mothers we must part, / and if I never see you any more, I love you with all my heart. / And if we land on shore, we'll be free forevermore."

In spring of the following year, I began work on *All Roads Converge,* the dance component of an all-day participatory event sponsored by the North American Conference on Christianity and Ecology, called "Journey of Dance and Sacred Architecture." For the architecture segment, painter

John Freda and his wife, Sandra Wells, did a visual and ceremonial workshop in which participants built "small cosmic temples" from light materials. The dance segment used three groups of dancers: four professionals, who rehearsed for a few months in advance; a larger group of dancers with some experience, who met for four Saturdays in advance; and people who came for the day, no preparation or experience required.

The videotape of *All Roads Converge*, which I view today, shows the bare gym of a Methodist church on Chicago's North Side. The core group of four stands out in bright jumpsuits with wide waistbands in contrasting colors: pink on purple, blue on green. The intermediate group is in white, uniform in color but varied in style. The third, the participating audience, wears whatever they put on that day. We've all learned two circle dances after a morning spent in embodied reflection on creation, a combination of meditation and improvisation, and everyone is gathered for the final event. I introduce the performance without mentioning my father, leaning back on a piano, hands folded, and my voice is calm and assured: "The dance expresses faith that those who have been separated by sin or death will meet again. What gives us this conviction? A story that we tell in the middle part of the piece. It begins with creation from mud and holy breath. Then borders arise to separate parts of self, to separate me from you, to separate people of different religions and cultures. We suffer, always and everywhere, but somehow, through suffering, through the cross in our world, we find hope of redemption, hope that we can sing and dance our faith that all roads converge."

I envy the person that I was that day, secure in her faith, happy, if struggling, in her marriage, and ignorant of the extent to which the whole fragile edifice depended on the existence of her husband, how her whole personality and its situation in life might crumble without his presence, leaving her like the last survivor on a bombed planet. But that spring Eric was perfectly healthy, and we were just recovering from my slide toward my father's rational relativism and Eric's consequent anger. As always, he attended my work and spent the day at the church where we had the workshop and performance.

The event is structured in concentric circles, beginning and ending with community dances to the two folk songs, fun to do but tedious to watch. In the middle, I do a solo in which life emerges from mud, using the original Trapezoid group's song "Cool of the Day." During this, the intermediate and community groups become an audience, sitting on one side. Lorraine Duisit's liquid soprano solo seems to fly in and through the reeds and grasses, flowers and trees of a well-watered garden, as she sings a text based on Genesis 3:8. "My Lord said to me, 'do you like my garden so clean? You can live in the garden, if you'll keep the water clean. I'll return in the cool of the day.'" Urgent percussion interrupts this solo midway, and the core group jumps against the walls and rebounds, crawls and huddles to survey the horizon. Another Trapezoid song, "Borders," accompanies:

> Across the bloody border
> Along the barbed wire fence
> The searchlight in the towers couldn't shine,
> Are you keeping freedom in?
> Are you keeping freedom out
> With your guns and dogs along the border line?

The second half of the creation solo follows: "Now is the cool of the day. This earth is the garden, the garden of our Lord, and God walks in the garden in the cool of the day." The piece concludes with the final community dance, *All Roads Converge*.

Participatory movement has an incredible power to arouse emotion, and people believe what their bodies feel. Warmth, cold, pain, hunger, satiety: no one doubts the reality of these. The body shares the grainy, rock-bottom reality of bread. Emotion aroused by movement is only a hair removed from sensation in the conviction it induces. You can say "we'll meet again" and you can sing it, but when you sing it and do it at the same time, it's like stepping from shadow into sun and makes you realize how fractional, how pale is intellectual assent. At the end of the performance and the journey, people felt they'd arrived on a free and brand-new shore.

"These songs of secular faith," says a program note, "are for my father, 1909–1987." I had not told Eric about this dedication in the printed program, and later I asked him if he had noticed it, knowing he hated the word "secular," as well as the concept. He nodded yes, as though he took it for granted, expressing a strangely intuitive understanding of Daddy and me that belied his antagonism. With a similar sort of empathy, Eric gave me a pair of Zuni earrings shortly after Daddy's death, the sort of gift Daddy might have given. He signed the card with both their names combined, "Phileric," for "Philleo" and "Eric." When I told him about the dream I'd had where the blowing garden turned into music, he understood before I did: "It's your father," he said. I think these sudden flashes of intuition were instances of selfless love, the kind that enables a person to rise for a moment above personal need and desire and simply be with and for the beloved, as Eric did when I was in labor.

With *All Roads Converge,* I tried harder to accommodate and approach my father than I ever had during his lifetime. Would we have understood each other better had I loved him this openly before he died? I'd always hoped there would be a moment of reconciliation, a moment when we connected on a deep level, and all that had been unsaid came to the surface. It was not to be. When my father entered hospice, driven by a friend and alternately chatting and napping, I considered going to visit. Eric said my father wouldn't want us to see him flat on his back, and I thought possibly he was right. Still, I asked. "No," my father said, "just come for my birthday," about a week away.

I could have gone anyway, without Eric, though this would have provoked great conflict in our marriage. I could have told my father, "I'm sorry I married someone you didn't get along with, and I'm sorry I turned to religion," thus opening a door never even cracked between us, but it didn't occur to me that the moment of connection might depend on my initiative. I really wanted my father to say he was sorry, to admit he would have preferred me single and childless, devoted only to him and deprived of my full, adult life.

I often read or hear criticism of how a parent died, a wish that he or she had stopped denying death and discussed the scenery while walking the narrowing path. I wonder how such critics imagine the living can teach the dying, the ones whose whole selves perform what survivors only mouth in words. I think the criticism masks a wish to dictate what last hand should be stretched across the sea of separation, to finally wrest from the parent what the child has always wanted. But dying parents now face frontiers unknown to their children and have new vistas to explore. It's not our province to tell them how to die.

Daddy did not speak willingly about his condition, but when he did, it was with calm. We visited once after he was diagnosed but still active, and Eric asked, "What do you think happens after death?"

"Long sleep," Daddy said, "but dreamless."

The last time I saw him alive, he had already entered that sleep. He lay in the hospice bed under a sheet, pink and a little flatter than I remem-

13

A Thickening Veil

Aｆｔｅｒ ａｎ ｉｄｙｌｌｉｃ ｓｕｍｍｅｒ vacation in 1988, when Anton, at twenty-two, joined us and nine-year-old Erica on a train trip to the Southwest, Eric began to notice pain on his right side. Soon an ultrasound revealed a hole in his liver. From then on, through the month of tests he designed to give some information but avoid the worst news, the fatal and the trivial linked arms in my mind, so that a misplaced book and a dog that wandered off carried equal weight with Eric's declining condition. I logged ridiculous hours and miles searching for the dog, even bringing home a look-alike substitute, so that when the original was returned, I had two dogs to care for, as well as a sick husband.

I failed to mark the day in September when we made love for the last time, for of course I didn't know it was the last, and only a later credit card bill showed me our final dinner out. On Erica's tenth birthday, October 19, her cat gave birth to five healthy kittens under the bed where Eric lay, and we took it as a sign of hope. He came out with us to the local coffee shop for dinner, but had no appetite.

Hallowe'en was his next-to-last night at home. He'd had a port for chemotherapy implanted as an outpatient that morning, and the surgeon had said to me, "Make him take you out to lunch."

"He's much too sick for that," I said. By then Eric had stopped eating entirely and needed to lie down, and I hated the surgeon's "cheerful doc" attitude. That evening, I took Stefan and Erica out trick-or-treating, and Eric tried to come along, then felt too weak, so we took him home and set out again. I asked Tom, twenty, to come with us. On the street I said, "I need you now; I need your help."

"Don't count on me," he said. I was nonplussed, not believing what I'd heard, having no idea how to respond. There was nothing I could do but pretend it hadn't happened and hope he would be different the next day. Later I asked him what had been going through his head, and he said only that he'd been upset. When we got home, I found Eric desperately exhausted from answering the constantly ringing doorbell, and a few days later a liver biopsy revealed metastasized colon cancer. *I won't have anyone to talk to,* I thought and panicked, suffocated by my own stifled voice. I called my closest friends: Joe and Madeleine, with whom Eric and I had long spent New Year's Eves, as well as many other occasions, and Beth, my sponsor in the catechumenate. They all came immediately to the hospital and stayed in close touch with me, but none could listen to daily minutiae the way Eric had, providing the reflection as necessary to me as air.

On Election Day, Eric failed to vote for the first time in his life as a naturalized citizen and even declined my offer to bring a ballot to the car, showing me how sick he was. I drove him to the hospital and began a monthlong vigil, trying to calm his frenzied moods, singing him the hymns of the St. Louis Jesuits and fetching ice. Drops of water were all he could swallow. At three each day, I left him with a strong male nurse and returned to the children. Eric's oldest son, Richard, also a physician, took leave from his practice in Vermont to sleep in Eric's room at night. I brought Erica to visit a few times early in the month, then thought better of it as Eric grew sicker and woke only briefly, battling weakness and his need to take charge. Byron, Eric's second son, visited from his home near Chicago, as did Anton, who played chess in a corner.

Sometime in the third week, Tom entered the hospital room, tears in his eyes. He came close to the bed where Eric lay, unable to sit up or pay attention for more than a short time.

"Dad, I forgive you," he said. Eric was puzzled and troubled. He turned to me.

"What does he want?" he asked. "I don't know what he wants."

"I want you to know I forgive you," said Tom. I was torn. I knew Tom was upsetting Eric, but I would not deprive Tom of access to his father at this crucial time. Eric turned back and forth on the wheezing airbed, designed to prevent bedsores, as he struggled for competence and control. The more helpless he felt, the more agitated he got, and Tom kept trying to communicate his message, growing ever more emotional. Finally he left.

"What did he want?" asked Eric.

"I don't know," I said. "He said he forgave you, but he should have been asking *you* to forgive *him.*" I don't know whether this made sense to

Eric or not, or whether Tom ever saw it that way. Eric asked for ice, then sank into restless sleep.

Numerous priests from St. Thomas and St. Basil came to pray with him. Visitors streamed in and out, sometimes comforting and sometimes confusing him, and cards and plants accumulated on the windowsill. Colleagues and friends acted as though a mythic king lay sick, his dying a drama that might shake the world. It seemed that only Richard and I saw him as human, in need of love and comfort. Days and nights became an endless progression of seconds, as he slept and woke equally round the clock.

Deep inside, I was shocked that faith did not ease his passage. "It's much worse than I thought it would be," he said, reminding me of how much he'd talked about death and dying, seeking safety by facing facts. His constant terror contrasted sharply with my unbelieving father's equanimity and peaceful death the year before, and I had to admit that faith might not provide the reassurance I had hoped.

Eric raised his mouth to kiss me before I left on November 28, the last time I saw him alive, and I whistled softly with surprise and pleasure. Richard called me with news of death in the middle of the night, then picked me up and drove me slowly, slowly through the snowy night. A scream that must have been my own echoed remotely in my ears, but urgency had given way to endless, empty time. At the hospital, I found Eric still and somehow hard, but warm. I crossed his forehead with my thumb. Striving for meaningful action in that sterile environment, I accompanied him on his wheeled cart as far as the elevator.

I did not think to tear my clothes as I had when Natasha died, for Eric's death threatened my sanity in ways that could not be contained in any ritual gesture. Returning from the hospital, I went up to my third-floor studio, my usual place for prayer, but all I felt was a cold knot of fear in my stomach that no tea could warm. I'd considered myself a dancer first, wife and mother second, but now I curled up and thought *wife, wife . . . that's what I was, and now I'm nothing.* I may have thought Eric was man, not myth, but now I realized I'd lost more than friend and lover. It *was* as though a mythic king had died, and the old chaos came to roost on my shoulder, like a dark, sharp-beaked bird. All the attachments of my busy life evaporated into a great, gray cloud. When I went to change the title on Eric's car for Tom, he asked, "Do you have time?" For the first time in my life, I had nothing but time, for I had no reason to do anything.

Erica woke up in my bed the morning after Eric died. I sat next to her and told her.

"I'm glad," she said. "I wanted him to stop being sick. I wanted him to be well or be dead." The next morning, a flash of memory: "Daddy was so soft," she said, clearly touched by a grief she pushed away. Thus began her growing up of sorrow lived into and denied, leaving her cheerful for days, then sneaking up to catch her by surprise. I told her she could stay home from school and busied myself with cleaning up the room, sorting out papers and all the junk I'd let slip during Eric's month in the hospital. Stefan did not appear to react to Eric's illness or death at the time, though much later he would say "Daddy's dead," without affect, at unexpected moments.

Eric's funeral was a magnificent mix of friends, family, medical colleagues, faculty from CTU, and poor people he had helped or treated— some four hundred people. The choir sang the Catholic folk-style songs of our usual liturgy, and I mourned him within the ritual as intensely as I had prayed for him in the days and weeks before. The Church was a matrix that held me up and released my tears during the first intense year of grief, when I found myself once again alone on a rock in space. But over time I had to face a confusing truth: Natasha's death had opened the crack between the worlds, and Eric's had squeezed it shut. Where once my sense of connection had crashed through brick, now it merely brushed up against a thickening veil. The fire of my faith gradually subsided to persistent embers.

If I learned one thing from this experience, it was that I didn't understand myself. I had always thought I knew where I was going, whether the path was artistic or spiritual. Now I had to recognize that self-understanding was one more illusion, a last gasp of self-sufficiency. I could choose to be faithful to my spiritual experience, but no act of mine could produce or renew that experience. My closeness to God was out of my hands. All I could do was try to remain awake and aware, to stay on the path and notice the incarnate beauty of every squirrel and bird and flower along the way. Eric's death had sent me reeling still further back toward my father's secular position, and I realized that my conversion, which had felt so personal, so independent, so authentically my own, was at least partly Eric in me, a rebellion against my father. I did not know if I could go it alone.

Had my father been alive when Eric died, I suppose I might have become more religious. The two deaths left me to resolve political and religious polarities within myself with no one else to blame, no one to fight my battles for me. I continued going to Mass but gave up parish ministries, needing to lie low while I acquainted myself with new territory.

One month after Eric's death came Christmas. Somehow holiday traditions told me what to do, got my adrenalin up, and kept the most painful feelings at bay. On the day before Christmas Eve, Anton came from his nearby dorm to help Erica, Stefan, Tom, and me select a tree. We reenacted the old debates about the height of the living room ceiling and chose the most symmetrical tree we could find. After the older boys set it up, we all began to decorate. Eric had always liked the lights and ornaments partially hidden inside the tree, and I began to weave the lights among the branches.

"You're doing it wrong," said Tom. "That's not the way Dad did it."

"Wait and see how it looks," I said. Anton and Erica hung some glass balls.

"That's not the way it's supposed to be," said Tom, morose. I continued adding ornaments for a while, then went out to the kitchen while Anton and Erica moved to the front room to watch TV. When I came back, I found Tom had removed all the ornaments and wrapped the lights tightly around the trunk, making a sort of dissonant parody of Eric's style. I was stymied.

Eric would have opposed him directly. Shortly before he got sick, Eric had agreed to pay Tom's rent in order for him to live elsewhere, giving both some distance. After Eric's death, I discontinued the arrangement, thinking it more important for Tom to pay his own way. I didn't mind having him in the house, and I did enforce household rules, like no smoking, but I couldn't confront him when he got mad. I was angry, perhaps as angry as Tom, but anger had always frightened me, and I couldn't stand up to him.

On Christmas Eve, we attempted to repeat the old rituals: reading the Christmas story from the big illustrated book Eric had made, singing some carols, and opening presents. To me each step in the process was an accomplishment performed on a high wire, brittle and risky, and I remember stretching out on the gray rug before the fire when it was over and feeling energy seep from all my muscles. This year I would not make it to Midnight Mass, and I put Erica and Stefan to bed after our late dinner. Later, when I went out to the kitchen, I found a favorite serrated knife broken in half. I asked Tom what had happened, and he said again, "I was upset."

A few days later, we all went up to celebrate Christmas week with Mama in Wisconsin. Now that the central part of the holiday was over, my heightened energy was gone, and I felt depleted, wounded, like part of myself had been ripped out. One night, Erica and I were up after the others had gone to bed, and I joined her as she began to cry, crying myself.

"*You're* not supposed to be crying," she said. I understood that these were important instructions. She would have her grief when she was able to feel and express it, and I would comfort her, keeping mine to myself.

Eric's death left me a single parent to Erica, just ten, and Stefan, seventeen. Anton soon went to graduate school in California, and I clung to all the children, mourning the loss of family life as much as I'd sometimes wanted to get away from it. I remember seeing the movie *Parenthood* shortly after Eric died and weeping as the children in the car sing about diarrhea with the same dumb hilarity I remembered from our car trips. Later the Steve Martin character is making love to his wife when a child interrupts them. When they return, he says something like, "Oh, is that where we were? Yeah, there." The sight of that language of touch and the way they knew it by heart brought fresh tears.

Other signs of married partnership could catch me unawares and shock me with the roughness of my torn edges, my difference from other people. One night I stood at a reception following a performance of my group, drinking a glass of wine and talking to a fellow dancer. His wife came up beside him, and he handed her his glass without a pause or break, as though she were part of him—his wine, her wine; her sip, his sip. I ached for that communion.

One day in June, I ran down from my studio to join Anton, my oldest, for a graduation event at his university, hopped on the scale, saw my ten-pound weight gain, and suddenly thought, "I've never felt this bad in my life." The sunny day turned into chunks of color, vibrating and unnatural, the world an alien place I didn't belong, and I recognized the ancient chaos I hadn't known since my teens. I held my panic in check by clenching palms and biting lips, while my body went along to the event and behaved normally. The terror came and went for weeks, and I tried to tell a friend or two about this trap, but no one knew of a way out.

Sometime in that first year of grief, my mother arrived for a visit, alert, verbal, intelligent, and well informed as ever. She told me about her writing group and community arts foundation in her hometown, then about a recent trip to South Africa.

"How are you?" she asked Stefan.

"How you?" he said.

"No, you say 'I'm fine,'" she said.

"I fine," said Stefan.

"Isn't that marvelous?" she asked me and then inquired about my grown sons, Anton and Tom. We had drinks and dinner, and I settled her in our back bedroom, equipped with a double bed bought specially for her, then sat on the floor nearby.

"How are you?" she asked me. By now it was seven hours since her arrival. The floor seemed to tremble and with it my bones, as a hot stream of fury shot up my spine and stopped at my voice, not knowing where to go. How could she ask me how I was after all this time, when I was living in such a black pit of alienation, fear, and despair? What kind of infinitesimal interest in me was this that occurred to her after she'd considered my children, her travels, her group, and her whole life? The volcano inside me forced open a tiny valve.

"It's too late for you to ask me that," I said and stomped out the door, amazed and a little scared by the new, fiery explosions that filled my head, straightening my back and making my hands tremble. I knew my feeling was wrong. Mama had always been kind and generous, if distant. How could I be mad at her?

At the beginning of Advent, I took this feeling to Confession, sitting face to face with the priest in Calvert House's carpeted study. He suggested therapy.

"What kind?" I asked.

"You can see a person in training at the Institute for Psychoanalysis," he said. "That's what I'm doing." I was thrilled to think I might be worthy of real, analytically oriented talk therapy, like Eric, like my mother. No one had ever suggested this to me before, but the water was rising, and I flashed on my earliest investigation of sinking and swimming, an oft-told story in our house.

I must have been two or three when my parents took me out in a rowboat, and I reached over the edge to drop my gold necklace in the water. I observed it "swims like a bish" before it sank out of sight. As I reached toward it, my mother grabbed the crossed back straps of my seersucker sunsuit. I replaced her hand with mine, grabbing the straps, and assured her that I could do it "by my delf." I'm sure my parents laughed at my odd estimation of fall, float, weight, and restraint. From then on, however, whenever I announced that I would test the world and do it "by myself," my parents let me go, confident that I could hold myself above the flood, knowing the difference between sink and swim. Now I was not so sure. My grief for Natasha had been hot, deep, and desperate, but Eric's death threatened my equilibrium. Alive, he had provided a nest so big I thought I was flying free; dead, he revealed the dark and empty space through which a flightless bird might fall.

"I've never even considered doing that," I told the priest. "Could I really get that kind of help?"

"Think of it as education," he replied. "You wouldn't turn that down." In effect, he gave me permission to do what I needed, and thus began again the saving of my life.

14

Warm Snow, Dark Sea

A YEAR AFTER ERIC's death, the older boys, now men, gathered for the holidays. One morning, they joined me and the younger kids in the kitchen, drinking coffee. The room seemed small, as the lumbering male bodies stood or leaned against a counter, on their way to someplace else. Stefan worked at spreading bright yellow mustard on bread, and Erica reached for a glass to get water. I wondered what they would say to my news.

"I've decided to go into therapy," I said. Anton and Tom paused and looked at me, startled. I was supposed to be the sane and stable mom, while they were the ones who dropped out, violated curfew, lay in bed until they dented the mattress, or holed up in a closet in the fetal position. Erica, always observant, probably noticed a shift in the air, and Stefan went about his business.

"What kind of therapy?" asked Anton.

"Psychodynamic," I said. "The talking kind. I got a recommendation of someone from Joe." I had considered a trainee, but my friend Joe, now a psychiatric social worker, had suggested someone he knew. I felt giddy, almost wicked, about to embark on a new, self-indulgent adventure.

"Who is this person Joe knows?" asked Tom, always a little suspicious of Joe, whom he seemed to view as embodying, or wanting to embody, a remnant of Eric. I didn't know much yet about the psychiatrist and couldn't answer.

"Are you OK?" asked Anton.

"Yes," I said and quoted the priest. "Think of it as a form of education." I smiled, pleased to break the mold others had made for me. I would be whoever I wanted to be.

The day of my first appointment, I was in the grocery store when the floor started to seem too far away, the light too bright, the aisles too long and telescopic. I hadn't felt this scary sort of disconnection for six months and dreaded its return. Feeling shaky, I went home, then made my way downtown.

"Hi," said Dr. M., stepping into his waiting room and extending a hand. He was tall, with pale skin and thinning brown hair, and his forward-angled torso reminded me of Miss Clavel in Ludwig Bemelman's *Madeleine*, when she rushes headlong down the hall, fearing disaster, running faster. I saw white, Protestant, Midwesterner . . . like Daddy? But this man was a doc, like Eric. Time would tell. Hi, I thought, as I shook his hand. What a strange way to greet a patient, as though you were passing a friend on the street. I entered the neutral inner office with its long couch, tank full of fish, shelves of books, and two comfortable chairs. "Sit anywhere," he said, and I took a chair. He sat opposite on a couch with pen and pad and gathered basic facts, "data," as he called them, asking me routine questions about age, family, and place of birth, which I disliked. I was not a datum, and I would not be routine.

I told him the central fact of my existence, that my husband had died the year before.

"Was there a goodbye?" he asked. What kind of a question was that? I'd heard of saying goodbye to the dying but found the idea offensive. Real goodbyes were not forever; they were blessings for a temporary separation: God be with you, wave bye-bye, until tomorrow, *hasta la vista, au revoir, auf Wiedersehen*. I wanted to tell him what Eric really said, six feet deeper than goodbye, but it was too emotional, so I saved it for next time. I told him the second most important fact of my existence, that I was a recent convert to Catholicism.

"How does that make you feel about talking to me?" he asked. "I belong to a U. U. community, Unitarian Universalist." I thought of my Unitarian grandmother, whose religion was high-minded and idealistic but did not prevent her from managing her home with fierce and determined control, insisting all arrive precisely at six for dinner and ruling equally against alcohol and onions. I saw no connection between her and Dr. M., and I said something vague and probably obscure about symbols: how they can point back, the way symptoms point to earlier trauma or psychic conflict, but they can also point forward to realities we can't see or touch, like bread and wine to God.

"Can you accept that possibility?" I asked. I think he said he could live with that.

"What brings you to therapy?" he asked. I told him I was angry with my mother.

"How angry?" he asked. "Angry words? Fighting? Physical violence?" I liked the range of intensities Dr. M. suggested, so far beyond what was possible for me, and the way he located me on a scale. I wondered if I could ever stop assuming that others were like me and assess where they stood the way Dr. M. assessed me, with a range of possibilities in view and an open mind.

I told him about the panicky feeling I had had earlier, and he asked, "How do you feel right now, in here?" A frisson of excitement and fear: we were going to talk about feelings in the here and now, without time for preparation or concealment? He offered me a prescription for Valium, which I took and saved but never filled. We agreed to meet twice a week.

The next time I walked in and handed him a feature from the *Reader*, Chicago's free paper, about Eric's life and work. Later he would comment about this—"You came in here and handed me Eric"—and it was true. I needed Eric as a buffer between me and the world; I was still trying to hide behind him or speak through him. I couldn't step forward and say, "This is me."

On the next visit I summoned my courage and said, "A day or so before Eric died, he said, 'I suffer it so you won't have to.'"

"Maybe it wasn't true," said Dr. M., now Ron to me. Fireworks exploded inside my head and heart. How could Eric's words be judged true or false? If Eric wanted to offer his suffering for my benefit, who could deny him? It's not that I thought he could actually save me from anything, but his words interpreted his experience, and who knows better than the dying person what that experience means? I found Ron's words inappropriate, challenging, arrogant.

The next time I came in, I asked, "What does true and false have to do with it, and how can you question what the dying have to say about their death?"

"I apologize," he said. This disconcerted me. Eric never apologized and criticized me if I did, because he believed that every apology carried within it the seeds of the next transgression. I'd accepted his opinion without thinking much about it, probably because it saved me from admitting wrongdoing. "You were obviously intelligent," continued Ron, "and I wanted to impress you. I was trying to say something smart, and I apologize." Even the word sounded strange, like part of an outmoded ceremony, something done with swords and capes. I tried it on, imagining myself saying something similar. Gradually, I enlarged my repertory of possible responses the way I enlarged my view of how others could be, and in times to come I would find the apology worked wonders with people I'd offended.

Ron and I discussed this interchange at length, and he told me of French psychoanalyst Lacan's view that the initial exchange between psychiatrist and patient holds the seeds of the entire relationship, and so it was for me. Ron would be different from Eric, as well as from my father: not overwhelming, not dominating. But he would also challenge my division of men into Eric-types and Daddy-types by being himself: a rationalist with spiritual interests, a person unafraid of anger but able to talk about it calmly, a person of authority who did not need to exercise control. Or so he seemed to me, but of course the person I perceived was a character I concocted from what he chose to share of his own personality and the traits of the important people in my life.

Including my mother. I showed him the photos of Mama and me as a six-month-old infant, where I sprawl on my back across her lap, and her hands fall by her sides, eyelids drooping with depression's lethargy.

"I'm amazed you've been functioning all this time without help," he said. We looked at pictures of me on my feet at one, chunky and determined.

"I look so tough and muscular," I said. "They used to call me 'Mussolini,' not very flattering in 1939." He shook his head in disbelief, and I basked in empathy's warmth, even though I knew he was establishing it deliberately, becoming my good mother. Looking back, I see this as the moment when therapy found its true point of origin, not with present grief but with an infant and her mother. And as Ron and I untangled and rewove the strands of my story, it found its own direction, far from anything I'd thought in that first year of sorrow.

Soon Ron moved to the chair he usually used, with a footrest that allowed him to stretch out his legs or fold them up close to his body. I was entranced by his lanky ability to fold, like an accordion, so different from my own well-stretched but compact body, with its joints growing stiff. I liked looking at him, but soon I discovered that if I closed my eyes and leaned back in my chair, I could enter a sort of watery space where my body floated and thoughts rose to the surface like bubbles.

One night I dreamed a companion and I were plucking fish from the sea in Alaska and storing them in a snowbank. But instead of being cold, the snowbank was warm and dark, as was the night. Even the sea was warm, and the fishing was easy: shared and intimate. Later someone put my foot in a machine, like the fluoroscopes shoe salesmen used to use to check whether shoes fit properly. Then I was in a swimming pool with Stefan, trying to get out and falling back in, over and over.

I told the dream to Ron. "The part about the foot sounds sexual," he said. Again the frisson: we were going to talk about *that*? I wasn't ready to point out that going fishing in the warm, dark snow was infinitely more sexual than the foot, and I let it go. "The part about Stefan in the swimming pool sounds like he's holding you back," said Ron.

"He's not holding me back," I protested, suspecting Ron of low regard for the mentally handicapped. "He's in school during the day, and I have a sitter for when I teach dance in the evenings." When Eric was alive, we often left Stefan with his siblings, but now the older boys were away, and Erica, at eleven, was too young to handle an eighteen-year-old.

"The dream says otherwise," said Ron.

Shortly thereafter, I began looking for possible homes for Stefan. At first it seemed impossible to find a place warm and supportive enough for him to live as an adult, and Stefan's opinions on this were clear. If we drove up to a place that looked forbidding or institutional, he began to scream. If a place seemed careless or lacking in stimulation, I crossed it off.

At the same time, I began getting Stefan approved for residential placement by the Department of Mental Health. I became his legal guardian, a process that involved evaluation of my suitability by a court-appointed lawyer. Then came incredible amounts of testing for him and red tape for me, funneled through an incompetent case manager who recorded each bit of information on a sticky note, until her entire desk, lamp, phone, and outbox had become a piece of dotted Swiss.

After visiting all the homes I could find within a radius of fifty miles, I came upon El Valor's Intermediate Care Facility, or ICF, and knew I'd found the answer. A freestanding house in Chicago's Pilsen neighborhood, not far from where I lived in Hyde Park, it was home to twelve adults, six men and six women. They slept two to a room and shared well-lit living, dining, and kitchen areas, as well as a large basement recreation room.

The twenty-four-hour staff seemed caring, attentive, and more patient with the clients' circular conversations than I could ever be. Delighted, I went with Stefan to meet the director of residential services. Carlos, a dark-haired, Hispanic man, rose from his desk and greeted us.

"What's your name?" he asked Stefan. Stefan answered appropriately and shook hands.

"What do you like to do? Go for walks?"

"Go for walk, yeah."

"And what do you like to eat?"

"Eat, ya."

"Hamburgers?" asked Carlos.

"Ya, hamburgers. French fries. He like it." They were hitting it off, and Stefan would have been glad to talk all day. Carlos asked me a few questions about Stefan's life at home, his skills, and his sleeping habits.

"We want him," he said. "We want people who've grown up at home, who are socialized, like Stefan. Clients who've grown up in institutions have behavior problems, like taking off all their clothes or throwing themselves down the stairs." He explained that he was required to take clients assigned to him from institutions first, but he acted confident, and I suspected he knew how to work the system. I pictured him like a clever rodent, working back along the red tape and untying the knots until he got to the point of origin, where admission actually took place, then crawled through and pulled Stefan in after him.

"Can he still go to Esperanza for the day program?" I asked. "It's really been good for him."

"Certainly. Their bus will pick him up here. We have another client who goes there already."

"And what about his gastroenterologist? He's had periods of diarrhea and weight loss for several years, and they think it's Crohn's, inflammatory bowel disease. He's been seeing someone at Northwestern."

"We take our clients to all kinds of medical appointments. Northwestern will be no problem." Within weeks, Carlos had penetrated the maze, and in November 1990, Stefan went to live at El Valor. The first month they encouraged me to call but not visit, and I felt bad for abandoning him. I did call frequently, though Stefan never had much to say on the phone, and they told me he was doing well, getting two hours daily of one-on-one training in showering and dressing. When I picked him up at Thanksgiving, he looked great. More important, he was happy and excited to come home. After the holiday, I was relieved to see he was equally happy to go back. He continued to live there, coming home for family birthdays, holidays, and vacations. Tom remained his special brother, developing a fine rapport with all the clients at El Valor.

My conversation with Ron about the dream of Stefan in the swimming pool was not typical. Usually he said little, though he was never the utterly abstemious, silent analyst of times gone by. Nonetheless, his quiet listening was markedly different from Eric's active intervention. And Eric's analytic thinking had been outdated, as I began to see.

"Can you imagine," said Ron, "the head of the Institute for Psychoanalysis writing a book called *The Prison House of Psychoanalysis*? Prison house!" and he laughed. "Something had to change."

"What's the prison?" I asked, fascinated.

"It's the prison of silence," answered Ron. "Traditionally the analyst isn't supposed to even cough or yawn or move in the chair. Now we're realizing that the honest interaction of two human beings can be therapeutic." I gobbled up these nuggets of information and asked about his training, ambitious to have the real thing, in-depth psychoanalysis.

"I've been trained in both, psychoanalysis and family systems," he said. "But I'm becoming more known as an analyst." I nodded with satisfaction.

Before the first month of therapy ended, Ron asked me if I was finding it ordinary, unimportant.

"Once people get into it, they often wonder, 'Is that all it is?'" Not me. I wanted him to love me; I envied him his marriage and friends; I was contemptuous of the gullible way he repeated rumors about gangs and crime, barely a step away from urban legends. When I occasionally heard something about his life, it gave me the illusion of friendship, though bitter tears often followed my realization that it was friendship for pay. I wondered how the small room could keep from disintegrating, rocked by battling feelings, outside of time and detached from space. Ron asked me about friends, and I hated the replies that indicated my isolation. No, there was no one that lived next door, or within a block, not more than one on the South Side. I was on the far side of friendless. He made me feel like the child who fails to play well with others, who should have more friends her own age.

"People are thrilled," said Ron, "—that's too strong a word—but people are more than glad to listen if you tell them what you feel." I doubted it—I still do; most people would rather talk than listen. But that day as I went to rehearse with my colleague Jane, preparing for our trip to a sacred dance conference in Hong Kong, I tried it out. I don't remember what bad feeling I confessed, but as I spoke to her, I felt a knot inside untie itself; my mood lifted, and the world became a kinder place. I doubted Jane was thrilled, but we became closer, and she, Erica, and I made the trip to Asia together. There we performed *Women at the Well,* a dance I had made with Jane's help, based on the story of the Samaritan woman in John's gospel. We taught together, and I presented a paper on liturgy and performance.

After the conference, Erica and I toured Beijing and Shanghai with others from the conference, while Jane traveled briefly alone and then returned home. Riding in a bus with Erica and near strangers, I felt again that veil between me and the world, that slight nausea and sense of hollow at the core, even as Erica and I ventured by ourselves to Beijing's shopping street, proud to navigate the purchase of a great resonating gong, a gift for Tom.

That fall Erica started sixth grade and became fearful of school, wanting to stay home all the time. She pointed out that staying home had been my idea in the first place, and she was right; I'd told her to stay home the morning after Eric's death. I hated Ron's term for it, "school phobia," as though it were totally irrational, like claustrophobia. Investigating, I discovered how socially difficult middle school was at Lab, compared to lower school, where she'd been the year before. Some kids wrote hate letters to a boy with a mild physical handicap, and others ganged up on each other. A pair of twins worked the pizza scam on Erica, ordering pizza and giving her name and address. Erica's eleventh birthday party was a sleepover disaster, with girls separating into warring camps at two in the morning. Fortunately, Anton was there and kept the peace while I slept, ignorant, until daybreak. I met with Erica's teachers and the school psychologist, and she stayed in school, but transitions from vacation to school remained difficult.

I continued to attend Mass all this time, and she came with me, but my participation became more and more attenuated. Just as conversion had made no radical change in my way of life, neither did this dimming of passion. I never lost hope or became angry with the Church (though

I often became angry with particular stances or particular priests). I needed to wait, wait a long time, to rediscover my relationship with God. Ultimately, I had to recognize that I knew not the day or the hour, that my ways were not God's ways, and God's ways were a secret.

Anton moved to Berkeley for graduate school in physics, and Tom traveled to Johannesburg, where he'd been hired to set up a studio with a Synclavier, an early digital synthesizer and sampler. The big house held just Erica and me, a dog and some cats, and she hated it when I referred to us as a "family." The first few summers we spent alone were hard. At first I tried to re-create camping trips, driving cross-country with Erica to visit Richard in Vermont. Despite money worries, we didn't camp out more than a couple of nights. The challenge and glory of outdoor living had lost its savor, reduced to discomfort tinged with fear. Nature's night noises felt more like threat than invitation, and I was feeling too depleted and abandoned myself to make a safe place for Erica.

Another summer we headed out to California to visit Anton and stayed in his student apartment for a week. He was struggling with roommates and grad school and surely found our visit much too long. One day we searched for the zoo and got lost, and Erica's upset showed me how grief was carving subtle, steady pathways in her mind and body that she would only slowly come to recognize. At the same time, I saw her growing empathy with me, which seemed to come as naturally to her as patting my back when she was an infant. She noticed everything.

"You don't like that," she would say, after I tasted something, or "You don't believe that," at something I heard. No one had ever found me transparent before. I liked it a lot and only hoped I didn't take advantage of or exploit her gift.

Around this time I was dismayed by a dream where I looked in the mirror and saw the shadow of a penis, and I waited a couple of sessions before I admitted this to Ron. Having rebelled for years against the stereotype of "penis envy" with its patriarchal assumption that women want to be men, I was furious with my dream life for producing this unwanted image. To my surprise, Ron interpreted the dream and the concept as a sign of injustice, not inferiority. Patriarchal society oppresses women, he said, and thus they sometimes want what men have. And in my case, where my father had a full, enjoyable life and my mother was sad, it was hard to think highly of being like her. Slowly I realized how important his approach was for my whole sense of personal worth. If I had gotten an old-school, authoritarian analyst, I would simply have repeated my efforts to gain identity through a strong man: father, husband, therapist. Looking back, I think Ron's egalitarian and feminist approach may have been the most important aspect of the therapy. Loss had launched the storytelling, but now it was weaving a new character, one who could embrace the way she was made and did not need Eric's reflection to be whole.

But at the time, emotion dwarfed understanding. My admiration of Ron's foldable body gave way to overwhelming attraction, to hopeless and agonizing desire. Each visit revitalized and intensified the conflict between what I imagined and what was real. Ron assured me that the more I felt, the more likely I was to benefit from therapy, but it was hard to believe. Fortunately, progress depended more on relationship than on belief. Somehow, I continued to find more satisfaction in real life, which took place on a sort of parallel track to the imaginary drama of therapy, where everything desired must be renounced.

In the mid-'90s, I began teaching dance at Valparaiso University in Indiana, as well as choreographing and producing organ-and-dance concerts at St. Thomas in Hyde Park. My second year at Valparaiso I added a section of freshman seminar, developing a curriculum around the sacred and secular in fiction and film, so I was making connections professionally as well as personally. Slowly I replaced a single, intense connection with many more diffuse: dance colleagues, friends from college, fellow teachers, later writers.

By now I was feeling significantly better, and Erica had grown from fascination with the movie *Dirty Dancing* to obsession with the English rock band Jesus Jones. She wanted to go to London, and I located a reasonably priced B&B in the North End. We rode the double-decker buses, careening through the sky, and shopped the Kensington market, perhaps past its '60s prime, but full of gothic, punk, and funky stuff. We waited in the half-price ticket line and saw some great theater, including Ariel Dorfman's *Death and the Maiden,* which impressed Erica enough that she read the script, as well as the musical *Carmen Jones.* After penny-pinching our way through this expensive city, eating from grocery stores and Indian curry shops, I was furious to come home and find that Tom's car had been booted. This VW, formerly Eric's, was still good, and I had no choice but to pay for its recovery.

As long as we all had Christmas together, it sent Tom on some kind of rampage, usually about whether we were following Eric's traditions correctly or not. As a result, Erica grew to her teens hating the holiday, and I regretted deeply that she was deprived of that joyful time. Often we were joined on Christmas Day by Eric's second son, Byron, his wife, Joan, and their son, Timothy, and the added presence diluted the family tensions. We'd been acting out presents ever since Eric invented this strategy to slow down small children, and we encouraged Stefan to guess as well. I remember firelit afternoons with Tim at eight or nine pretending to toss a salad with graceful, fluid gestures or winding up to throw an imagined ball to Stefan with perfect ease. Symbolic representation was hardly Stefan's forte, but once in a while he'd come up with "ball," and everyone would cheer.

Until he met Carole, his future wife, Anton came home at Christmas to see friends as well as family. After presents and dinner on Christmas Eve, he would join his friends at the Tiki, a local bar, while I took Erica and Stefan to Midnight Mass, then put them to bed. At one or two in the morning, I would meet up with Anton in the kitchen. Now I could ask him about his new postdoc fellowship, his apartment in Berkeley, his life and friends. For me this was a charmed time, talking to him at leisure while I tidied up, a time without the pressure of the holiday or the demands of children, a time to feel the special closeness to him I'd known since he was born.

Two or three years into therapy, Ron and I agreed that I would benefit from the deeper analysis made possible by four meetings a week. Just at that moment, Mama resolved to sell the cranberry marsh she'd inherited at Daddy's death, of which I was part owner, and the money I received enabled me to pay for the visits. Four times a week meant the couch. Sounds simple: just lie down. It felt more like jumping off a cliff. In that charged space where details all carried weight, it was the difference between the visual assurance of another's presence and the vague and distant sound of a disembodied voice that could come from anywhere, like radio replacing television. When I lay on the couch and couldn't see

Ron, he turned into my distant mother, and I the two-year-old who stands at the edge of a chasm when she's left the room. I knew this, and yet my feelings were as real as the situation was artificial, friendship warming to love and fear twisting to resentment and rejection, all inside therapy's fantastic capsule.

Soon Ron got a new couch, a long leather one that must have cost thousands. The first time I saw it, I found little cotton doilies, like the antimacassars my grandparents used to protect furniture from hair oil, at the head and foot. I always took off my shoes before lying down and never put sticky stuff on my hair, and I was offended. Was my body too dirty for Ron's new couch? His fastidious care was stingy and fearful, like his stories about gangs, and I became a free-spirited bohemian to his materialistic, leather-conserving bourgeois. Actually I was a woman who needed reassurance that her body was OK, and Ron got the message, removed the doilies, and picked them up from then on before I arrived. A few years later he moved his office, and the configuration of furniture in the new office left me on the couch with the precipice on my left, where before it had been on my right. I was used to chasms on my right, for that was my side of the bed when Eric was alive, but the chasm on my left side left me flailing, clutching at roots.

On the couch, listening to the disembodied voice behind my head, I learned that Ron had been raised a conservative Lutheran, and he'd rebelled against the "unscientific nonsense" that was stuffed down his throat as a teenager. Like many, he considered Catholicism a dogmatic, authoritarian system of belief. Wandering in the space behind my eyes, I felt a great desire to share the insights and understandings I'd found at CTU.

"We're not required to believe everything we say in church," I said. "No one can do that all the time. And much of liturgical language is metaphorical."

"Yes, but the creed says Jesus rose from the dead, and I can't believe that."

"Look," I said. "All Christians believe more or less the same thing, and none of them think God has literal hands. So when we say 'Jesus sits now at God's right hand,' the language has got to be metaphorical."

"I never heard that before. Are there other Catholics like you, or are you out on a limb?" Parameters again.

"I'm telling you what I learned at CTU, and that's a mainstream seminary. It comes back to symbols," I said, warming to my subject. I'm not sure where the heat came from, but every time something moving happened in church, my fantasy put Ron there beside me. If I couldn't have him there, I'd tell him about it, and these discussions became a magnetic nexus in our relationship. "Those words of liturgy that upset you so much are not propositions for us to accept or reject," I continued, "but aspects of a Kingdom we aspire to, a Kingdom we rehearse during liturgy. They are symbols, and symbols don't work by telling me something I can understand intellectually. They work by drawing me in. They present me with something sensory—like a spoken word or a piece of bread—then move me from their outside to their imperceptible inside."

"I can see what you're saying," he replied, "as it relates to visible symptoms of invisible disease or art that points to invisible meanings, but Christians do believe in resurrection, and that's nonsense. I don't see how a soul can exist independent of the complex human brain."

"My body points to my soul, the way the visible part of a symbol points to the invisible. Everything I am or do is expressed, pressed out, through my body. You're right in a sense—you can't unscrew body and soul."

"Then how can the soul survive death?" asked Ron.

"That's a question of faith," I said. "I have to rely on St. Paul, who says, 'We shall not all sleep, but we shall all be changed.' It's a big change."[1]

"That's beyond my experience," said Ron.

Was I trying to make contact with my unreachable, secular father? I don't think so. I may have been trying to convince myself, for religion was fading from its central place in my life at the time. Or I may have sensed a chink in Ron's psychoanalytic detachment. I wanted so much to have something to offer him besides pay for his work. Like a mouse sniffing for cheese, I nosed around for a need I could meet, some way I could become important, even necessary to him. I sensed, or thought I sensed, a hunger for God in him, and I yearned to show him that faith didn't have to be irrational.

I think that Ron was a searcher and inquirer, more like me than like Daddy, but he was also a committed rationalist. Despite or perhaps because of all the time he spent exploring people's twisted thinking, his view of rationality was more all-encompassing than mine and did not leave space for the essential, nonrational aspect of religious experience. More important for me, our discussion embodied Ron's egalitarian approach, which made it acceptable for me to become the teacher. His honest engagement in the dialogue may have been a psychoanalytic prison break for him; for me it turned grief into a catalyst for change.

On the dialogue went, interspersed with the rest of my life, as Erica began and finished high school, Anton finished graduate school, and Tom began a collaboration with choreographer Randy Duncan, composing scores for the Joseph Holmes Chicago Dance Theatre and the Joffrey Ballet. I was proud of his music but dismayed that he used the name Tommy Mother, especially when he won a nomination for Outstanding Collaborative Artist from the Chicago Dance Coalition. Later he turned the skills he'd learned from the Synclavier to business computing and wound up at the Bank of New York with the rank of vice president.

Ron once likened therapy to a small change of steering on an ocean-going ship. The change at the time is infinitesimal, but later you can look back and see that you have arrived at a destination far from where you were originally headed. I wept throughout my last visit, but I was ready to travel on my own.

"Do you want a hug or a handshake?" asked Ron as we parted. I opted for a hug and noticed how narrow were those shoulders I'd never touched before.

Rhonda Fleming and Leigh Richey
at St. Thomas Apostle Church, Chicago.
Photo by William Frederking.

Rebecca Phillips and Rhonda Fleming
at St. Thomas Apostle Catholic Church.
Photo by William Frederking.

Members of Kast & Company at St. Thomas Apostle Church.
Photo by William Frederking.

Rhonda Fleming, Rebecca Phillips and Leigh Richey
at St. Thomas Apostle Church.
Photo by William Frederking.

Christy Bennett, Rebecca Phillips and Jenny Kobylarz
at St. Thomas Apostle Church.
Photo by William Frederking.

15

Still Dancing?

I WAS STILL TRYING to locate myself between sacred and secular poles when I started thinking about ways of dancing in relationship to an architectural site: the church building. I wasn't sure whether art would serve or seek to appropriate the sacred. Working with organist Thomas Weisflog, I recruited a large group of professional and community dancers to develop a series of organ-and-dance concerts at St. Thomas, with the support of the pastor, Father Jack Farry. These concerts, presented outside of liturgy, used the pathways of the church as a basis for site-specific choreography. I began to read, think, and write about the impact of sacred space on the one who moves through it and the way the architectural path affects the story the dancer tells. We used every part of the church building—elevated pulpit, communion rail, pews, and long aisles—and we rigged rope ladders to the balcony at the back.

At two moments in a piece with music by French composer Jehan Alain, the central figure assumes the shape of a cross, echoing the many crosses already found in the church. In the first, the entire company carries the figure aloft, at arm's length, down the central aisle to the sanctuary. In the second, the same dancer climbs to the balcony and assumes the shape in silhouette against the stained-glass windows. Such images, already suggestive of death and resurrection, are further interpreted by the space in which they are performed, what architect Thomas Barrie calls the "built myth" of the church.[1] Since they are performed outside of liturgy, however, their interpretation is not limited by doctrine or rubric. An audience member may think of Jesus, of the music's dead composer, Alain, or of someone else when she or he sees the processional figure, and music makes the procession seem triumphal as well as mournful. The figure at the end suggests hope, but the hope pales compared to the tempestuous struggle taking place on the rope ladders below, as the entire company struggles to gain the balcony, and most fall repeatedly to the ground. I continued making site-specific dance in churches for several years, first at St. Thomas and then, with organist Martin Jean, for Valparaiso's sky-piercing Chapel of the Resurrection, using the pulpit that flies some fifty feet from the floor.

Anthropologist Victor Turner distinguishes between symbols that refer only to each other and symbols with an external referent, symbols that posit "the reality of the object of faith."[2] Liturgy, of course, does posit this reality, and performance, in itself, does not. Performance that uses religious symbols and takes place in a sacred space perhaps teeters on the brink, and many interpretations are possible. The "reality" question will probably be different for each performer and audience member.

The dancers developed the pieces through workshops in which participants improvised in the sacred space, then rehearsed, developed, and finally told the story as a community of performers. They said repeatedly that to touch, or sit on, or walk on a part of the church structure was to experience in an entirely new way the meaning of this communion rail, that pulpit, this altar. Physical contact with the church building, the dancers' bodies with the body of the Church, was an experience of becoming what they touched. As the dancers walked the church's path and physically entered its built myth, they had a heightened opportunity to assimilate their personal stories to the Christian one.

Even as I made these complex dances, working with several different groups at a time, a part of me remained with Eric, reaching into his ancestral past, stretching my hand across seas and centuries with desire as strong as I'd felt for him in life. I returned over and over to images of the polyglot, winding streets of Czernowitz, in the province of Bukowina, where his grandfather Isidor Katz had been born. Eric and I had always known that his maternal grandparents had been married under the traditional Jewish *chupa* but only much later discovered that his grandfather had changed the family name from Katz to the gentile Kast. Eric's mother never knew this, or if she did, she didn't tell. She was a Kast and proud of it. In fact, she appended her maiden name to her husband's when they became U.S. citizens. They were Schwarz-Kasts, but Eric dropped the Schwarz, thus giving him (and me) his mother's maiden name. He shared this name with his mother's father and brother, both physicians and more significant mentors than his own father.

Searching through boxes of photos, newspapers, and military medals, I tried to breathe the air of Czernowitz and pick apart the tangled strands of oppression, aspiration, and sometimes self-hatred that formed the milieu in which Isidor and his descendents had grown. Slowly, my tidy categories of religion and nationality eroded, and I began to understand the separation of Jews from Austrians, Czechs, and Poles that had puzzled me in the concentration camp memorial at Ebensee. Illuminated by the past, I grasped the traditional fusion of identity and faith that goes to make a people and a way of life, so different from my family's traditions of tolerance and even-handedness.

I pictured Isidor and his wife called, as Abraham was, to leave familiar parts. They took to the air like Chagall's green and purple dreamers, a wedding bouquet in her hands, his head twisted around to kiss her as they fly. Bravely they swooped in ever-widening circles, tending westward, to land with a surprised thud in a strange European city. Isidor shaved off *peyas,* if he ever had them. They forgot the Yiddish they never knew, learning to call it "bastardized German." They started a family, put up a tree at Christmas, and began attending a Lutheran church. No one noticed when they changed their name from Katz to Kast, since they'd been using Kast ever since they arrived in Vienna.

But entering Eric's world in fantasy made my loss too real to bear, and only after several years of therapy was I strong enough to sit with these images and let them ferment into a performance piece. I began to improvise with symbols of Vienna and its charged, repressive atmosphere, using Federico Garcia-Lorca's poem "Vienna" and Leonard Cohen's adaptation of the poem for a song. Chicago artist Susan Michod designed and painted a table and chairs in the style of Viennese painters Gustav Klimt and Egon Schiele, providing a *Kaffeehaus* set for the dance; Caryn Weglarz designed lavish costumes in the same style; and Scott Silberstein developed a score around the Cohen material and some melodies the performers sang. Erica had started studying photography and made slides of the patterns on the table and chairs to project during the performance. The piece was well received, but I knew in my heart of hearts that the music, costumes, and set were primarily responsible for its success. I'd not captured the drama of Vienna, and the movement remained constrained.

My practice of liturgical dance had opened a new genre and new venues for me but also put artistic excellence in second place. And while I was directing the organ-and-dance concerts, I realized I was using less and less of my own movement and more of other people's. There's nothing wrong with this practice, common to many choreographers, but for me, a connection between my own body and the body of my work was an essential part of the process of dance making. As I stiffened with age, I lost my ability to "think movement," to find physical solutions to physical problems.

For decades, people have asked me if I were "still dancing," and I've laughed at the "still" as I got older. The answer was always "yes." But a series of "no's" was also present below the surface in some essential reluctance to move, a fear of disturbing the air with my presence that competed from the start with the great joy I found in physical pattern, rhythm, and awareness of my body in space.

I am reluctant to be seen, to be blamed, to be found wanting, to stand up or out. Natasha's death made me bold by relativizing my aversion—no punishment could equal that worst thing. In a different way, my entry into the Church also made me brave. The danger of exposure became petty in the face of religion's great hope, and Eric was surprised and pleased to see me marching and shouting slogans one day in protest against U.S. aid to El Salvador. Still, reticence continued to undermine my work, and I consider it a major cause of failure as a choreographer. One could well ask what I was doing on stage if I didn't want to be seen, but all I can say is that I wanted two contradictory things. I did fly and flew with pleasure, but I didn't fly free.

Reluctance to move may have been my first, essential, and lifelong failure, but other more practical ones followed. When my dance company moved from my home to the Body Politic, giving us both studio and performance space, we had a number of good dancers and choreographers who made new and exciting work, exchanging ideas and fertilizing each other. We got good and thoughtful reviews in Chicago's *Reader* from writers who were also getting their start. But after the initial production of *Tropical Juice* and the aborted pregnancy that followed, I put more value on my personal life than on supporting the company's work.

We had booked tours of Michigan schools to take place in deepest winter, when I was four months pregnant with Erica, and Eric didn't want me to go. He feared a cascade of dominoes—Stefan's condition, Natasha's death, the abortion—and he saw me slipping on a snowbank or tripping over a cable. On other occasions, I overrode his fears with my own confidence, but this time I acceded to his wishes and sent the company off to frigid rehearsal spaces, not-always-friendly hosts, and overscheduled performances, leaving Alida Caster Szabo, the administrative director, to deal with all the difficulties. I still regret abandoning the group.

Looking back, I see that I never succeeded in transcending two limits in dance making, one physical and one emotional. My movement never attained the energy that could make a room sizzle with speed, height, or precision, nor did my intimate gestures discover the deepest complexities of feeling. Whether these were failures of nerve or skill, talent or perseverance, I don't know, but when audiences flagged or critics were unenthusiastic, the outside world confirmed my inner suspicions.

Erica was seventeen in 1995, the year I won a Ruth Page Award for Outstanding Contribution to the Field, and we shopped together for dresses for the awards, mine black lace over satin, with skirt well above the knees, and hers bronze-colored, form-fitting silk. We stopped in the Chanel store on Michigan Avenue for gold-flecked nail polish, and the salesperson turned out to be Ruth Ann Koesun, a former dancer with the American Ballet Theatre and a heroine of my ballet-watching childhood. The coincidental meeting seemed to point to the importance of the event, like stars aligning.

The awards ceremony was held in a downtown hotel. A cocktail party for award recipients, Dance Coalition board members, and event cochairs preceded the dinner, and I was nervous, finding myself vis-à-vis Richard Ellis and Christine Duboulay, also slated for an award. I still revered and almost feared these ballet teachers from my early days in Chicago. At the dinner I sat with family and friends: Joe, his wife, Madeleine, and Sister Bernardine Karge, a Dominican lawyer and close friend of Father Bill O'Connor, the priest at St. Basil's, site of Eric's Free People's Clinic. Mama had come from Wisconsin and Stefan from El Valor, formally dressed in suit and tie. I was still nervous, anticipating the award and the speech I would give. After dessert, we rose and milled out into an anteroom, where rumbling sounded from behind double doors in front of us. I put my arm around Stefan's shoulder, knowing the sound would excite him.

The doors swung open, and the rumbling rose to articulate, complex drumbeats, as the dancer-musicians of Jellyeye were revealed in theatrical light, jumping over instruments, spinning between beats, juggling drumsticks. Stefan went ballistic. This was his rehearsal basement multiplied tenfold, a huge, brilliant room filled with live, percussive sound and enough action to rival ten of the front-loading washing machines he liked to watch. I thought of someone getting their first hit of heroin—nothing would ever again be that good. He roared and bounced and clapped his hands, all his sounds drowned out by the music.

Inside me, a voice said, I'll get this, and then I'll quit. Jellyeye had created the stage of my life, where I could walk out and accept adulation without raising false expectations. I couldn't lose—because my entrance would also be my exit. Stefan shouted words I didn't catch. Laughing, I hugged him. Both he and I had arrived at some kind of culmination, and I guided him to a chair.

When it was time for me to accept the award, nervousness disappeared as I thanked Mama, identifying her as "a Wisconsin writer," Eric, the kids, and all who'd danced with me, crediting the supportive Chicago dance community for whatever I'd achieved. I don't remember now any more of what I said, but everyone was pleased with it, especially Mama. For once, I'd done right by her. My dancing continued but diminished over the following six years, and I never produced a concert of my own work again. And I doubt that Stefan ever had a greater thrill.

Part Five

16

God Has No Grandchildren

A T FOUR IN THE morning on March 8, 1998, in the middle of a raging blizzard, my phone rang. The nurse at El Valor said Stefan was
vomiting "coffee grounds," a sure sign of intestinal bleeding, and they'd
rushed him to the hospital. I threw on clothes and drove through howl-
ing winds and whiteout to this unfamiliar place. First, the struggles that
came to be usual with Stefan in the ER: they want access through all of his
portals—IV, nasogastric tube, urinary catheter—and he screams, resists,
and pulls out the tubes. An X-ray heightened the emergency, and they
raced his gurney through halls, shouting, "free air, free air." I jogged after,
dimly realizing that it must mean air in his abdominal cavity, a sign of
perforation. Where air can escape, so can intestinal contents, risking massive infection. Soon I gave permission for surgery: Stefan had an intestinal
abscess and needed a colostomy.

"Will it be reversible?" I asked.

"No," said the surgeon.

By now it was day, and I wanted to call home, but a tree had blown
down in our yard across the phone lines, and it didn't occur to me to try
our first cell phone, now sitting in its cradle in the front room. Eventually
I got hold of a neighbor, who notified Erica and Tom, living in an apartment nearby. They came to the hospital, along with staff from El Valor,
and we spelled each other through Stefan's time in the ICU. At first it was
chancy—he failed to oxygenate sufficiently and had to be reintubated—
but gradually he improved, moved to a floor, and was ready for discharge.
There was no way he could return to El Valor, for he had an open wound
from nipples to pubis that required packing every four hours. His first
week at home was a nightmare for me, a nightmare of worry as well as
interrupted sleep and difficult management, for Stefan often resisted
handling, and changing the colostomy bag threatened to contaminate

the wound. With each packing change, I feared the wound was dehiscing, opening like an earthquake's fissure, sand and gravel avalanching down the slope of the ravine. Tom was not squeamish and good help; Anton came from California and sat with Stefan, keeping me company as well, but did not deal with the wound. Twice in those first weeks, I bundled Stefan up and rushed him to the ER, seeing leakage from the colostomy into the wound, but Stefan recovered without serious complications.

After a few months, when the wound was healed, El Valor took over. To their tremendous credit, they trained every staff member in colostomy care, enabling Stefan to participate in all activities as before. He continued to be treated for Crohn's, now at the university hospital where he had had surgery, and his condition flared about once a year. Then he needed hospitalization for intravenous antibiotics and steroids, and his care reverted to me. I learned to avoid the ER by phoning the GI fellow on call and bringing Stefan to the GI lab, but often there was no choice. Twenty-four hours could pass in the ER before Stefan was sent home or admitted and moved to a floor. At first staff from El Valor helped out, and one night Erica took over from midnight to dawn, but I continued to dread the phone calls that signaled the beginning of those long nights. Fortunately, he never got sick when I was away, and over the years, I wrote in Slovenia, biked from Warsaw to Prague, and studied Spanish in Spain and Mexico. Now that surgeons had peeked inside Stefan's belly, I considered the diagnosis of Crohn's confirmed, and so did his gastroenterologist.

That fall, Anton and Carole got married in San Francisco. With incredible generosity, El Valor gave us a staff member, Carmen Mendez, to care for Stefan on the trip and at the wedding. Carmen was a special friend of Stefan, had often invited him to her home, and had come to our house during his recovery to help him relearn how to shower, brush his teeth, and trace the letters of his name.

The wedding was held in Stern Grove, a huge park in a canyon in San Francisco's Sunset District. A hundred people gathered in the dark ravine, waited, and drank tea, and the crowd mixed people the couple knew from the Burning Man festival, where they had met; scientists from Anton's study and work in physics; lawyers from Carole's practice; and both families, including Tom, Stefan, Erica, Mama, and cousins who lived in California. Fog rolled down the canyon's steep slopes, rose and fell like blown fabric, and white mist glossed the towering redwood and eucalyptus trees. Soon it began to drizzle, and we went inside the lodge, where a wood fire burned, for the ceremony. Carole's father, a Methodist lay minister, had written the service and presided. He called Carole's mother, Donna, and me to stand. Feeling suddenly exposed, I took her hand.

"Do you promise to support this couple and not to come between them?"

"We do," we said in unison, over the laughter of the crowd. Carole's father turned to the assembly.

"And do you promise to support the bride and groom?" A hundred people shouted "We do," voices resounding in the drafty lodge before the fire. Gay men in costume circulated quietly, setting out food and wine: the Sisters of Perpetual Indulgence, an activist group who catered the event. The Sisters provided rat-themed decorations in honor of Carole's great love for the animals, which she kept free-range at the time. Black rubber rats adorned the tables and climbed up the cake. A photo shows one of the sisters in bright purple dress, billowing pink shawl, elaborate turban, and huge pendant cross, arm around Stefan. Stefan looks up, not quite at him, neat and short in suit and tie.

Food, wine, and cake flow into Klezmer-inflected punk rock music: the Polkaholics. The newly married couple takes the floor. Knifelike, Anton dances, entwined with his billowing bride, and in my mind, she swoons, her tattooed breast stark white against black bodice, above blood red taffeta, which falls in bustled layers to the floor. They fly across seas and centuries, joining hands with ancestors who once flew West, and in their dreamlike flight, the lodge becomes a *stetl* (by Chagall) and he a yeshiva student whose long limbs flow with awkward grace and hold the drifting body of his swirling wife.

Carole once said Anton was "a diamond in the rough" when she met him, and it was true. Not only was he bearded and shaggy-haired, but he had no idea how to be responsible to another person the way a husband is to a wife. Now he was not only neatly trimmed but ready to care for her and the new lives they would make. He'd found what I'd wanted most for him, a chance to realize his full humanity as husband and father. But they would fly to their own destination, far from any *stetl* by Chagall, and my fantasy of connection to Eric's ancestors would evaporate as quickly as the couple swept out of the canyon. The wedding was over. The last few guests gathered bottles and dishes, shoved back tables, swept up leaves and grime. The fire burned out. Wind and fog blew through the chilly lodge.

The next year I applied to Vermont College's low-residency MFA-Writing program, then set out cross-country in my car, headed for the Senior Institute at the Liz Lerman Dance Exchange in Tacoma Park, just outside D.C. An audition would follow the institute, and Liz, well known for using older and younger dancers together in her company, was looking for seniors. If I didn't get into Vermont, I wanted a new challenge. Around Ohio, I got a call: I'd been admitted to Vermont in fiction.

At the institute, I immersed myself in Liz's approach to changing ingrained and habitual movement patterns. Company members taught classes in styles ranging from Tai chi to Afro-aerobics to gestural solfège, a charming hand language that accompanied the familiar singing of "do-re-mi-fa-sol." After the audition, Liz invited me to join the company part-time, working twenty-six weeks out of the year. Unlike most dance companies, the Dance Exchange offered a contract with benefits. I took the job, went to Montpelier for the June–July residency, and met the Dance Exchange in Tucson, where Liz's multiyear, multicity *Hallelujah* project would have one of several working periods in that city. Though "hallelujah" means "praise God" in Hebrew, the project was not explicitly religious. As a whole, it articulated Liz's commitment to celebratory dance for and by communities. Sections of the piece were performed from Los Angeles to Eastport, Maine, each one based on local lore and personal stories.

Thus began a year and a half in which I stripped my life of everything but dance with Liz and writing. I found it glorious, a new beginning and a second chance all at once. My first residency at Vermont was like rebirth, as lectures, readings, and workshops drew me in, awed by how much I could learn and how much critical attention my work would get. In Tucson I rose at five every morning and watched the sun rise over the mountains beyond the hotel's pool. There I wrote until the day's work started, around nine. All day I was with the company, warming up or learning existing *Hallelujah* sequences, improvising with the wonderful music of Bob Een's cello, or working with a community group to help them respond to the project's questions: "What are you in praise of?" and "What is a little hallelujah in your life?" If we had no evening work, I was in bed by eight thirty, preparing to rise and write.

After Tucson we went to Gdansk, on the Baltic Sea, for an International Theatre Dance Festival. In my plain room in a dance school, I wrote, then performed in a beautiful bombed-out church, light visible through the ceiling. While I was in Poland, Carole gave birth to Iris, my first grand-child. I got the news in a phone message left by Tom. Frantic to talk to Anton and Carole, I raced up and down stairs, tried to place calls, failed with the phone card, tried again. I knew I couldn't have been there physically, because Carole had ruled out visits from anyone for the first two weeks, but still the separation seemed to stretch my nerves to attenuated threads, and my heart overflowed with a need to embrace them all. It was at least a day before I got through on the crackly phone.

"You got a baby girl!" I said to Anton.

"Yes, and everyone's doing fine."

"Was it very long?" I tried to squeeze myself through the phone line.

"Yeah, it was twenty-four hours, and I couldn't make it."

"What do you mean?"

"When they gave Carole the epidural, I fainted. After I came to, the nurse said, 'This is when we always lose the fathers.'" I thought of how hard it must have been for Carole, just at the moment of transition, to have to curl up for that procedure. How much easier it had been for me to give birth without interference! Anton put Carole on the phone.

"Congratulations," I said. "How great you got a baby girl!"

"I'm glad it's over," she said, sounding tired but happy. They had made a deal that girls would carry Carole's name and boys Anton's, so the baby was Iris Morrell, named for Iris Murdoch, one of Carole's favorite writers. Back from Europe, I went to San Francisco for a week, staying in their spare bedroom, and I held and changed Iris and took her for walks. The visit was much too long for Carole, who always felt uncomfortable around me, and over time we evolved a compromise: I would visit for a weekend every three months and stay at The Willows, a B&B of which I'd grown fond.

Work with the Dance Exchange continued to feel like a reprieve, a little unexpected extension of my dancing time. March in Tucson brought the culminating performance of *Hallelujah: In Praise of Ordinary Prophets*. Prayer by a Tohono O'odham tribal leader began the piece, which continued with sections of *Hallelujahs* developed in other locales. From Tucson itself came stories about rain in the desert told by a nun and embodied by students from the Hebrew school, music by a mariachi band and a gospel group, and a rousing circle dance that brought the prayed-for rain, falling from above the stage while a group in the center lifted its members up to praise the drops.

Much as I enjoyed the scope and power of these complex, community-based projects, their unfinished and thrown-together aspects and Liz's lack of control over the details disturbed me. Even more disturbing was my lack of control over my own body. Liz found my movement all of one piece and too abstract, and I never was able to produce the kind of detailed, theatrical movement she liked. Once when I was improvising with a younger company member, she said, "Could you imagine that at least one of you is human?" She pointed out that I was mourning the dancer I used to be instead of finding the one I could become, and she was right. I was always trying to move bigger, stronger, and faster. After a year and a half, I left the company and began my final semester at Vermont.

I had just gotten off the plane from my last residency when my cell phone rang. El Valor had taken Stefan on a group excursion to the mammoth shopping mall at Gurnee Mills, and midafternoon, he'd wandered off and disappeared into the crowd. The staff had hunted for him, growing more anxious by the minute, and then enlisted the help of security officers. Finally, despairing, they'd called to notify me that he was lost. Fortunately, they found him before I got off the phone, and the sequel turned out to be more interesting than the incident.

On the way back to El Valor in the van, Stefan said, "I'm sorry."

"What are you sorry for?" asked the attendant, as always kind and in touch with the residents.

"I got lost," said Stefan. Both the attendant and I marveled at this development. Improvements in Stefan's behavior were important, but his emotional and moral development was more profound. Over his twenty-odd years, he'd gone from failure to notice a sibling's death, to jealousy, to acknowledgment of fault and apology—a complex negotiation. Stefan would never be able to scheme like Nixon, but he'd learned to know when he was wrong and to say so.

Eric was adamant that the whole family show Stefan respect and never be ashamed of him in public, never care about what other people might think of his strange noises and sideways-looking eyes. We taught the boys to care for him, and they often had babysitting duties. Much later, so did Erica. If Stefan wanted to go to the Laundromat to watch clothes churn, we could leave him there while we went next door to the grocery, trusting that other patrons would soon get used to him, even look out for him. Eric was right: people often befriended Stefan, talked to him, and bought him candy. I agreed with Eric but did not have his fortitude; sometimes I couldn't help but care what people thought, and after Eric's death, I faltered.

It's a summer day, a couple of years after Stefan's surgery, when I pick him up from El Valor and drive with him to the Field Museum for an outdoor performance of music and sonic sculpture. Now in his late twenties, Stefan has outgrown washing machines, and I think he might enjoy this show more than any other human being on earth. It has everything he likes: strong rhythms, deep vibrations, large-scale mass movement.

Music is the subject of his talk as we drive. "He like music. Rock-n-roll too. He like music, yeah." I know I'm doing the right thing, but small ripples of apprehension spread outward from a knot in my stomach. Eyes turned on me and Stefan are always a test. I park, and we walk toward the museum, me wishing that Stefan would get the hang of walking next to me, instead of right in front or far behind. I hate stepping on his heels, and I shrink at the thought of how I must look, standing and waiting for him, calling his name and telling him to walk faster. He pauses to scratch the sidewalk with his fingertips, tries to lick each lamppost we pass.

"We're going to hear music," I tell him.

"Good music," he says. "I like church. I'm fat. I gotta fourteen. Neighborhood." I've learned to decipher some of his nonsequiturs. "Church" goes with music. "Neighborhood" is a shortening of my habitual response to his request for Burger King: "We don't have one in our neighborhood." "Fourteen" is a mystery. Wind from the lake has cleared the air, and the sun soaks it with warmth and brilliance. The museum's splendid stone facade rises before us; an intricate jumble of red and gray skyscrapers lies on our left, like a cubist painting; and a bright expanse of lake and sky opens up on our right. The city intoxicates me. It sings with little joys: the profusion of produce at the farmers' market, the lapping water of the lake. I float through it, blending into the colorful background.

But I can forget blending in today; today is for Stefan. Everyone can see me as I circle the museum, my son still lagging behind. A huge black metal dinosaur skeleton stands starkly in front of me, glinting with tiny points of sunlight, and I hear the seductive call of drums. Stefan starts to bolt toward the music, and I put a hand on his shoulder to slow him down. *You don't have to hang onto him,* says Eric's voice in my head. He liked to remind me that children are bound to their parents as tightly as parents are to their children: let them go, and they'll cling to your side.

Here comes someone: Tom. He has zoomed down the lakefront on his in-line skates to meet us. Stefan examines Tom's black wrist guards, and Tom undoes the Velcro straps and fastens the wrist guards around his brother's arms. Delighted, Stefan pretends to skate, following Tom around the garden. Stefan calls the wrist guards "muscles." "See my muscles?" he asks, gliding from foot to foot.

The performance begins. A man sits down on a chair placed on a picnic table and proceeds to bow an amplified cello. Deep, multilayered sounds flood out of the instrument, which is soon joined by the beat of drums. Hundred-foot strings are stretched from a wooden frame on the ground to another mounted on the roof of the museum. Musicians with gloved hands reach up to stroke these strings with strong pulls, using their whole bodies, setting off low vibrations I can feel in my gut.

I look over to see how Stefan is reacting. The excitement will probably agitate him, making him growl and bite the back of his hand, leaving red welts. Maybe it will be all right at an outdoor performance, where extraneous noises are less noticeable. Stefan's eyes jump around, and he twitches, but so far he remains engrossed. *He's OK. Don't worry about him,* says Eric.

A dancer undoes her huge red-silk shirt and trails it behind her like a cape, running between the musicians. A man spins something that looks like a top and makes tiny, squeaky sounds when he touches it with a stick. Another man in blue jeans runs in a big circle, blowing on a conch shell. When the music pauses, the running man stops and tells the audience about the enormous ground-to-rooftop stringed instrument, a sonic sculpture called the earth harp. When the show is over, Tom starts to head for home on his skates. He decides to let Stefan keep the wrist guards.

"Just until he goes back," I say.

"No, he can keep them," says Tom. "I'll get some more."

People are lining up to put on cotton gloves and try out the earth harp. Stefan will not ask to play; he doesn't even know that he can. I should encourage him, I should take him and get in line in that revealing sunlight and show him how to put on the cotton glove and stroke the strings. Maybe he will try it; maybe he won't. *What are you so worried about?* asks Eric.

But I know Stefan will hold everybody up. He will say, "Glove?" And laugh and bite his hands, afraid to try. People will wait politely, indulging him and me, and I'll shrink, aware that we are taking two or three times as long as anyone else. If someone in line coughs, I will be sure people are losing their patience. I will put on a glove myself and show Stefan how, sliding my hand on the overhead string and startling him with the sound. I will look only at him and the string, avoiding the spectators' eyes, imagining that no one can see me. If Eric were standing next to me, he wouldn't dream of leaving without Stefan's playing the earth harp. Neither would Tom, but Tom has gone home. I see myself balancing on a seesaw with Eric: he jumps off, and I crash down, tumbling over backward until I come to rest in a place I never intended. He would not be pleased if he could see me now. I realize for the thousandth time how much I need his counterweight. I contemplate leaving but fear Stefan wouldn't consent to go without a fuss. What am I doing to do?

I wrote this story originally as fiction about shame. My narrator's "I" ducked behind a "you," the "you" who left the performance without giving her son a chance to play. Then I revised it, still in second person, but with a joyful ending, the son finally playing to the crowd's applause. It made a better story. Now, the truth.

As I stood vacillating, Stefan gave me an out. "Liptauer," he said, referring to the cheese spread made with paprika that his father loved. Alone of all my children, he often remembered and asked for it. He liked to help buy the cream cheese, blue cheese, and green onion and to add the spices himself: a drop of Worcestershire, a dollop of mustard, and lots of paprika—hot and sweet. I knew that if I said, "Sure, Liptauer, let's go make it," he would leave without a struggle, and I did. We shopped and made the spread, and he never made the earth harp sing. The fictional version still plays in my mind, supported by a character I invented to encourage me, but the fact of my cowardice continues to haunt me. Had I met someone's eyes and enlisted help, the fictional companion might have become real, and the story would have earned its celebratory ending. In fact, Stefan enjoyed the shopping and the stirring, and I was left alone with the knowledge of what my shame had cost him.

On a Palm Sunday in San Francisco, Anton and Iris come with me to a church I love, the old Mission San Francisco de Asis, popularly called "Mission Delores" for the Mater Dolorosa, Our Lady of Sorrows. The sun is bright, and Anton has pushed Iris, now three, down their steep hill to pick me up at The Willows. Iris pretends to talk on a cell phone, using an old one of Anton's, as we make our way toward the Mission District. We pass the coffee shops and restaurants of Church Street, and I admire the profusion of flowering shrubs, bright blossoms, and thick succulents that Anton takes for granted, San Francisco's April sun warming my still-frozen Midwestern bones. Iris is lulled by the stroller's motion, and Anton and I talk about the war in Iraq, the group of dads with whom he goes out for beer, and his hopes for another child.

I am delighted to have Anton and Iris with me this morning. They are coming along primarily for the walk and the outing, not for the service, which is of no particular interest to them. Iris has had no religious education, and we plan that Anton will take her out to play from time to time. We arrive at the church just after the blessing of palms in the original mission church, dedicated shortly after the Declaration of Independence. With four-foot-thick adobe walls, it's the only church that survived the 1906 earthquake and fire. The place is packed, and only the ceiling is visible: redwood logs lashed with rawhide, painted in Ohlone Indian zigzag patterns with vegetable dyes. I pick up some of the long green fronds, distribute them to Anton and Iris, and join the procession, my heart speeding up at this way of doing it: from old church to new, from origins to modern parish, remembering Jesus's entry into Jerusalem and acclaiming him with praise as eternal king. I am thrilled to see that people in San Francisco feel free to raise and wave their honorific greenery, unlike many in Chicago who hold palms timidly at waist height.

Anton takes Iris out of her stroller and stands her on a pew where she can see, and I watch her. She seems captivated. She looks around at the brilliant stained-glass windows and the big blue domes overhead, fingers of gold fabric reaching like sun's rays from them to the crucifix in front. She reaches out to touch the large bunches of palm that bookend each pew. I know she likes red, the color of today's vestments and draperies, and wince to think that Iris's favorite color stands for martyrdom. The big choir on our right is singing "All Glory, Laud and Honor" as we arrange ourselves, and Iris seems absorbed in the sea of sound.

Today's Palm Sunday liturgy will fuse calamity and triumph, Jesus's joyful entrance followed by an account of his suffering and death, read in its entirety. I doubt that Iris will be able to last through that long reading, but somehow, she does. She sits on Anton's lap or in the pew between us and pages through the hymnbook, pretending to join in the congregation's parts.

They say that God has no grandchildren, and it's true that each generation must discover or reject God for itself. The missionary impulse is famously destructive, and the term itself has been so damaged by colonial practices and cultural imposition that many in that work have stopped using it, calling themselves instead "missioners." Mission Delores is making a worthy effort to make up for its history. This year, for the first time, the church's curator will be a descendent of the Indians by whom and for whom the mission was built. The curator jokes about a sign that might say "Returned to Former Management." Today the mission sponsors a "Day at Chutchui," the settlement San Francisco replaced, exploring Ohlone history and influence on the church's architecture.

I view Iris's presence as a gift and have no intention of exploiting her interest to teach her about religion, something both her parents would resent. Raised in a fundamentalist tradition, Carole was taught as a child that her occasional illness was punishment for failure to pray. This and the many sins of Christians have long since turned her against the faith, and she will soon request that I stop bringing Iris to church. I am unwilling to risk the fragile contact I have with Iris and resentful that Carole can't see the harmless nature of these outings, but I will comply.

The long reading is over, and the Mass moves on to preparations for Communion. Iris remains entranced, serious, maybe awestruck. Anton lifts her up to watch the gifts process up the aisle, and I marvel at what attracts her, what overcomes her natural three-year-old restlessness. She's exactly the same age Natasha was when she died. Eric did not live to know Iris, but I know he would recognize and rejoice as I do at the movement of the Spirit within her. We both always noticed and respected the special receptivity of children, the way they can respond to the Spirit without words or intellectual understanding. Iris continues to look and listen, a well being filled, and my joy overflows into tears, seeing that despite the distance and differences between us, she seems to feel what I feel and want what I want. There's no way she could name what calms and charms her, but her focused patience is clearly visible and amazing to me. I hope she doesn't view my tears as signs of distress. When Communion time comes, she wants to join the procession, and Anton carries her up the aisle for a blessing from the priest. We walk together, differences in our beliefs and practice temporarily reconciled by our steps.

After Mass we walk out to the walled cemetery and garden where Iris can run around, a haven of quiet and fragrance in the middle of the city. Tombstones equalize city founders and infants, roses bloom, and a grotto memorializes the forgotten dead whose markers have disappeared. Iris runs along the stone paths, among the markers and statues, and Anton picks her up to smell the tall roses. I read the inscriptions and enjoy Iris's release from stillness into motion, as she runs round and round the statue of the mission's founder, Juniperro Serra. I think of the thirsty pioneers who traveled the Camino Real from Mexico City to here and the respite they might have found in a cool garden such as this. Their timeless presence blesses me as the Church's communion expands to include the garden and the generations: a stream of communicants all walking toward the God embodied in this place. The divided is united, then springs open, as though cleaved by an ax. Iris picks up pebbles and makes a small pile, a brave little girl exploring the world, carrying the seeds that unite a succession of grandmothers and mothers, the living and the dead, down to Natasha, Erica, and the children Iris will bear.

17

Separations

NOT UNTIL THIRTEEN YEARS after Eric's death did I move. As I grieved, the old house became a snail shell around my fragile body, then expanded and echoed with absence as children grew up and moved out. Despite regular repairs, the house decayed around me, tomorrow's ruin. I knew the house I wanted; I could have drawn it, but I couldn't figure out where on the planet to set it down. While dancing with Liz Lerman in D.C., I decided I didn't want to return permanently to the city where I had grown up. San Francisco appealed, with Anton's family and two granddaughters now living there, but my friends were all in Chicago, and the city I'd wanted to leave as a student had become my true home. Finally I found a perfect house and snatched it up; then began the process of divesting myself of the past.

The remote cupboards of the old house held more than baby shoes and memories. There were boxes filled with tatting worked a hundred years before, heavy volumes of advice in German on household management, a multivolume art encyclopedia that had crossed the ocean during wartime. Finally the detritus of thirty-five years of living was spread across the alley, two garages full of discards to be fork-lifted and compacted, Eric's Uncle Ludwig's silver-backed, monogrammed set of brushes and combs abrading street signs stolen by teenagers, until everything was reduced to indistinguishable particles, crumbs at the bottom of a cookie jar.

At first, unpacked boxes filled the new house floor to ceiling, and I inched around the walls in search of a cup or a spoon. Later it seemed barren, too clean and too new. Important survivors claimed their places: the ceremonial sword Eric's grandfather wore as a general in the Austro-Hungarian Army; his mother's Russian tea glasses, reminders of the family's Eastern origins. Objects from the old house still surprise me by turning up, as if they had a will that brought them through the flood and fire of that garage.

Propped in a corner between the kitchen and the large entry foyer is my father's guitar. When did it come to me? I don't remember, and I've never played myself. Now I've had it restrung, and I hope each Christmas that a guest will take it from its black case and play for my assembled guests to sing. In a bottom drawer: the shorts and shirt I was wearing on the hot day when Natasha died; Eric's baby book, of course; a box marked "Brod und Salz" (bread and salt), a souvenir of his mother's wedding. This remnant of the time when her name was Katz, accompanied by a note, "from my parents when we married, 1912," testifies to the Russian customs of her parents.

I pick up flaking reproductions of the Sistine Chapel frescoes, the edges crumbling, and picture the brittle, teenaged girl who discovered those images, teetering on an edge and snatching at straws to keep herself upright. She's slight and undeveloped, but her hair is already showing the hereditary salt-and-pepper that will turn it white in her twenties. After school, she rehearses in the studio past the dinner hour, then comes home to eat the meal her mother has saved in the oven. In the basement she gets out her books, surreptitiously stashing some celery sticks stuffed with cream cheese in the drawer. She sits, and her mind wanders, but she won't let it get to the moon. AB–Celt., Celt.–Drool. The arbitrary headings defend her against the night sky's magnetism, and she tries to recite them with her eyes closed. Drool–EFG, HIJKL, MNO–Phar., Phar.–Q, R–Sals. She's tired, but she still has work to do. She decides to sleep for two hours, then study for two hours in the middle of the night. She sets the alarm. Waking, she eats some rice and soy sauce, but still the emptiness inside her threatens to connect with the great emptiness of space, and she shudders. There's no way out of everywhere.

Then, one afternoon, at a moment that's more than opportune, *Life* magazine arrives in the mail with prints of the Sistine frescoes. She pores over them, searching out details and reading the stories. Without knowing how, she finds herself saved from the moon, the stars, the void, and all the useless tricks she'd used to fight them off.

In a closet: the Christmas book we made for the children when I was still my parents' secular daughter. I lettered those pages with the infancy stories, King James Version, while Eric drew fanciful illustrations. I haul the book out of the closet. Its two-by-three-foot surface is dotted with spots of brown mold, and shiny blue paper peels away from the cardboard on the edges, while frayed black and white velvet ribbons hold it all together. The title, "The First Christmas," stands over a reproduction of a medieval painting in which a two-dimensional Mary holds an infant in a boxlike cradle, while Joseph ponders, chin in hand, and an ox and an ass look on. I open the book to see Eric's drawing of a terrified Mary, kneeling on one knee alone on a mountain, assaulted by an arrowlike Spirit. This is no gentle Annunciation in a garden, but a manifestation as awe-inspiring as a thunderstorm or a burning bush. In the distance and far below, palm trees, a tent, and a camel localize the event, while three crosses on a small hill prefigure the end of the story.

On the next page, chickens peck in a courtyard, a little boy pees, and a donkey balks while an innkeeper refuses Mary admittance, and an angel points the way to the barn with waiting manger. A big golden star illuminates the scene and lends its brilliance to Mary's swollen stomach and the guiding angel. Every child can read this color-coded holiness. On the next page, shepherds throw up their staffs and fall down in fear of the announcing angel (gold, of course), while the sheep, a dog, and a camel, already friends of God, remain calm under the palm trees.

Each Christmas Eve, while candles burned on the tree, we read this book aloud, the children taking turns as they learned to read. For me, for many years, the repetition awakened memories of Christmastimes at school, but the story did not embody any truth. Now it seems clear to me that the book itself was a manifestation of Eric's faith, a subterranean stream that grounded the many layers of his personality, ready to surface at any moment, whether in tears or in joyful and humorous images. And perhaps my participation in making the book prefigured my later awakening.

Mama turned ninety in July 2004 and began to feel ill shortly after. She'd never been seriously sick before, though she often responded to conflict by retreating to her room, pleading indigestion or a low-grade fever. But this symptom had gone on too long, and I was alarmed.

"I keep calling, but I only get the nurse," said Mama to me on the phone.

"Tell her you want to see a gastroenterologist," I suggested.

"You can't do that. The insurance doesn't allow it."

"You can just make an appointment and pay for it yourself."

"That's not the way it works up here." She'd been living for many years in central Wisconsin. "I'll keep calling. It'll be all right."

I refrained from pushing her further to go outside the system, knowing Mama feared making waves more than illness. Well-known in her community as founder of a writing group, patron of the arts, and philanthropic supporter of liberal causes, Mama still avoided anger, grief, and any intense emotion. If feeling threatened to break through, a single tear might roll from eye to chin. Those outside the family often interpreted her remote responses as celestial forgiveness; they could confess to betrayal, incest, or anything short of murder, and Mama would nod approval: "That's all right." But to me, Mama's reassurance was a sure sign of something amiss.

By now I was teaching writing and rhetoric at Columbia College and began going to see her Wednesday through Friday, the days I didn't teach. I found her in bed but able to walk, uninterested in food, and very glad of the visit. Her face was drawn, bringing out the elegant bone structure that had made her resemble Nefertiti in her youth, and her gray hair was still thick and curly. We talked about books—she was reading James Weinstein's *The Long Detour* and liked the parts about people she'd known on the Left—and I encouraged her to resist the friends who tried to tell her she needed a nurse or a nursing home. She'd had a personal staff for many years—part-time writing tutor, secretary, and household help—and she intended to manage without additional care. I'd observed the tendency of adult children to criticize the way their aging parents faced disease and death, and I resolved to respect Mama's wisdom about her own journey.

On the surface, we conversed sensibly. Mama loved me, in her cool, detached way, and I feared the loss of her current, companionable self. At the same time, I hoped for the warmth she'd never been able to generate, and inside I clung to the mama of my childhood. I remembered her cool hands, elegant fingers, and black curls, the way she sang me to sleep every night, stroking my head. "Nice pussy, soft pussy, little ball of fur. Sleepy pussy, happy pussy, purr, purr, purr." My sister and I used to curl like spoons with Mama in bed and scratch each other's backs. Sometimes she made us delicious bowls of rice with butter and sugar, and there was always more. I loved the sexy jazz songs she used to sing at late-night parties, accompanied by Daddy's guitar. Still yearning for what I'd never be able to have, I imagined myself the mother, doting on my infant self. I longed to smile and coo, to fill that baby's well, as Sylvia Plath does in "Child":

> Your clear eye is the one absolutely beautiful thing.
> I want to fill it with colors and ducks,
> The zoo of the new.[1]

Each of my children made trips to Wisconsin to see their grandma, Anton and Carole bringing the girls from California and Tom bringing Veronika, the Russian woman who would soon be his wife and lend stability to his life. Erica came with me a few times. Soon a biopsy showed lung cancer, and my shock vied with a sense of inevitability, as Mama's path was obviously narrowing. Back at the house, Mama filled her staff in on the morning's events, always a bright storyteller.

"They did a CT scan first," she said. "And I asked for Dan to do the biopsy, so we had to wait for him to be free, but he came and did it himself, even though it took an hour. I had to hold my breath, and they took a few samples, and a lady raced them to the lab. And then we came home. Pretty tiring." She didn't mention the results.

Mama's composure served her dying well. Calm and determined to maintain her independence to the end, she never lost her acuity or interest in the world around her. She adopted the words of Jane Kenyon's poem "Let Evening Come" as a symbol of her acceptance and read it aloud to visitors. Any time her world began to crack, threatening vision that might break the bounds of speech, she got out her can of putty and quickly patched up the break.

Finally she fell through. We discussed the moon's eclipse just hours before she died, me talking on my cell phone as I walked to a movie in Chicago, Mama looking out her bedroom window. I was glad I helped Mama die the way she wanted. Though sad and shaken by the death, I was not overwhelmed by grief.

On the day of Mama's memorial service, in early December, I felt sick, sad, disoriented as well as congested, unable to distinguish grief from my bad head cold. The service was distant, full of strangers, and I spoke to person after person I didn't know and wouldn't remember. The ceremony, arranged largely by Mama's staff, reflected her rich public life. Two well-known Wisconsin writers spoke, as well as a commentator for Wisconsin Public Radio, a professor of American Indian Studies, and a member of Mama's writing group. The presider was a liberal lawyer I had not met before, and the impersonality of the service was painful to me. Only the end seemed to embody Mama's private spirit, as a small combo played the Dixieland tunes she'd always loved. Stefan was predictably enthusiastic, bursting into applause and clapping along as the saints marched in.

Now I miss her and often want to share an idea or a book. I am more like her than I would care to admit. The very coolness that entranced Eric came from her, as well as my fear that conflict will condemn me to isolation. We were both bystanders, letting others fight our battles. She talked to me all the time when I was a baby, using chatter to hold me at arm's length but giving me words. Like her, I write. At a later memorial service for her at the independent school she once directed, I learned that she had offered teaching jobs to many young and drifting people who credited her with rescuing them and starting them in lifelong careers. Her smooth, distant words comforted strangers more often than they did her sticky children. But this story is about the tectonic shifts and eruptions she could not allow. When I began to see the world as charged with God, the face that shone on me was not my mother's, but my child's. My mother gave me the words to write my story, but no colors, no ducks.

18

A Delicate Affair

Eric died to me a second time through that process strangely known as healing. With Ron's help, I rebuilt my psyche from square one, filling in the long-missing parts that Eric had provided, so that ten years later I could put gas in the car, make a friend, or care for a sick child on my own. But Eric has continued to live for me in the vibrant domain where fact gives way to fiction, pretending makes present, and the imaginary trumps the real.

I stand in front of my house on a misty autumn evening. A column of vapor eddies upward and glistens with reflected light, then thickens with drizzle. Shining drops of water are trapped in what looks like a beard, and a wet face takes shape to frame it. I imagine Eric emerging from the fog, smiling above his bushy beard, and his warm body solidifies. He walks toward me, ready for a big hug, raising his arms overhead in greeting, as he always did when we met on Wednesday afternoons to go grocery shopping—filling two carts and organizing a week's menus on a yellow legal pad—at the Hyde Park Co-op. I embrace him, warm inside his habitually unbuttoned coat, and press my face to his yielding flesh, then step back and see he looks unchanged. A crazy hope for reunion makes my heart race, as it does whenever I dream him up, and I begin again to piece together a contradictory story: how the wife I was has never stopped yearning to reach across the unbridgeable divide and join him, while the single, solitary widow I am now has become a person who could never be that wife. Eric takes up a conversation he might have started long ago.

"It's not that you've forgotten me," he says. "My voice and words and touch are just as you remember. My hand still shakes. It's yourself that you've forgotten. You've changed so much I wouldn't know you." The truth of what he says brings real tears, and I brush them away.

"How?" I ask, reaching out to touch his soft brown hair. He covers my hand with his, and I feel myself succumbing to his gravity, drawn into the planetary system of "us," two orbs in playful balance that comprised a universe, spinning off children like meteors. I long to enter that powerful field and attach my center to his by bonds so strong they make him my male self and me his female self.

I pull my hand out from under Eric's and point toward the house. "I live here now," I say, eager to show him. "I had to throw out a lot, but I have your mother's Russian tea glasses, and your grandfather's sword hangs over the bookcase—you'll see it as soon as you walk in."

"Good," he says. "Evidence is necessary, also memory. I hope the sugar game served its purpose." I picture a cafe in Hyde Park, four children aged three to fifteen sitting at a Formica-covered table waiting for Cokes and burgers, a glass of water in front of each. Eric corrals the supply of sugar packets and starts asking questions. To the youngest, "What's my real name, besides 'Daddy'?" The reply, "Eric Kast," wins a packet. He addresses the next, the disabled one. "What's your name?" If the child can say "Stefan," he wins. Now it gets harder. "Where was I born? What was my father's name? What did he do for a living? Who was the chancellor of Austria at the time of the Anschluss?" Than an orgy of packet tearing and stirring, sweet water the reward.

"The children are all grown and gone," I say, knowing I can never communicate the fullness of two weddings and two granddaughters or the emptiness of years in which I corrected, bit by bit, the erratic motion of a comet out of orbit, when I found myself sitting on a rock in space, the people around me only passing Martians.

"Tom married Veronika, from Russia," I say, without the heart to tell him his beloved Soviet Union broke into smithereens, "and Anton has two daughters. Erica finished college. You wouldn't believe how fluent Tom is in Russian."

"I tried that long ago," said Eric. "Remember 'Ochen horosho'?"

"Oh yes, the teacher: 'Very good.' Your silly names and games outlive you," I continue. "Tom and Veronika actually dust off chocolate before they eat a piece, the way you used to do with the kids to teach them patience."

"Do they make you sit and wait, butt on the floor?"

"Hardly. Maybe they will when they have children. And Tom tries to sing the Austrian national anthem while dousing the candles, just like you did when the boys were little. We all still act out presents."

Eric relished *The Honeymooners,* especially an episode where Ralph invents a can opener and develops a TV commercial to sell it. The plan is that Norton will try to open a can and fail, and then Ralph will burst on the scene in chef's whites, one finger in the air, to demonstrate his invention. The plan fails, but it became the model for our gift-giving charades: the failure, the arrival of the "Chef of the Future" with finger raised, the gift that solves the problem.

"That's cooking with cookies," says Eric.

"I see you're still talking nonsense," I say.

"Funny joke," he says. "It's just a funny joke."

"You should see the house. It's exactly my size."

"I'd never fit," he says. Already Eric is receding into the rain. Drops of moisture glisten in his beard like crystals before his substance dissolves into streaks. "Time to blow this joint," he says, and I hear a familiar enthusiasm in his voice. "Hey, stupido!" The sound is faint, directed elsewhere, then stronger as he turns back to me. "I've got to go order some crumb-bums around."

I look behind me at my real, brick house, where I've lived since 2000. The house is small enough for me to clean by myself, located close to friends, the train, my yoga class. My groceries fit in a handbasket, and I only plan ahead for company. Sometimes I appall myself with the oddly assorted leftovers I eat in my bright kitchen, remembering the slow-cooked winter soups I ate with Eric, the long conversations by candlelight. Often I yearn for companionship, always for deep connection and intimacy.

Writing fiction was a way to bring him back. With pen and paper, I could take us on a trip we never took or inhabit his point of view. I turned to memoir when I suspected I was hiding behind him, as I'd sometimes done in life, and I wanted to see with my own eyes and tell the truth I saw. But writing truth challenges me with a third and unexpected loss. If I'm to make him live for others, I have to give up my imagined listener and lover. The contradictions I ignore in memory must be rendered on the page to make him believable, and with his lumps and kinks, of course, are intertwined my own.

With rare exceptions, Eric could not tolerate collaboration with men of equal age and standing. Both in private practice and at his free clinics, he was in charge, surrounding himself with younger or less powerful colleagues. Charismatic and visionary, he attracted a loyal following and was aware of his priestly role. I considered myself different from these acolytes, for I dialogued with him as an equal. To me he was husband, not mythical figure, and I knew his fears and weaknesses.

The person I didn't know was myself. Occasionally I regretted the loss of a friend antagonized by a tactless remark of Eric's, but I failed to notice how our circle narrowed over the years. I let relationships fade and did not develop new ones. Eric hated and feared women who walked ahead on the street or "looked elsewhere," as he said, seeing the wandering eye as a sign of infidelity. I stayed within the limits he set, considering our closeness and relative exclusion of others to be part of the terms of the marriage, like vows of fidelity. The force of the soft bars of that cage was my need for a listener. It was I who initiated the daily recital while Eric responded patiently.

I also failed to notice the extent to which I relied on Eric for a sense of self, as well as adult love. Now, fifteen years later, I talk to many friends and all my children, but only in my dreams and fantasies of Eric do I re-create that deepest exchange of heart and mind. My memory may have airbrushed him, but, as Woody Allen says of the delusion that his brother is a chicken, I need the eggs. So I'm holding him close and putting him out there at once, always amazed at the myriad ways in which the dead come to life.

Eric often made fun of his father's rigidity and insistence in restaurants that "everyone order the same thing," yet Eric the rebel retained some of this same rigidity, essentially a fear, I think, that he would be found lacking in the sophisticated world of food and wine or be shown up by a knowledgeable waiter or sommelier. Eric never claimed consistency, and this was one of the many contradictions that made him who he was, easy to forget when I've lived so long with my imagined version.

Only toward the end of his life would Eric allow me or the children to order for ourselves in restaurants or ask the waiter questions about the food or wine, though this was my territory: I did the cooking and also wrote restaurant reviews for a neighborhood paper. I'd long since exchanged the transparent cage of my upbringing for this visible one, and I pushed against its velvet bars until I could squeeze through. I remember Eric's discomfort the day a waiter brought me the wine to taste, but by then the whole thing seemed silly. I patted his arm. "We'll both taste it," I said.

I rarely got angry. Eric often faulted me for denial of anger, a skeletal remnant of my childhood cage, where anger threatened permanent loss. But I did get angry when our boys were in their teens and it was time to put Stefan to bed. Eric would go limp, saying, "I can't." I'd be ready to clear supper and wanting him to take care of bedtime, but he couldn't tolerate the lengthy and frustrating process of coaxing Stefan up the stairs. If I insisted, he'd turn off the downstairs lights and wait for Stefan to come up on his own. I was sometimes exhausted, and any sign of indisposition on my part reminded Eric of his mother's hysterical illnesses. He tried to ignore both. I seethed and sometimes complained but never exploded, possibly disturbing Eric more by my failure to admit or even recognize anger than I would have by an outburst.

I remember only a couple of times that I was frankly angry, like when Eric failed to make good sense, demanding, for example, that I shift the car into a higher gear when I was on the highway, with no place to shift but down, and then my anger burned my face and jerked my hands around, so I couldn't fail to claim it.

Now I wonder whether I could write were Eric alive. The price of the reflection he offered for all my thoughts and feelings was just that: *all* my thoughts and feelings. To write, I would need the freedom to explore murky depths and inappropriate attachments. Had I tried, I fear I would have reined myself in before I went far enough to threaten him. Though I still write to get him back, both as listener and as lover, I suspect I couldn't write at all were he alive today.

But I also suspect the opposite. Eric was infinitely adaptable and much quicker to change than I. And he was willing to go further than any man I knew or imagined for the women he loved, especially after the birth of our first daughter. One day when Natasha was three, she brought her three-legged stool into the bathroom where Eric was in the tub. I sat on the toilet seat.

"Your body has a wonderful secret," said Eric to Natasha. "You can't see it—it's on the inside—but you have a womb and tubes and lots of fancy connections. Someday you can grow a baby in there. I wish I could grow a baby."

"I wish I could color inside the lines," she said.

"I wish I had a vagina, like you," he said. I tried to write this scene once as fiction, but my readers insisted it was too far-fetched. Now, the privilege of memoir: I can tell the truth. He may not have meant it, but he said it, for Natasha.

"Sadie can behave yourself," she said, speaking of a friend a year older. "I can't behave yourself."

"You can have a baby," repeated Eric. "I wish I had a vagina."

Remembering that, I think the burden of daring to write may have been on me. If Eric could dream up "vagina envy" for Natasha, might he not have accepted deeper and darker explorations from me? If I had conquered my own timidity and fear of conflict, perhaps he would have tolerated my writing after all.

Over the years, we discussed and reworked and finally eliminated those dated categories from our worldview: "castrating mothers" and "competition with men." Not long before Eric's death, I began to read feminist theology and tried to get him to do the same. I pointed out its critique of racist and classist biases, as well as sexist ones.

"It's radical," I said. "Like you."

"Yeah. Sure," he said. "Sometime." I reminded him of his happy discovery of Marxist interpretations of the Bible and liberation theology. "Men and women getting along together . . ." he said. "It's such a delicate affair. Why would anyone want to mess around with that?" His wistful question made me smile, and I let it go. For me, feminism ultimately meant learning to embrace the way I was made. For Eric, it threatened being manipulated once again by someone with the power to support or destroy his entire sense of worth.

As I reflect on Eric's compelling need to take the initiative, my imagined meeting with him reveals an intrinsic flaw. No passivity in life could equal the one he suffers now, as I put words in his mouth and steal his volition altogether. Whatever I remember, dream up, or write reflects *my* will. If I once seemed to be Eric's puppet, now he's mine. And if he once was my exotic "other," now he's a part of me.

There's bound to be some triumph in survival, and I enjoy making Eric walk and talk. As his tone of voice comes to life, my excitement rises, but my creation is bound to disappoint. Without the little shocks of difference, there's no risk and no discovery. The Eric I invent can never satisfy.

Though my waking fantasy robs Eric of his will, the Eric I meet in sleep is someone I can't shape or move. Night after night he comes to me, returned from the dead, and the scene seems real. One thing, however, is always lacking: in fifteen years, he's never made love to me. I protest, "What's wrong? How can you have changed so much?" But nothing I say or do intrudes on his indifference: the dead don't fuck.

Centrifugal force hurls us apart, sending Eric into invisible realms and transforming him in an instant, entirely. Like the bride in the Song of Songs, I've no choice but to "seek him whom my soul loves" (Song 3:2), looking beyond my remembered Eric to the greater reality of which he's now a part. The same centrifugal force launches me into solo flight, unburdened and unattached, and I keep changing as I fly in ways that are also rich and strange. The hours in which I think and write are no longer stolen from sleep or other's needs, but stretch, suspended, like a child's endless present. I gobble my freedom with heady greed and defend it against intrusion or obligation. No distraction shields my senses from the menthol smell of rosemary growing on my porch, a summer cherry's burst of juice, or the surge of power in my pedaling legs as I outrace a dog that barks and nips. I sleep alone, awaiting the early-morning hours that give me time to write before I speak, allowing words to condense slowly from the images of dreams, and I pray that Eric's life in death will illuminate the path on which I walk. Solitude nourishes the private, contemplative person I always was, inside.

19

No Pity

STEFAN IS THIRTY-FOUR WHEN he, El Valor staff, and I meet on a hot July day for an appointment at the GI clinic. I'm apprehensive, knowing he's been losing weight. For the last six months, he's been trying to make himself throw up, sticking his slender hand down his throat to the wrist, and he can't tell us why. He knows he shouldn't. He will even tease us with a hand-to-mouth feint, a crafty look in his eyes, but he can't say what compels him.

"Hi, Pumpkin," says a nurse. "How are you?" She knows him from the four-hour intravenous infusions of Remecade he has periodically to control his worsening Crohn's.

"Hi," says Stefan. "How you?" He steps forward to shake her hand, less than five feet tall and beardless, hair gelled into little spikes. In the examining room, he begins to shiver in a way I've never seen anyone do before—deep, bone-shaking tremors that run through his whole body—and I'm aghast. His gastroenterologist appears in the doorway, takes one look, and says, "ER—now." We hustle Stefan, frightened and screaming, into a wheelchair, grab the hands he's trying to put down his throat, and hurry down the hall. The doctor explains as we go that the chills called rigors (pronounced "rye-gores") are caused by an immune response in which the set point for body temperature in the hypothalamus rises, and the body shivers in an attempt to warm up.

"Can't we go directly to admissions?" I ask the doc, hoping to avoid the ER.

"It wouldn't be fast enough," he says, explaining that rigors are a common symptom of septicemia, or blood poisoning, and require immediate treatment. Blood tests soon confirm that diagnosis.

"How do you get septicemia?" I ask an ER nurse as she hurries by our curtained cubicle.

"From infection in any part of the body," she says. "Often from hospitalization." Vaguely I remember hearing about resistant organisms living in hospitals, but I can't stop to think that the help Stefan needs might come bundled with lethal exposure. It takes all my strength and concentration to keep Stefan's hand out of his mouth. We're both scared, and sometimes I think swallowing his hand has become a response to fear in addition to whatever is going on in his stomach. Soon his heart races out of control, and an ER doctor comes in and starts massaging his carotid artery, watching the wall, not looking at Stefan.

"I'm not trying to choke you," he says. "I'm just trying to get your heart rate down." I don't understand how this works, and Stefan even less, but he lies fairly still, eyes searching for escape like the eyes of a horse in a fire. His usual patter in the hospital—"Almost finished? Go home soon?"—is oddly absent. The bottom falls out of my stomach and my world as I realize that he's sicker than he's ever been before.

Ten days earlier, Lupe, a staff member at El Valor, brought Stefan for a consultation with an older, well-respected colorectal surgeon.

"I don't think he has Crohn's," said the surgeon. "I see no evidence of it. His scans show a shadowy area, possibly an obstruction. We'll remove a section of diseased bowel and reverse the colostomy." Lupe and I were flabbergasted. Could he really do this? How Stefan's life would improve without the constant need for colostomy bag change and cleanup! We looked at each other, breathless. Was it possible that he didn't have Crohn's, after so many years of treatment? Though I feared surgery, we were all hopeful of cure and even betterment of his life when septicemia changed a well-thought-out plan into an urgent rescue operation.

After eight hours in the ER, the staff decides that Stefan should be admitted to intensive care, and a doctor comes down to explain the requirements of that unit. Stefan will need a central line (into a large, centrally located vein), an arterial line (for constant monitoring of blood pressure as well as blood gases), and a urinary catheter (a patient in the ICU is tied to so many devices it's nearly impossible to use the toilet). In the unit, Stefan scrambles to climb over the bed rails, nearly succeeding, then bites the back of his hand where a brown callous has formed. He growls and swears rapidly under his breath, revealing a surprising mastery of foul language. I worry about the loss of his independent-living skills—toileting, dressing, and feeding—as well as his human connections and sense of self, so easily destroyed by the machine-driven life of the ICU.

After three days with nothing by mouth in the ICU, Stefan is moved to a surgical floor, starving. "I'm hungry, Ma," he says as I arrive. "Ven acá." His sharp ear has picked up bits of the Spanish spoken by staff at El Valor.

"Here I am," I say. "You can't eat now, but soon. What would you like? Hamburger?" Before he moved to El Valor, Stefan was a cosmopolitan eater and even used chopsticks, always articulate with his fingers, but now he sticks to the all-American diet of the group home. "French fries?"

"Yah, fries, yessir. I'm hungry, Ma. I'm hungry." He's wearing the big, spongy boxing gloves the hospital uses to prevent pulling of tubes or the hand down the throat, and he calls them "mittens." Though he can easily undo the knots and ties that hold them on, he says "Mittens?" if he feels the urge to make himself vomit, the same way he says "Gotta take it, gotta take it" to himself when confronted by pills. But his self-monitoring gives way to impulse in a flash. I leave the room for ten minutes to eat, for I couldn't possibly eat in front of him, and come back to find mittens off, IV line and catheter pulled out, bed wet.

"I don't see why he can't eat," says the surgeon. "Give him a full diet." The gastroenterologist opposes feeding, and the difference between the two doctors seems melodramatic, almost farcical. I begin calling them Dr. Pessimist and Dr. Optimist in my e-mails to family. Dr. Pessimist isn't writing the orders, and I want to believe Dr. Optimist, longing to feed my famished son. So far as I know, they do not confront each other over this, nor do I confront them.

In the beginning I think it's good they disagree, so discussion and argument can reveal the truth. This turns out to be my first mistake. Though they confer at the start, they are not even once both present with me, and my hope for conference by e-mail turns out to be stupidly naive. Pessimist says he can't type. Their differing views lead not to discussion but to management that ricochets from one pole to another.

So Stefan eats with pleasure, and I am shocked to find forbidden foods on the tray, kernels of corn or tomatoes with seeds, things we've avoided for years, told they could cause mechanical obstructions for people with Crohn's. When I question a nurse about this, she says, "We don't have any no-corn diet. We only have clear liquid, full liquid, and full." Stefan eats one or two meals, then loses appetite and wants to throw up. Usually we prevent him, but he's quick. A minute alone in the shower, and his hand disappears down his throat.

On my way home from the hospital, I stop by Esperanza, Stefan's day program, where live jazz percolates through the summer evening and barbeque smoke thickens the air. I stroll among the clusters of people eating on the grass, but the festive scene feels unreal and out of place, as though viewed on a small television screen in the middle of a vacant lot. Only Peter and Diana White, the parents of Benjamin, Stefan's roommate at El Valor, can know what's in my head and heart. I greet them, relieved by sharing the unspoken, then head for home.

Dr. Optimist postpones surgery until Stefan's blood counts improve and he's weaned from steroids. The first day's urgency fades to hours that accumulate like beads on a string. Along with the surgery, my real life recedes, replaced by the hospital's beige halls, blue gowns, and stagnant air. I don't see Pessimist for a week, and he fails to respond to messages. Frustrated, I contemplate finding new docs but fear losing the communication I have if the current ones find me fickle or histrionic. So I stay put and intervene to save Stefan as much suffering as possible, refusing permission for all but the necessary needles, tubes, and tests, using permission as currency to get information. Tears come at night, making me hate myself for this girly meltdown of anger, when a man would put anger to work.

I know if Eric were alive, he would use his authority and forceful character to demand attention and get second and third opinions, breaking the hospital rules that say only staff physicians can see a patient. I picture him storming into this hospital and raising hell, then despair of even beginning to find my way through the medical tangle alone.

On the weekend, the hospital becomes a warehouse, so I don't even think about doctors or plans. Stefan sits in a chair, legs neatly crossed, so thin now they make two perfectly parallel lines, a pair of pipe cleaners. With him is Nancy, one of several nurse-techs who stay with him when I'm not there. She finds his position adorable and points it out every time he assumes it. I get out the supply of puzzles we've accumulated and line them up on Stefan's tray.

"Which one do you want?" I ask. Stefan points, and I spread out the pieces.

"What's for dinner, Ma?" he asks.

"I think you'll get some broth and Jell-O," I say, "in about two hours."

"I'm hungry," he says. He's expert at puzzles and keeps his mind on the task, picking up each piece with precise fingers and trying it with each other one, regardless of color or image. I work on the edges and make suggestions, sneaking a peak at the picture on the cover for clues.

"Try this one," I say.

"OK, Ma." We do four puzzles before he tires. I've bought him some new CDs and old favorites from home: songs by Pete Seeger, *Satch Plays Fats*, a Beatles album, *Bluegrass from Heaven*, a Leonard Bernstein compilation that includes "Pomp and Circumstance," and *Soul Hits*, very popular with the nurse-techs. He slips a disc in with his usual skill and presses "play." Nancy and I begin to clap and dance to the bouncy, circus rhythm of "Tears of a Clown," by the Miracles.

"Oh yeah," says Stefan, swaying from side to side, roaring and clapping. "I like that."

"You like music?" asks Nancy.

"Yes, I do," he says. "Yes I do."

"Go for walk?" asks Stefan as I arrive.

"He's been walking all morning," says the nurse-tech, and this becomes the new routine. Up and down each corridor of the floor and across the no-man's land that connects East and West, where the service elevators are, pushing his IV pole, with me or one of the sitters. He peeks into a room and gets excited when he sees a young man with shaved head.

"Hi, Tom!" he says, so pleased to see his brother, and I explain to the stranger that Tom also has a shaved head. I place my hope in the promised surgery, and this is my second and more serious mistake.

After three weeks in the hospital, they open him up and find an inoperable tangle of intestines and mesentery, the blood vessels that supply the gut. They try to biopsy the mass, start runaway bleeding, and close him in less than an hour. At first they call it a Desmoid tumor, a mass malignant but noninvasive; later they call it simply unknown. The diagnosis of Crohn's recedes in importance, as Stefan's body refuses to speak the language of medical science.

Following the useless surgery, Stefan is at first heavily sedated, then weak. Nurses who saw him walk before surgery are shocked to see him so passive and debilitated, and nurses who meet him now ask if he's ever been able to walk. Optimist orders full diet again, and Stefan, restrained, vomits at night and aspirates, causing pneumonia. Back to intensive care, now on a ventilator. He's learned to bite on the flexible tube to prevent suctioning, and they've responded by adding a rigid, plastic airway. Sedation is wearing off, and he's choking. A respiratory therapist enters. I point out that Stefan needs more sedation or extubation, and he says, "I haven't heard anything about pulling a tube." I ask for a doctor, and eventually one orders removal of the tube. "You win," says the respiratory guy. I wonder with horror what happens when *he* wins. Freed of the tube, Stefan says hoarsely but with perfect articulation, each word separate: "I—need—help. I—need—help." I think if he must die, it shouldn't be here.

Friends who live nearby invite me to dinner. The evening is warm, and we sit on the porch above a garden, a luxurious tangle that seems to extend without limit in the setting sun. I am held by their welcome and the care they've taken with the meal, their care of me, for me. We have a glass of wine and tapenade on crackers, as I tell them Stefan's news.

"You seem to be doing all right with this," says my friend.

"That's because I've left the hospital," I say, with a sharp laugh. "I always feel worse in the morning, before I go." This is true, but I hear the rapid clatter of my voice and realize I've taken leave not just of the hospital but of much of my feelings. What happened to Stefan today was unspeakably cruel and heartless. If I let myself feel its full impact, I couldn't go on, and I've instigated what my late husband used to call "martial law." You give yourself orders, and you carry them out.

And you take comfort where you can. Right now, in a classical pesto Genovese, the basil-and-garlic-flavored sauce mixed with spaghetti, potatoes, and bright green beans, accompanied by grilled asparagus. Then a platter of red and Green Zebra tomatoes, ripe when green, fresh from the shadowy garden. By candlelight we eat espresso ice cream with raspberries and brownies from a nearby bakery, talking late about Stefan and books and writing and painting in the thick, embracing dark.

Calling to leave a message for Dr. Optimist, I discover that he is gone. Gone, altogether and permanently. To London, says his secretary, and if he comes back at all, it will only be to tie up loose ends. Stefan and I are not among them. Though I try to contact his team repeatedly and tell Dr. Pessimist how unconscionable I find their behavior, I never meet a single one of the surgeons again. I demand a conference with Dr. Pessimist, who points out that Stefan's blood counts must improve before he could survive further surgery, then says, "You know, you're his advocate . . . if it weren't for you . . ." and trails off. Through his unspoken thought, the silence of the surgeons speaks loud and clear of Stefan's disability and their own distaste for a hopeless case.

Little pleasures grow in importance: movies on DVD, the weekly farmer's market. I'm beginning to understand what taking care of yourself means. I've always thought it a "me-generation" antidote to guilt or excuse for self-indulgence, but now it feels like a triumph of the selfish gene, a biological imperative with a life of its own. Ambivalence has never felt so much like two people inside me, as the pleasure-seeking one elbows its way past mother love and compassion with the willfulness of a two-year-old and a diver's demand for air.

After two months in the hospital, Stefan begins working with Kelly, a young physical therapist, who teaches him to use a walker. I time my visits to coincide with hers, though she communicates perfectly with him, because it's so satisfying for me to help with something constructive, to see him make progress and to have company while doing it. Blond and cheerful, she coaches him with an ideal blend of demand and patience. The nurse-techs cheer him on. As he gets stronger, he slowly resumes his habitual role as life of the party, chatting after his PT sessions.

"I gotta wife. You gotta wife?"

"No, sweetheart, I gotta husband." Laughter.

"Oh, husband, yeah. Husband. I'm hungry. I gotta girlfriend."

The Whites invite me to dinner at RoSal's, a family-run restaurant near the hospital. As I walk there, the blue sky grays, and the incandescent lights of Taylor Street, Chicago's little Italy, come on, welcoming me. The hospital hasn't retreated, but the embrace I sense is big enough to hold the institution, Stefan, and me as well. The Whites order a round of Prosecco, and I tell them what's up with Stefan. Then Peter asks, "What do you want to do when you retire?"

I haven't thought beyond Stefan for weeks, and now we begin to discuss how to live the last third of one's life. We share a salad and eat rich pasta dishes like ravioli with Gorgonzola sauce, drinking a bottle of wine. Frozen parts of myself stir and stretch, engaging in conversation ordinary enough in its content but exalted in its power to revive.

Soon I discover that Stefan's blood cultures show VRE, vancomycin-resistant enterrococcus. I barely register the acronym at the time and don't know what it is but can't miss the defensive outfits now worn by those who enter Stefan's room: blue disposable gowns, masks, rubber gloves. These precautions are intended to help prevent spread of the organism, but most of the docs don't observe them, and neither do I. I ask a resident if there's any cure, and she says, "Once you've been colonized . . ." I think of organizing a rebellion or demonstrating for home rule.

Later research tells me that vancomycin is a powerful antibiotic, usually used as a last resort again bacteria resistant to penicillin and other drugs. First identified in the United States in 1989, VRE is spread by direct contact with body fluids, the hands of health care workers, and environmental surfaces, in addition to lines. Like friendly fire for the military, this organism is modern medicine's dirty little secret, the danger you don't hear about until it's too late. The vague understanding of resistant organisms I had on Stefan's first hospital day was probably based on conditions before '89, and now VRE seems like today's leprosy. I am outraged that Stefan has become three times untouchable: handicapped, inoperable, colonized.

Finally discharged to a barely adequate nursing home, Stefan continues physical therapy, always hungry. I work with sitters to restore his ability to dress and toilet himself. Nine days later, his temperature rises, and I meet him in the ER at midnight, find him shaking like a jackhammer and blubbering nonsense, delirious.

The next day, he's back on the floor in his hospital bed, and I am worn out. Every cell in my body resists return to this place. It's a Saturday, and I resolve to visit for only one hour on my way to dinner with a friend who lives nearby.

"Wha's for brea'fast?" Stefan asks as I enter. I respond as usual by talking to him about food, painting word pictures of cereal, pancakes, or eggs. "I like scrambled," he says. I tell him soon he'll get some broth and Jell-O, and he repeats, "Broth, Jell-O," then starts over. "Wha's for brea'fast?" I go to dinner and on to a concert where I turn off my cell phone, then go home. The flashing red light on my answering machine tells me that while I was breathing the air of freedom, Stefan breathed his last.

One hundred and two hospital days become part of the time when Stefan lived, the time my children numbered four. I walk the still-warm streets, wanting to go on doing things for Stefan and wondering where the summer went. At first I was glad that they couldn't reach me. They wouldn't have let me get near him, I thought. Later I regretted it deeply, not to have held his hand, at least, as he died. I still do. I grieve that Stefan will have no more music to clap to and Cokes to buy, no more pets to annoy or candies to unwrap and stash in his pocket. I grieve that his innocence will no longer point to the goodness of things as they are. But I'm relieved that he's escaped the trap of hunger and nausea and do not grieve for myself. Each day I wake and think: *I don't have to go to the hospital today.*

Two months later, I received a note from a friend whose son suffers chronic fatigue. She said, "How lucky our children are to have found us as parents." I'd never thought of Stefan as lucky, least of all during his illness, and I was moved by this reversal of priority: not that I gave birth to a handicapped child, but that Stefan existed a priori and might have ended up with any parents. The thought was like forgiveness; he could have done worse.

Erica came from Austin, Texas, where her boyfriend, Brent, was in graduate school. She took a few days off work and kept me company, made a vivid and varied photomontage of Stefan, and designed the program for the funeral. Together we arranged flowers and planned the reception afterward. Tom and Veronika flew in and stayed overnight, Tom open and friendly with Stefan's housemates but otherwise silent and withdrawn. Anton brought Iris, to my delight, for she'd never been to Chicago. At six she was young for a funeral, and she'd scarcely known Stefan, but she'd insisted on coming until her parents gave in. I plotted shamelessly for her pleasure, arranging play time with neighbor children and giving her and Anton my bed with access to cable TV, hoping she'd want to come back.

Stefan's funeral was as eloquent as the hospital was incomprehensible. Held at St. Thomas the Apostle, the big church he'd attended while living at home, it was filled with his housemates and staff from El Valor, the childhood friends of his siblings, teachers from his day program, and people he'd befriended in the neighborhood as he grew up. Stefan's housemates passed the photomontage around, touching and feeling him again in his image. "Ooh, it's Stefan," said round-faced Karen, blond hair in barrettes, dressed in her best. "Let me see," said Kim, with short black hair, articulate. She gave me a hug. "I have to give you two more, she said, "for my sisters," and she did. "Hi, David," I said, and he looked at me, wordless as usual, in suit and tie.

One hundred and two days of isolation melted in this community's warm embrace. I remembered Dr. Pessimist saying, "If it weren't for you . . ." and thought, *No, if it weren't for his friends and staff, neighbors and siblings and his six-year-old niece who came all the way from California . . .* This vast network had touched and shaped his life, as it would for any well-connected person. Though I was his flawed but present companion for those 102 days, these communities had provided so much more for the time of his life.

At the start of the Mass, we invited people to speak. Diana White remembered the strange sounds that used to come from two sides of the church, as Stefan echoed the last lines of prayers, and her Benjamin sang. Subdued rustling and murmurs lay like a carpet under a neighbor's tale of Stefan's trick-or-treating and continued as two teachers sang:

> Peace is flowing like a river
> Flowing out through you and me
> Flowing out into the desert
> Setting all the captives free.

"Now?" asked muted voices.

"Is it time?"

"Should we go?" A ragged procession wound its uneven way to the front of the church and back, as each of Stefan's housemates placed a white rose on the coffin, shy or proud, shuffling or striding, until the white drapery was piled high with flowers. The next day two roses accompanied Iris back to California, where she brought them and their story to her kindergarten's show and tell.

After the roses, I stepped up for the Mass's first reading, but people weren't through, and the stories continued. Erica said she'd intended a plea for Stefan as a person of depth and feeling, not merely sick or handicapped. "You can tell by all of these speakers," she said, "even interrupting the Mass, that people found Stefan uniquely equipped to lead a happy life and to make others happy. I feared that you would remember him as handicapped and sick. I wanted no pity in this celebration, and now I discover I needn't have worried—there's no pity in this room."

A funeral serves only the living, and no music can rouse the dead to dance, but we clapped as well as wept, following the coffin out of the church to the upbeat tune of "This Little Light of Mine," knowing that Stefan would have burst into applause and little yips of joy.

Erica and her friends took care of the food at the house, baking hors d'oeuvres, making endless pots of coffee, emptying garbage, and opening wine, with El Valor staff pitching in. All of Stefan's housemates came, as well as my friends and those of my kids. The night was unseasonably warm for October, and I sat late on the front porch with Erica and her generous friends, drinking wine, as the funeral flowed out of the church and knit us together, young and old, dumb and smart. Early the next morning, buffeted by cold rain and blowing leaves, Anton, Iris, and I headed for the car and the airport, Iris delighted by the Midwest's extremes of wind and water.

"It's 'smarch' weather," she shouted into the storm, quoting Homer Simpson's reading of a misprinted calendar. Cheerful despite being hustled out of the house at dawn, she hoisted her backpack and twirled down the street, raising her face to the scowling sky. "It's 'smarch' weather." I hoped her presence in Chicago had set a precedent that might soon bring her back.

20

The View from Here

Now that I no longer "think movement," inventing complex choreo-graphic structures, I return to the simple pleasure of dancing to the music, letting it move my hands and feet. I sing and clap in church, a little dance going on inside me. The swinging and twirling of barn dancing, with its shared weight, feels as risky and satisfying as catching a trapeze in midair, while my feet delight in marking the rhythm of its string-band accompaniment. But I often fail to pick up the complicated figures of the lines, squares, and circles and hate to confuse a whole room of dancers. Sometimes there aren't enough men, and I no longer have the wit and adaptability to dance a man's part. So I bike, do yoga, and dance at wed-dings, and when I need to make something I pick up a pen or fill my hands with yarn, vegetables, or flour.

Natasha's ashes have found a bright home on a top shelf in my new study, and the heart-shaped pillow sewn and stuffed for her by Tom still lies next to them. When Eric died, I figured he would want light as much as he'd wanted it for Natasha, and I placed him next to her, held in square brass. Now Stefan has taken his place next to father and sister.

The pool and fountain we built as a memorial to Natasha met a wrecking ball, and memory became the unreliable curator of the past. Aware that I'm forgetting things and searching for evidence, I haul down a scrapbook with Natasha's pictures. Inside I find Tom, at six, one front tooth missing, holding the tiny fourth finger of newborn Natasha in his hand as they lie together on our big bed. I peer at her face, turning the picture in the light, and see only the fat cheeks and closed eyes of any healthy, sleeping infant. Unbelievable, but I've forgotten her. I page through the scrapbook, bottomless love searching for its object, but all I find is a stranger. Flipping faster, as though I were hunting for a lost child on a crowded street, I hit a dead end. Three years, two months, and fourteen days of life provide only so many images.

This blank space is a new kind of loss, not a rupture but an erasure. Ashes become an empty placeholder if my heartless mind can't remember the person for whom they stand. For years, I thought she was clear in my memory, but now it appears those memories weren't real, if reality is what photos reveal. A picture of Anton holding her in his lap reminds me of the infant with three big brothers, but not the baby Tom called "Herman" for her first few weeks, after a schoolmate he liked, unable to imagine anything but another one like the others. I do remember the way she sang "Sewanee River," her voice meandering up and down the refrain, "Oke soke say, oke soke say," but I still can't remember her heart or soul. I search her image at eight months and recognize her long head, but it fails to give me "Tasha the terrible," the cruel czarina I invented in lullabies, giving her power to send her rebellious people to the dungeons. Where once it seemed she and I were parts of one organism, cell next to cell, as closely bound as arm or leg to torso, now I've become the stranger who sees a baby from a distance and never really knows her.

Photos of her first camping trip and last summer show me a person I begin to remember more clearly, tall for her age and serious, as though she were conscious of the power and responsibility of being the only girl-child in the family. I turn another page and see a photo of her at two running away from the camera, holding my father's hand. Slowly, the picture brings back a visit to a farm. As the adults were having drinks on a porch, looking out at a field turned nearly orange in the late-afternoon sun, a small vehicle rumbled round the corner of the house, carrying Natasha's brothers. They took off across the field in a cloud of dust, dogs following, yapping and nipping. She jumped up and ran from the porch, saying, "Wanna ride, wanna ride, wanna ride!" My father grabbed her hand, and together they chased after the boys across the glowing field, his strides doubled by her sturdy, churning legs.

After two years in Austin, Erica and her boyfriend, Brent, returned to spend a month in my basement apartment before moving to Pittsburgh for her graduate school. My preparations for a farewell dinner threaded through the days after they arrived, as I made soup, rolled piecrust, and stewed rhubarb. The day of dinner I picked and washed lettuce from my bountiful garden and roasted new potatoes with garlic and homegrown rosemary, sliced asparagus, and brined some pork. I built the fire and roasted onions in the coals, slipping off the charred outsides to heat them with butter and chives. It had been the sort of perfect day—the sky deep blue, the air so cool it made me seek the sun, the sun so hot it made the shade feel soft—that always makes me think of loss. Perfection cannot last.

Time grew short as I assembled the pie, spreading rhubarb and dotting it with strawberries, pointed ends arranged in circles, then covered it with meringue and baked it till the shiny points turned brown. As we settled on the porch, our voices were an orchestra tuning up; the soup was overture, and then the curtain rose.

Big-bodied Brent and Erica sat massed closely behind the new, brushed-steel table; Erica's friend Kristin sat slim and stylish on my left in black tunic with rainbow stripes around the breast, my friends Madeleine and Joe on my right. I sat just beyond the table on the wicker trunk that holds my garden tools. For this moment all were here, Erica, boyfriend, girlfriend, and my oldest friends, gathered round the table, burnished surface shining softly as the day grew dark.

My heart lunged for my camera, to hold the quiet pause when glasses were still full and plates still neat arrangements of brown-edged meat and red-toned salsas, crisp leaves, and green-specked globes. I cried inside "Please wait!" but would not spoil the moment by begging it to stay. Impending loss felt needful because tied to so much good. We rounded the corner, and the play began, enacting love and leaving as the feast wound down to red-stained glasses, smeary plates, and pale, congealing fat.

On a recent Holy Thursday at St. Gertrude, the church where the children danced and lit the Advent candles, the veil of the present rested lightly on the impassioned time of my conversion, and the glow of that time shone up to the present like lights from the bottom of a pool, illuminating details of this year's Mass like bits of shiny flotsam or fluorescent fish.

At St. Thomas, a group of dancers had dressed the altar, preparing it as though setting the table for a meal at home, accompanied by a solo lute. No pirouettes, just purposeful, attentive action. During the entrance procession, the assembly sang an invitation to Passover: "Let anyone who is hungry come in and eat the Passover meal." The minor harmonies of the song portended the tragic end of a luminous night, reinforced by the aching allusion to Jewish history's hopes deferred. In the first reading, God instructs the community of Israel to celebrate Passover by eating a year-old sheep or goat, "[with] your loins girded, your sandals on your feet and your staff in your hand" (Exod 12:11). The brittle facade of modern life fell away to reveal my connection to ancient people on the move.

In the second reading, Paul, who never knew Jesus, passes on to us the story of the night when Jesus was betrayed, giving us the words we still use in the consecration of bread and wine, the Words of Institution of the Eucharist: "This is my body, which is for you. Do this in remembrance of me. . . . For as often as you eat this bread and drink this cup, you proclaim the Lord's death until he comes" (1 Cor 11:24, 26). The final words of the reading give the symbol its bottomless depth, its ability to hold together absence and presence, death and life. Father Tom Seitz at St. Thomas used to reinforce this synthesis with the words he used for the invitation to Communion: "At this table are both light and dark, grief and balm. We who eat here must change."

At the end of the Mass, a cantor sang Esa Eynai, Psalm 122, in Hebrew in a setting by Max Janowski, a renowned Jewish composer in residence at a nearby temple. While he sang, the dancers who had dressed the altar took it apart, folding cloths, extinguishing candles, and carrying every movable object into the sacristy. No matter how many times one sees it, this dismantling, almost trashing, of the sacred space makes it look like a firebombed city or a drowned island.

After Communion at St. Gertrude's, I suddenly smelled incense, then saw the altar servers lighting a big bank of candles at a side altar decorated profusely with flowers. The present dissolved into the past, as I realized that the generous day was giving way, as it does each year, to abandonment, emptiness, and death. Good Friday approached. There was nothing to do but watch disaster come and pray. "Stay with me, abide with me, watch and pray." We sang the Taizé setting of Jesus's plea to his friends in the garden of Gethsemane. They fell asleep, and then they abandoned him. A deep shaking began in my bones and proceeded out to my shoulders, as tears streamed down my face. I hadn't fasted or observed Lent in any deliberate way; I'd not changed my often critical attitudes, but the Good News had reached me anyway. Was I closer to God when I wept those same tears twenty years earlier? Ridiculously rigid at that time, I ate no meat, fish, eggs, or cheese during Lent, but satisfied my appetite by cooking for Easter. The rich traditions of Orthodoxy appealed, and I made the tall, cylindrical Russian fruit bread called kulich and pascha, a sweet, molded cheese, long before Tom fell in love with Russia and Veronika.

Now I question the purpose of this subtle dance between permission and restriction. I never told anyone what I was doing, thinking I was following the biblical precept that you should "go into your room and shut the door and pray to your Father who is in secret" (Matt 6:6). Today my practice seems to me furtive and obsessive. However unbalanced my dance, it did lead to rich reflections of the liturgy in household ritual. After Lent ended on Wednesday of Holy Week, I would make a round loaf of white bread with a cross incised in the middle and arrange it on a white cloth on the kitchen table, surrounded by candles and a bottle of red wine. On Thursday night, after the service, I would eat my first eggs since the beginning of Lent and drink my first wine. Eric joined the feast but not the fast, skeptical of my monitored self-deprivation and indulgence, happy enough that I had made his favorite dish from childhood: spinach and eggs. I would eat heartily, stoking my body for the fast of Good Friday and Holy Saturday. After the Easter Vigil, late on Saturday night, we'd celebrate resurrection with guests, food, and a big party, feasting on salads of egg and shrimp; chicken and homemade mayonnaise; breads baked with cheese or ham; and a big, pink dessert made of meringue, raspberries, Chambord, and whipped cream.

Sometimes I think my faith is in my body, in the boardlike reluctance to kneel I first noticed on viewing the silk-shawl woman at the Episcopal church, then the desire to prostrate myself I felt at the Words of Institution at St. Thomas, my body surrendering as surely as it had resisted the year before. My dance embodied the hope and zeal of the Sanctus in *Dies Irae,* while my feet took me to church in Tucson or Beijing, rain or shine, in belief or doubt, and my knee bent to the God who intervenes in history, the Absolute that enters the relative and opens the crack between the worlds, allowing me to glimpse the Eternal from the now.

I still trust in what I've seen through the crack. My conviction has waxed and waned and evolved ever since Eric's death, but I've kept faith with my original experience, recalling and probing it. I've kept faith with those who have guided me along the way: spiritual directors and faculty at CTU, a minister of communion whose touch said that "body of Christ" referred to me as well as to the cup, leaders with the courage to resist the culture of money and power. But I can't take responsibility for the cleaving open, the slamming shut. I slip into the passive voice when I describe these events, as though I were an idle bystander, but I believe that the

Real is always there, that God is always close, in the Treeness of the tree or the Meness of me, the organization of my neurons that lets me think a thought or speak a word. Each day I hope to find communion, to glimpse within a dusty tree or blowing leaves and dirt a source of Being: my own, the tree's, the dirt's, the solid earth's—behind every configuration of matter and motion, living and dying, constantly changing, the underlying ground revealed by the figures of the world.

When I was a child, I saw early productions at the Arena Stage in Washington, a theater in the round. We sat in the first row, only a few feet from the actors. I remember that their eyes were like windows into the characters they portrayed. When the actors came out to take curtain calls at the end, the shades on the windows had been pulled down. In the same way, the objects and people around me remain themselves, but usually the shades are down. Once in a while, they pop up, revealing an inner truth, a reality that cannot be contained in words. The Real doesn't appear with flashing lights or thunderbolts, but like an actor revealing a character, the world sometimes breaks open, the wood not so much cleaved as opening of itself to reveal its complex grain and time-honoring rings.

My understanding of what is real also mutates constantly, minute shifts echoing back and forward in time, but the Church continues to draw me, giving me a place and a reason to sing. The Church lets the amens resound, giving hope to sinners passing by, like Augustine, like me. If I had expected the Church to be better than other people, my unchurched parents, for instance, I never would have joined. I like to read about the impassioned torchlight parades of Nicea, in which the specifics of the creed were hammered out, when people really cared about religion. Often I'd like to have my own torchlight parade, advocating for ordination of women or full acceptance of gay people.

And yet I value the tension between the center and the edges, even when it defeats my personal wishes. To me the genius of the Catholic Church is this dynamic balance between central control and the embodiment of faith in thousands of diverse local cultures. Out on the edges of the worldwide Church is every kind of society, from my own individualistic, materialistic United States, with its capitalism and serial monogamy, to others as foreign to me as ritually beheaded chickens. The universal Church tries to hold all this together, laying down a framework for belief and rules for a moral life. The effort fails—how could it not?—and yet the tension holds. And in that crucible, I learn that culture's not a straitjacket, that I can question all that I hold dear, that I can change.

Non-Catholic friends sometimes ask me: how *can* you, given the Church's treatment of women or gays, given the autocratic dismissal of priests, the censorship of theologians, the '40s alliance with fascism? The last one stops me, for Hitler did have a Concordat with the Vatican. Under the leadership of Archbishop Cardinal Innitzer, Austrian bishops urged congregations from the pulpit to vote for Anschluss to Germany, and Eric lived through that, just before he fled. Faced with this history, I would not have joined the Church had I not discovered a powerful, alternate understanding of scripture and tradition that supported the poor and marginalized, as well as the primacy of conscience.

But when people ask or think, "How can you?" I want to say that it's not a political choice or any kind of choice at all. It's a response to a call, a call that comes from a place beyond my understanding of right and wrong. "God sends rain equally on the just and unjust," says Jesus, when commanding us to love enemies (Matt 5:45). The Church is both in and of the world, as deeply mired in sin as I am, yet it also draws me into another level of reality, which allows me and all that is to exist, and another level of justice, to which I can only aspire.

Today, thirty years after the car accident, I'm still trying to see cause and effect at work, to find a reason for Natasha's death, to invent alternate scenarios, to assign blame. Our trip to Jamaica seems hectic and fraught with ordinary difficulties, the kind that made me tense and flustered at the time but later seemed so routine, even desirable. Leaving Chicago's snowy spring for our first vacation without Stefan, I saw the trip as reward for all the work I'd done to raise the family. Without admitting it, I also hoped it would cure the sudden emptiness I'd discovered in my store of dances, the threat of nothing to show for spring season at the Body Politic. I'd dreaded to be revealed in all my naked incompetence, and fear had slid into mild depression. Now I retrace our steps once more, searching for breaks in the linked chain of the past.

The day before the accident, we flew from Chicago to Washington, planning to leave Stefan with my parents, and Daddy met us at the airport. Eric and he sat in the front seat, four kids and I in the back. Eric turned and gestured to the back, showing off his progeny to his father-in-law.

"Quite a brood," acknowledged Daddy, rolling down the windows and starting the car on the humid spring night.

"Do you have airplane dishing?" asked Anton. The children's baby talk had been preserved by Eric's usage and become standard in the family.

"Sure," said Daddy, turning on the air conditioning with window open in his typically generous way, making Eric wince at the waste. As usual, the grating between them pained my stomach. We drove to the apartment, where my mother was preparing Mongolian hot pot, a moat of broth surrounding a cone filled with burning charcoal.

"You never eat on airplanes, right?" she asked me. I had, but I didn't admit it and ate anyway, worrying about my weight. We sat around the table until late, dipping, cooking, and eating. Excused from the table, Tom sat Natasha on a horse with wheels and pushed her down the apartment's long halls. In my last photo of Natasha, Tom looks at the camera, glazed with late-night concentration, while she looks down, trying to balance, neat in her diagonally striped dress with white collar and cuffs. Excited by the new environment, she stayed up late, and I resented the fact that Eric and I couldn't make love.

The next morning, we hurried to get everyone dressed, packed, and out. The two boys each had a suitcase, and Natasha had a backpack. Daddy drove us to Friendship, the ancestor of Baltimore-Washington International Airport, where the children threatened to get lost in the crowd. I was holding Natasha, who wanted the gum promised for the flight, and I'd gotten stuck somehow with Anton's small bag. I saw Tom's curly head at my side.

"Would you take care of this?" I asked.

"Sure," he said, and took his scatterbrained self off into the crowd. Checked in, we settled in a waiting area where Natasha jumped around the carpet's multicolored squares.

"Now I'm on red," she sang. "Now I'm on green; now I'm on blue." On the plane to Montego Bay, she chewed her gum and drank a Coke but never ate. The air was hot and moist when we arrived, a shock even after Washington. My lightweight brown jersey, with turtleneck and long sleeves, had never felt so stifling. Natasha and I went back and forth through immigration repeatedly to the only bathroom, shedding piece upon piece of clothing, as we waited for the missing suitcase. Finally, we filed a claim for lost luggage. My heart ached for Anton, the careful brother, deprived of clothes and a favorite stuffed animal, and I chastised myself for trusting the suitcase to Tom.

Anton had nothing cool to wear, so we went to a shop and bought him a bathing suit. By the time we got in the rental car, the day was winding down, and Eric was anxious about driving on the left. We had a reservation at the Bonnie View, a hotel perched between the Blue Mountains and the sea in Port Antonio, the hometown of my first dance partner, Neville Black, and a place we'd visited several times before. The car had no seatbelts, and still the children hadn't eaten. We piled them in the backseat and stopped at a street vendor for ice cream, then continued as voices quieted and hands and mouths grew sticky.

The road twisted and turned, following the coast, and half an hour later, Natasha threw up. Miles from any facilities, we pulled into the road to a farmhouse. The kind inhabitants brought us a bucket of water and paper towels, and we washed her up, then retrieved new clothes from the trunk and changed her. She never complained. I put her in my lap in the front seat and sang to her as we drove on.

Later, Eric would think he'd been punished for the competitive pride with which he'd displayed the kids to my father, and I would think, ridiculously, that Natasha had died of chewing gum, ice cream, and a Coke. For years I went back and walked that car safely around the bend, slowing down, avoiding the oncoming truck.

Yes, I was angry with Eric for driving too fast, my fury escalating as the car hit the embankment, reared, and began to roll. But by the time we got to Santa Maria, Natasha's condition had bled me of anger. I knew Eric loved her every bit a much as I did. After months of grief, blank and disheartening, I remembered my rage like an outgrown, childhood hatred. It belonged to a lost order of existence, like appetite and love.

If I couldn't undo the past, I wanted a cause. Natasha did not, of course, die of chewing gum or pride. Perhaps Eric had seen enough of physical cause in his medical career, for he did not need to know the facts, but I sent for the medical examiner's records from Jamaica and did not turn away when they arrived. Recently, I searched my files for the records and discovered I'd saved every piece of paper connected with the accident, from deceptively ordinary to-do lists about airline tickets (change them) and ambulances (to get Anton to the airport), to a medical certification (that Anton was safe to fly), to extremely polite letters to police, mortuary, and constable (how long after that did we both become angry with everyone?), to death certificate and coroner's report, typed with uneven letters on a bleak, colonial form.

What was I hoping to preserve with all that paper? Some essence? Some funereal sequence that would lend order to her death? I lost her smell soon after she died, when someone threw her blanket in the washing machine. The only part of her that I can hold is her long-dry blood, soaked into the short-sleeved shirt and denim shorts I was wearing, saved in a plastic bag in my bottom drawer next to the small, square-toed sneakers that made her look so resolute we used to call them "combat boots."

She did not bleed to death, as I'd suspected. The medical examiner's report does describe the long gashes in her jaw that connected with her mouth and turned my white hair red, but the cause of death was "shock resulting from fracture of the cervical vertebrae and damage to the spinal cord in the neck." I could have saved her in a thousand ways, by avoiding the vacation or the ice cream, by keeping track of the suitcase, by overcoming my fear of hen-pecking and insisting that Eric slow down, by anything that would have altered our presence at that one time and place. But once her neck was broken, there was nothing I could do.

A couple of years ago, I made a video transfer of my father's super-eight movies. As I view it, images rise from the depths to fill in the missing surface. Eric, Tom, Anton, and Abiyoyo, our German shepherd, are in the Wisconsin River, on the banks of which my parents had a simple, two-room log cabin. Just before or just after the video was shot, Eric would dance, holding the boys in the water, singing a Strauss waltz at the top of his lungs, but now they are jumping up and down and on each other, while Stefan, Natasha, and I sit in the boat moored to the dock. Natasha is naked, with curls brushing her shoulders and wisps of brown hair in her face. Someone is reading "Goldilocks" to Stefan off-camera, and I am lifting Natasha to stand on the edge of the boat and look over.

"It's the water," says Mama, off-camera, in an artificial voice intended for children. "I don't want you to fall in the water."

"Why?" asks Natasha, impish face telling me she knows perfectly well why but senses something not quite direct in my mother's speech.

"Because you'll get all wet." Another off-camera voice talks about teaching Stefan to take the stairs down to the dock instead of tumbling down the precipitous hill. I am not active in the scene, though I'm caring for Natasha and overseeing Stefan, but I am filled with all the commotion around me: dog paddling, boys swimming and shouting, voices reading and discussing, Mama advising. Natasha begins to wrestle with the boat's steering wheel, throwing her weight against it. Again I hear Mama's voice: "That's it, Natasha. Drive! Drive!" Now, for a moment, I do remember Natasha at three, her vivid intelligence and desire to do all her brothers did, her fierce energy, her determination and her pluck.

The video is over, and Natasha recedes, figure blending into ground. The door that she opened swings on its hinges, only occasionally allowing me a glimpse of what lies beyond. Other births have partly healed the rift in my world: Erica, now grown, and my granddaughters. But when I look back on that liminal time of not knowing and almost seeing, I remember the whirlwind that exploded my faith in "facts," then forged grief into hope with the heat of a fiery furnace. I both want and fear to know that place again, and I still hope to follow the little girl I can't quite remember as I hear that noisy engine roaring just out of sight—it's a go-cart with tractor wheels, a child's delight, rounding the corner of the house, and Anton—yes, it's Anton—driving, Tom and a younger child riding in a wagon attached behind, two older boys running beside and shouting, motor revving, dogs barking, insects buzzing, Natasha's resolute legs trampling the incandescent grain and her voice rising clear through the evening air: "Wanna ride, wanna ride!"

Epilogue

SPARROW IN THE HALL

A BIRD FLIES THROUGH darkness, spies a bright door, and flies into a warm and well-lit room, then out a window into darkness again. Maxwell Anderson and Kurt Weill adapted this traditional story for their song "Bird of Passage," used in *Lost in the Stars* and proposed for a secular funeral service. The story captures my imagination for the proportion it gives to the time and space of my life, the ignorance it confesses about the time before birth and after death, and the sense of continuity it suggests among past, present, and future. The bird still flies.

Hunting up its origins, I discovered that the story concerns the conversion of the Northumbrian King Edwin and is recorded in the Venerable Bede's *Ecclesiastical History of England*, written in the eighth century. As King Edwin debated converting to Christianity, one of his followers made this speech:

> Your majesty, when we compare the present life of man on earth with that time of which we have no knowledge, it seems to me like the swift flight of a single sparrow through the banqueting hall where you are sitting at dinner on a winter's day with your thanes and counselors. In the midst there is a comforting fire to warm the hall; outside the storms of winter rain or snow are raging. This sparrow flies swiftly in through one door of the hall and out through another. While he is inside he is safe from the winter's storms, but after a few moments of comfort, he vanishes from sight into the wintry world from which he came. Even so, man appears on earth for a little while, but of what went on before this life or of what follows, we know nothing. Therefore, if this new teaching has brought any more certain knowledge, it seems only right that we should follow it.[1]

As is apparent, the meaning I took from the story is the reverse of the original, which shows not continuity through the ages, but the plight of darkness and ignorance without Christianity. After hearing this story, King Edwin did convert. His chief pagan priest, Coifi, noted that pagan gods could not be good for much since they had not rewarded his own careful observance, and the pagan priest advised conversion to more efficacious doctrines.

To me, the story of the sparrow holds up our life as a gift of light surrounded by mystery, mystery in the original sense of religious truth we cannot fully comprehend, mystery embodied in sacrament that offers us an opening to that truth. The story gives equal weight to the "before" and the "after" and reveals how faith and doubt, knowledge and ignorance, presence and absence, are bound together as inextricably as body and soul.

But the sparrow shouldn't fly alone. It needs other birds, the community essential to faith. So I would tell the story of a flock of birds circling above a rafter in the updraft over a boiling pot, surprised to find themselves in this safe haven. Warmed by the fire and by each other, they smell the bubbling stew and squawk noisily about where they've come from and where they're going. When they quiet down enough to listen to each other, they discover that they all know how to sing. They settle on the rafter and join their voices in a hopeful tune about what lies outside, drowning out the murmurous calculations of the thanes.

Or I would replace King Edwin's stewpot and his thanes with my parents' Mongolian hot pot, charcoal burning in the conical center, heating a moat of broth. Instead of birds, I imagine a gathering around that authentic pot, where all our dead join the living as we dip raw meat, shrimp, bean sprouts, and snow peas into the moat with chopsticks, cooking and eating.

The ancestors exclaim over the exotic pot, while the youngest are already skilled with chopsticks and rarely lose a morsel. Like the birds, we don't know where we've been or where we're going, but we have questions for each other. Eric prods the hesitant speakers of German. "*Ihr könnt dazu setzen,*" he says, addressing them informally and urging them to sit next to the shy speakers of English and French, then making introductions. Daddy offers a toast, and a bilingual Huguenot ancestor translates. All begin to identify and point out shared family traits: the Habsburg-like prominent eyes and full lips of the Austrian side, the prematurely gray hair and short stature of the Irish and French sides, the long bones and curly hair of the German Jewish side.

Children rise to play from time to time, and Eric corrals them to resurrect the sugar game. The children rejoice, discovering they now have all the answers. Mama sings, and soon others join in. Shoes come off, and everyone lines up their feet, looking to see who gave whom the twisted toes and who the straight ones. As the night wears on, adults in search of the bathroom discover the apartment's other side, a vast network of rooms extending in all directions, strange but also expected.

Gesture takes over from language as minutes and hours give way to a timeless present. No longer watching and waiting, we forget about what lies outside and sense that we've been here all along, sharing a meal whose meaning is now coming clear. Finally we dump noodles into the broth and divide the whole into bowls for a slurpy finish, seasoned with ginger, garlic, green onions, and soy, new tastes suddenly as old and familiar as home.

Notes

CHAPTER 1. THE OTHER SIDE

1. Adrienne Rich, *Of Woman Born* (New York: W. W. Norton and Company, Inc., 1976).

2. Leo Tolstoy, *War and Peace,* trans. Constance Garnett (New York: Random House, 2002).

CHAPTER 2. DANCE WAS MY RELIGION

1. *Collected Poems of Muriel Rukeyser* (Pittsburgh: University of Pittsburgh Press, 2005).

CHAPTER 3. SNAKE YEARS

1. Arlene Croce. *Writing in the Dark, Dancing in the New Yorker* (New York: Farrar, Strauss Giroux, 2000), 59–60 (first published in the *New Yorker,* Aug. 19, 1974).

2. Maxine Kumin, *Selected Poems 1960–1990* (New York: W. W. Norton, 1997).

3. William H. Gass. "Order of Insects," in *In the Heart of the Heart of the Country* (Boston: David R. Godine, 1981).

CHAPTER 5. CLEAVE THE WOOD

1. Albert Rouet, *Liturgy and the Arts,* trans. Paul Philibert, O.P. (Collegeville, Minn.: The Order of St. Benedict, Inc., 1997).

2. Catholic Church, *The Sacramentary* (New York: Catholic Book Publishing Company, 1974).

CHAPTER 6. OPPORTUNE MOMENTS

1. Alan Paton, *Cry the Beloved Country* (New York: Charles Scribners' Sons, 1948).

2. *Lost in the Stars,* book and lyrics by Maxwell Anderson and music by Kurt Weill (New York: Alfred Publishing Company, 1949).

CHAPTER 12. ALL ROADS CONVERGE

1. Fyodor Dostoevsky, *The Brothers Karamazov,* trans. Constance Garnet (New York: New American Library, 1957).

CHAPTER 14. WARM SNOW, DARK SEA

1. 1 Cor 15:51.

CHAPTER 15. STILL DANCING?

1. Thomas Barrie, *Spiritual Path, Sacred Place: Myth, Ritual and Meaning in Architecture* (Boston: Shambala Press, 1996).

2. Victor Witter Turner, *Dramas, Fields, and Metaphors: Symbolic Action in Human Society* (Ithaca: Cornell University Press, 1974).

CHAPTER 17. SEPARATIONS

1. Sylvia Plath, "Child," in *Winter Trees* (New York: Harper and Row, 1972).

EPILOGUE

1. *Bede's Ecclesiastical History of the English People,* ed. Bertram Colgrave and R. A. B. Mynors, Oxford Medieval Texts (Oxford: Clarendon Press, 1969).

Please remember that this is a library book,
and that it belongs only temporarily to each
person who uses it. Be considerate. Do
not write in this, or any, library book.